Sven Hedin (1865–1952) was one c
explorers. His travels through Russi
Central Asia, China and Tibet led
important discoveries and achieveme

produced the first detailed maps of vast parts of the Pamir
Mountains, the Taklamakan Desert, Tibet, the Silk Road and
the Transhimalaya (Gangdise today). He was the first to
unearth the ruins of ancient Buddhist cities in Chinese
Central Asia and in 1901 he discovered the ancient Chinese
garrison town of Lou-lan in the Taklamakan. The many manuscripts he found there are of huge historical importance. His
great goal – never realised – was to reach the forbidden city
of Lhasa. His books, which include *Through Asia*, *Central Asia
and Tibet*, *Overland to India*, *Transhimalaya*, and *My Life as
an Explorer* have been excerpted, translated and published in
dozens of languages throughout the world.

Tauris Parke Paperbacks is an imprint of I.B.Tauris. It is dedicated to publishing books in accessible paperback editions for the serious general reader within a wide range of categories, including biography, history, travel and the ancient world. The list includes select, critically acclaimed works of top quality writing by distinguished authors that continue to challenge, to inform and to inspire. These are books that possess those subtle but intrinsic elements that mark them out as something exceptional.

The Colophon of Tauris Parke Paperbacks is a representation of the ancient Egyptian ibis, sacred to the god Thoth, who was himself often depicted in the form of this most elegant of birds. Thoth was credited in antiquity as the scribe of the ancient Egyptian gods and as the inventor of writing and was associated with many aspects of wisdom and learning.

THE
WANDERING
LAKE

Into the Heart of Asia

Sven Hedin

Foreword by John Hare

TPP

TAURIS PARKE
PAPERBACKS

Published in 2009 by Tauris Parke Paperbacks
an imprint of I.B.Tauris & Co Ltd
6 Salem Road, London W2 4BU
175 Fifth Avenue, New York NY 10010
www.ibtauris.com

Distributed in the United States and Canada Exclusively by
Palgrave Macmillan
175 Fifth Avenue, New York NY 10010

First published in English in 1940 by George Routledge & Sons Ltd

ISBN: 978 1 84885 022 4

A full CIP record for this book is available from the British Library
A full CIP record is available from the Library of Congress

Library of Congress Catalog Card Number: available

Printed and bound in India by Thomson Press India Ltd

CONTENTS

LIST OF ILLUSTRATIONS

LIST OF SKETCHES AND MAPS
IN THE TEXT

FOREWORD

ON Easter Sunday, April 1, 1934, Sven Hedin's relief is palpable. After months of surviving hardship, bombardment and misfortune, vividly described in *The Trail of War* and *The Silk Road*, he had finally freed himself from the machinations of devious men, and set out with his Uighur and Swedish team on what was to be his final excursion into the Desert of Lop.

In 1900, Hedin had famously walked into this desert from west to east, along a dry river bed called the Kuruk-daria and had reached the dried-up lake bed of Lop-nor. He had accurately concluded that another lake which at that time was also known as Lop-nor and which lay many miles to the south-west had, as a result of the silting up of the Kuruk-daria, re-located from its ancient site.

As Hedin trekked along the river bed at the turn of the twentieth century Ordek, his trusted guide, mislaid the expedition's only spade. Having been sent back by Hedin to retrieve it, Ordek not only found the spade but also discovered the ancient city of Lou-lan, an important staging post on the Middle Silk Road. From manuscripts and coins collected at the site, Hedin concluded that the city had been gradually abandoned over a period of thirty years in about 400 AD, when the Kuruk-daria had diverted into its new channel. This diversion had left the inhabitants of Lou-lan without their only source of water which had come to them annually as snow melt from the surrounding mountains.

In his book, *Scientific Results of a Journey in Central Asia 1899–1902*, Hedin had written 'In the light of the knowledge we now possess of the levels that exist in the Lop desert, it is not too daring to affirm that the river *must* some day go back to the Kuruk-daria ... it is only a question of time ...'

In 1928, Hedin learnt that the river had, seven years earlier, reverted to its former river bed.

'I was thunderstruck at the news,' he wrote. 'It meant not only that my theories put forward twenty-eight years earlier were right, but also that my prophecy that Lop-nor and the lower Tarim [river] would return to their old beds in the north had come true.'

Now another six years later in 1934, he had at last set out to discover what had happened to the dried-up lake bed as a result of this momentous event.

The changes were startling, wild pig with huge tusks, sported in the reed beds. Herds of black-tailed gazelles were seen grazing by the river, in areas where hitherto they had been unable to survive because of a lack of water and vegetation. He sighted the Bengal tiger, today totally extinct in China, and fresh fish, up to two feet long, swam in the northern waters of the lake and proved easy prey for his Uighur canoe men who used their wooden paddles to stun them in waters no more than three feet deep.

Near hummocks known as *yardangs* and ancient land formations called *mesas*, his team discovered ancient grave sites and mummified corpses including one Hedin dubbed, the Queen of Lou-lan, who has recently been carbon dated as approximately 3,500 years old.

Hedin's restless pen is never still. Page after page of this wonderful book are enlivened with black and white sketches of graves and the numerous artefacts they concealed, graphic details of mummies that had lain undisturbed in the desert for millennia, and vivid and expressive scenic panoramas.

This section of the Middle Silk Road was abandoned long before foreign travellers such as Marco Polo made their historic journeys from the west to the east. Polo, for example, would have been oblivious of the Middle Silk Road, the ancient city of Lou-lan and the dried-up lake bed of Lop-nor. The road had been abandoned almost a thousand years before he undertook his journey along the Lower Silk Road, further to the south.

Hedin, having recorded so much of value, made his return out of the desert by motor vehicle—another 'first'. On this journey he had glimpses of the mysterious, elusive and shy, wild Bactrian camel. 'The lorry stopped. A solitary wild camel was moving slowly along to our right. He stopped short, raised his head, stood for a moment as still as a statue, and then set off to the north and vanished as swiftly as a shadow of a cloud. I was glad that no shot had been fired at the king of the desert.'

Hedin's official mission on this historic journey in 1934 had been to recommend to the Chinese government a site for a motor road which, as he put it, would link the 'Pacific with the Atlantic'. He mused that, 'the oldest and longest caravan route on earth, which in ancient times linked east and west, was to be raised from the dead'. However there was to be, 'no more camels, no tinkling caravans, no mail courier's horses with collars of bells ... First motor cars will come and then the railways.'

In 1996, I was extremely fortunate to travel to Lop-nor and Lou-lan. We trekked along a once again dead and dry Kuruk-daria as Hedin had done at the turn of the twentieth century. We became ensnared on hard and brittle rock salt which surrounds the newly dried-up lake of Lop-nor. There was neither a camel caravan nor a motor road. There were no more wild pigs, black-tailed gazelles or fish. In fifty years, the lake and its surrounding landscape had reverted to Hedin's 'region of death'. The establishment of a nuclear test site for nearly 30 years and the intentional diversion of the Kuruk-daria for irrigation 400 miles away, were beyond Hedin's forecasting abilities.

But the desert is not wholly dead, when I googled Lop-nor recently, a bulldozer was spotted on the dried-up lake bed, no doubt part of a gigantic kaolin mine which the Chinese are currently excavating in the desert. 'Develop the West' is the Chinese cry, but that development is a long way from the vision of Sven Hedin.

And yet, as Hedin rightly pointed out, a thousand years is but a second on the geological clock. The waters from the melting snows on the high mountains must flow some-where. When two or three more geological seconds have ticked away those cold, clear, icy waters may once again flow back into the old lake bed.

Hedin's great prophecy about the nature of the 'wandering

lake' was spectacularly fulfilled in his lifetime. The event is described with a unique insight and enlivened with fascinating discoveries. Hedin, in this book, no longer writes with the immediacy of a war correspondent as he did in the first two books of the trilogy. He is once again in full flow as an explorer without equal in Central Asia.

John Hare

THE START FOR LOP-NOR

EASTER Day, April 1, 1934, was one of our great days, for on it we were freed after a month's imprisonment in Korla. Ma Chung-yin, "Big Horse", and his Tungan troops had been defeated and fled westward, and the victorious Northern Army of Red and White Russians, Mongols and Chinese, under the command of General Bektieieff, was now master of the little East Turki town. The military governor-general of Sinkiang, Sheng Shih-tsai, had—so Bektieieff told us—proposed that we should move off eastward into the desert region about Lake Lop-nor and not go to the capital, Urumchi, until two months later, as the road to that place was still rendered unsafe by gangs of Tungan deserters and looting robber bands.

The governor-general, who, one can be sure, had never heard of Lop-nor, had no idea how welcome his decision was to us, and especially to myself; for I longed once again to see those parts which had been so flourishing 2,000 years ago, the region in which the Wandering Lake had returned to its old bed in 1921, at the same time as the lower course of the Tarim.

During the last days of March we had been occupied from morning to night making new light tents, buying and stowing away the supplies of flour, rice, fruit and eggs which were to be had in the villages, loading the cars with the petrol we still had left, and finally packing our own luggage. Everything we could do without was left in a sealed room in our former prison, where a damaged lorry was likewise left under a military guard to await our return.

As usual when starting on an enterprise of some dimensions, there were a quantity of small matters which had been postponed till the last moment: tailors, carpenters and

Bridge south of Korla, awkward for motor traffic.

smiths brought their bills ; peasants from outlying villages, who had heard that we paid well for their goods, brought spades, pails and copper cans.   Time went by, and it was past midday before we could get properly clear.   The gates opening into the narrow street, between low grey clay walls and houses, were flung open, and the inquisitive crowd made way as the heavily laden cars rolled noisily out into the dust.

In war-time, when most of the civil population has migrated to undisturbed regions, there is no one to regulate the flow of the irrigation canals, and stretches of high road were, therefore, now flooded.   The three motor-lorries rushed through these lakes with the water streaming round the wheels, but the small car got stuck and had to be hauled out with the aid of a rope and a few peasants from neighbouring farms.

We halted for a few minutes at the memorable place where the attack of March 11 had taken place, and found in the willow trunks some of the holes made by the Tungan bullets.   Now no danger threatened except the frail little wooden bridges, which, strange to say, bore the weight of our heavy loads.   The willow avenue came to an end ; we caught a glimpse of some women at a last farm ; a belt of steppe came next, without bushes and trees, and then we went on southward over barren *gobi*.

This belt of desert was narrow, and we were soon rolling again through clouds of dust over soft, gently undulating ground, covered with herbage. We crossed several canals, one or two fairly wide. A bridge gave way under one of the lorries, and it took some time to get the bulky thing on its wheels again. In the dusk we approached the out-skirts of the scattered village of Shinnega, now inhabited by a few Turki families. We drove through a maze of small overgrown clay mounds, infrequent trees, and gener-ally deserted farms, over canals with wretched wooden bridges, and sought out a suitable place for our camp no. 52 on the margin of a fair-sized irrigation canal.

The headman of Shinnega and its vicinity—called a *bek* in Turkish, in Chinese a *hsiang-yeh*—was a good fellow named Seidul, who immediately placed himself and his services at our disposal. He understood that we were distinguished people from Europe and China, and not savage Tungans, who looted at will and paid for nothing they took. He promised to get us as much flour and rice and as many eggs and sheep as could be found in the oasis, and he carried out his undertaking to our complete satisfaction.

It was a long time before the camp grew quiet that night. Our mechanics, Georg Söderbom and Effe Hill, and the two Mongolian chauffeurs, Serat and Jomcha, had as usual to examine the cars and repair defects here and there. In the middle of the night a few creaking ox-carts went by, and the drivers' shouts of exhortation to their beasts rang shrilly through the silence. They were refugees returning to their farms.

Next day Georg, the Chinese engineer C. C. Kung, the Cossack Gagarin [1] and I made a short preliminary tour of exploration to the Kara-kum region, rather more than 20 miles to the southward on the river Konche-daria. [2] The country was of the usual type—alternate strips of steppe

[1] The commander-in-chief of the Northern Army had given us an escort of four Russian Cossacks.
[2] Konchi, or Könchi, means " tanner ". Daria means river ; the common English transcription is " darya ".

and desert, clay soil, the road broken up by cart-wheels and the hoofs of cattle and horses into the finest dust, which was sent whirling up by the cars and formed impenetrable clouds. On both sides of the road rose clay mounds clad with more or less withered reeds and tamarisks. About the first farms we passed stood small groups of poplars.

One could see that it was war-time. Here the farms were mostly deserted. But after much humming and hawing, and the offer of a handsome reward, we succeeded in getting a young peasant girl to guide us amid the labyrinth of tracks and show us the best way to the chief town of the district, Yü-li-hsien, the Konche of the East Turkis, situated right on the bank of the Konche-daria.

The girl had plenty of pluck. She cried " Come along ! " and ran ahead lightly ; we followed slowly and cautiously— it was in any case impossible to drive fast on such ground, and we had not far to go. She had soon piloted us to the beginning of a willow avenue. She stopped there and declared that the avenue led to Konche.

Konche, a poor village sucked dry by the war, had never seen a car, and the whole population, a few hundred people perhaps, quickly assembled round the strange visitor.

It was not hard to find our way to the *yamên*, where the Chinese *amban*, or district governor, of Yü-li-hsien lived. This *yamên* was not a bad official residence, seeing how far it was from the main road. It consisted of several wooden houses in the usual Chinese style, separated from one another by small square courtyards. Kung and I, accompanied by the whole population of Konche, walked down the pathway of flat stones in the last courtyard and were met by the *amban* himself, a thin, pale little man with a serious, almost frightened expression. It was natural that he was astonished, and anything might happen in wartime. But Kung reassured his countryman, who courteously invited us into his simple reception-room. He seemed to be glad that we did not belong to the same band as the gangs of Tungans who had three times during the war plagued and looted Konche, and forced him to flee out into the desert to save his life.

The recollection of these strange adventures no doubt

explained to some extent the meekness and submissiveness he showed towards us. He did not even ask what our business was, nor did he ask to see our passports. At first, I expect, he thought that if we belonged to the Northern Army we had the governor-general Sheng Shih-tsai behind us, and if we were a patrol from one of Big Horse's detachments, he could escape into the desert for a fourth time if the place became too hot. But Kung handled him diplomatically, and in a few minutes he was promising to do everything in his power to satisfy our wishes.

When we explained that we needed a dozen canoes, the *amban* sent for a young East Turki, who assured us that there were no boats at Konche at the moment, but that there were sure to be some in the Chong-köl (Big Lake) region, 70 li or 22 miles away. If we could give them twenty-four hours, the boats would be at Konche with both crews and oars. They advised us to fasten the canoes together in pairs or in threes with crosswise poles, and lay down on these a plank deck for the baggage. A vessel like this, consisting of three canoes, could carry 1,500 Chinese chin, or 1,980 lb. Planks and beams for this purpose would also be provided in the time stated. A part of the provisions should be sent by cart a few days' journey downstream. We need not trouble about sheep, for shepherds tended their flocks on the banks of the river right down to Tömenpu, the point at which the new river, the Kum-daria, leaves the old bed of the Konche-daria.

We rose to return to the camp at Shinnega; but the *amban*, who was evidently glad to have met pleasant and well-disposed people in such disturbed times, begged us to stay and have a simple evening meal with him. A refusal would have hurt his feelings, so we promised to come back in half an hour.

We wished, before the sun gave place to twilight, to take a short walk down to the left bank of the Konche-daria, which was quite close by, and where we had to find a suitable harbour for the boats and a point of departure for our long journey by river to the new lake.

We came to a little creek where a couple of high-wheeled carts had driven out into the water to be washed, while

their horses had a refreshing bath.   Immediately above the
creek the bank formed a fairly steep wall running down to
deep water.   This place was chosen for the harbour, and it
was agreed that the canoes we had ordered should be lying
moored there at midday on April 4.

I thought of the strange and inexplicable chances of life
when I now saw this region again, which I had visited for
the first time in the spring of 1896.   I little dreamed then
that I should come there once again thirty-eight long years
later.

The river Konche-daria was quite imposing as it ran
between its well-marked banks, covered here and there
with trees and bushes, with a long-shaped island near the
right bank.   Only one canoe was to be seen, and that lay
waterlogged, all twisted and out of shape and condemned.
I longed to go on board the flotilla we had ordered, and be
carried by the current and paddles through the once waterless desert to our distant goal, the mysterious Wandering
Lake.

Meanwhile supper had been prepared in the *yamên*.   There
we were regaled with the East Turkis' favourite dish, rice
pudding boiled in sheep's fat with raisins, carrots and
onions, *pilmên* (minced mutton in suet), scrambled eggs and
boiled mutton—all solid Mohammedan dishes, none of the
delicacies of the more elaborate Chinese cookery.

When the meal was over we rose and took our leave.
The dusk had fallen, and a new night was approaching.
Georg assured us that he could see our old tracks and
follow them easily, even without headlights.   But we had
not gone far before he got stuck fast in the mud and vainly
endeavoured to get the car up on to firmer ground.   At
last he had to go on foot and collect a few peasants, who
quickly helped us to get the car out and put us on the right
road.   Then we lit our headlights, and reached the camp
after a successful reconnaissance.

We spent April 3 too at Shinnega.   The river party—
Dr. David Hummel, Kung, Parker C. Chen and I, with two
of the four Russian Cossacks and a couple of Chinese
servants—collected and packed our various belongings.
The cook, Chia Kwei, was busy with cooking apparatus,

saucepans, crockery, cutlery and provisions. We engaged an East Turki named Ibrahim, who had been in Bergman's service in 1928. He was a skilful antelope hunter. As he was leaving a wife and children and his father and mother-in-law at Shinnega, he asked if he might receive part of his wages in advance, to which we readily consented.

All the river baggage, including two months' provisions for fifteen men, was loaded at dusk on to three carts, which were to drive to Konche during the night and report to our new friend the *amban*. A fourth cart would convey two tents, our beds and the kitchen equipment by the same route next morning.

At daybreak the members of the boat party said farewell to the motor expedition. The latter was to make a detour inland and proceed to a familiar bend of the river, Sai-cheke, where I had encamped in 1896, and where the two groups were to meet. It was impossible to fix an exact time for the meeting; our routes, both by land and by water, were too uncertain for that. The party which arrived first was to await the coming of the other. It was important to maintain contact so long as we were not too far from inhabited places. When the boat party had left the motor people for the last time, we were dependent entirely on ourselves in regions where not one living soul was to be found.

At Konche we immediately called on the *amban*, who told us that everything we had ordered was in readiness by the river bank, and accompanied us thither. The place of embarkation we had chosen now wore quite a different aspect from when we had last seen it. There lay six large canoes and as many smaller ones, each made fast to a paddle stuck into the slope of the bank. A whole pile of planks was there too, as long as the breadth of two canoes, and a number of poles of the same length.

The *amban* introduced to us ten *suchi*, or boatmen. Sadik, Hajit and Rozi were from the Chong-köl; Seidul, Hashim and Musa Ahun from Konche; and Sajit, Aveile, Abdur-ahim and Osman from the village of Ak-supe, a few days' journey downstream. Seidul was appointed foreman.

The canoe, the ordinary means of transport everywhere on the Tarim, from the region just below Yarkend to the river's end, is cut with axes out of a single poplar trunk. A middle-sized canoe is about 13 feet long and so narrow that a man can sit at the bottom of it with legs outstretched and hands supported on the bulwarks, but has no room to turn sideways. The craft is round like the poplar trunk, and its balance on the water is therefore extremely delicate. Its natural inclination is to roll over with every movement of its cargo. But the paddlers are as safe and experienced in manœuvring their craft as our Norrland men floating timber on the rivers. The paddler stands upright or kneels in the stern of his boat, which he skilfully directs with his broad-bladed paddle. If in a hurry one employs two paddlers, and they send the boat fairly hissing through the water. It takes some days for a stranger to accustom himself to the sudden movements, and learn to adapt himself to them and help to trim the canoe.

But we were to work on board during a river journey of nearly two months. I was to make a detailed map of the new river Kum-daria, and Chen was to measure its volume, depth, speed of current, breadth, etc. Hummel's task was to collect plants and animals, especially birds, and prepare them. And as we had a large cargo of provisions, tents, beds and other equipment, we should have found these unsteady canoes of little use ; so we ordered the crew to fasten the canoes together in pairs and lay down a plank deck over them amidships. When working at my writing-table—an empty packing-case—I sat on the forward plank with a leg in each canoe. My rolled-up bed was made fast behind me and acted as a support for my back. One of my boatmen, Sadik, sat or stood in the bows of the right-hand canoe, the other, Hajit, in the stern of the left-hand one. They paddled for days on end almost without interruption, and as a rule we made more ground by paddling than from the strength of the current.

Chen had arranged his double canoe for his surveying work in a practical manner, and had made some low tables for his instruments out of boxes. Hummel's craft soon assumed the appearance of a laboratory. Kung, who was with us for the first few days, was generally on board Chen's boat and assisted him in his surveying work.

Our cook, Chia Kwei, a Christian Chinese from a Swedish mission station, and a young Cossack named Erashin Sokolenko occupied a fourth double canoe. They had with them the cooker, kitchen utensils and part of the provisions. Another Cossack, Constantine, a *solon* from Semirechensk, who spoke Turki and Russian and also Chinese and Mongolian, became Hummel's assistant in the preparation of bird-skins, and discharged his duties excellently.

, The rickety canoes, needless to say, lay firm and steady on the water as soon as they had been fastened together with crosswise poles and plank decks. The provisions proved too heavy a load for the double canoes, so they were stacked up on board two capacious vessels, each consisting of three single canoes made into one. Thus we bought in all fourteen canoes, and the whole proud fleet, which was to achieve the conquest of the river right down to Lop-nor, cost only about £3.

These preparations occupied the whole day, and our two tents were pitched on the river bank. Our men were out on the prowl in the Konche bazaars, and returned with another 800 chin or 1,060 lb. of flour, which was to be taken on carts, travelling by day and night, to the village of Aksupe. Among the goods purchased was a reinforcement of our supply of rice, also eggs, walnuts, rope, spare paddles and a few long poles. Nets and other fishing tackle were to be held in readiness for us at Ak-supe, but we never used them during the trip.

The poor peasants who came into Konche, and the merchants sucked dry by the war, were thankful at last to find customers who paid honestly for the goods they bought. The crew, our *suchi*, who had five silver dollars a month and everything found, received a month's wages in advance for the support of their families. It was discovered at the last moment that we had one man too few, and an eleventh *suchi*, Apak from Konche, was accordingly engaged.

It was not till late in the evening that the ranks of curious spectators began to thin, and we were at last able to retire to our tents and our night's rest.

Our hopes of being able to start at a reasonable time next

morning were not fulfilled, for innumerable little things remained to be done. We procured straw mats and poles to serve as awnings for Hummel, Chen and me on board our boats ; our boatmen came with their private luggage, which was put on board a double canoe allotted to them ; and finally Chen took his seat at the top of the bank and paid out Chinese paper *liang* (35 to a silver dollar) to our suppliers.

Not till the sun had run the greater part of its course on April 5, 1934, was everything stowed away and made fast on board, and the boatmen took their places, paddle in hand. The whole population of the little town, with the *amban* at the head, stood patiently on the bank for hours waiting to see our departure for the region whither the stream would bear us, and which no human being had penetrated before. None of them had seen anything like it in their lives, and no one could understand why we were going eastward into the desert along the new river with such a huge store of food supplies. A few merchants, who had travelled about the country far and wide with their caravans, had heard rumours that the river Kum-daria, formed thirteen years earlier, continued its course as far as the town of Tun-hwang in Kansu. It would be easy enough to go on through the desert as long as there was current enough, but how should we get back against the stream ? It would not be true to say that we ourselves did not give this question an occasional thought. But the chief thing for me was to get the whole course of the river surveyed to the point where it ended. What would happen to us after that was a question to be considered later. We had our cars, and if the ground was impracticable for them, we could in the worst event go back along the river, where we should always have water, fowl and fish at hand. There was a glimmer of adventure and risk about our journey, but that only heightened its fascination. For a little while to come our water route lay firmly fixed between our bases, and the great adventure would not begin until each new day was leading us farther and farther away from the last of them.

A few boys were sitting on the bank lapping dirty river water from their cupped hands.

" All right ? " I asked.

" All right, sir," came the answer.

" Let go ! "

Sadik, my forward paddler, put his blade upright in the river and pushed with all his might, while Hajit, astern, shoved off from the bank. The boat came free after a few jerks and glided out into the river, where the stream immediately caught her. The long-shaped island by the right bank disappeared to starboard, and the whole string of canoes, fastened together in twos and threes, followed in our wake. The cottages and grey clay houses of Konche faded away behind us, and the people, from whose silent ranks we had heard only a few isolated cries of " *Khuda yol versun !* " (God speed !)

II

OUR FIRST DAY ON THE RIVER

HOW wonderful, how glorious! No words can describe how I enjoyed it! We had spent a whole month amid a mob of Tungan soldiers, threatened with death and kept behind prison walls without a shadow of freedom. Now we were out in the wilds with no guard but the two pleasant Cossacks, for whom the boat trip was an agreeable interlude in their hard military service, and we should soon turn our backs on the last human beings in that part of the world. My days would again slip away on a river of Asia; I had preserved precious, ineradicable memories from earlier voyages of the kind. In 1899 I had drifted right down the Tarim in a boat, and in the following year I had made a canoe tour of the winding watery arms of the delta (as it then was) and mapped them. In 1907 I had made a very short but unforgettably beautiful journey, in a boat made of yaks'-hides sewn together, on the Tsang-po, or Upper Brahmaputra, in Tibet. Nine years later I travelled 600 miles down the Euphrates by boat from Jerablus to Feluja, and in 1930 I went in a Chinese junk down the river Luan-ho, from Jehol towards the coast.

And now I was starting another idyllic journey on a river in Asia. But this new journey was of greater importance than the earlier ones. It was to provide the final solution of the complex of hydrographic and quaternary geological problems which are connected with " the wandering lake ". For that reason this voyage on the Konche-daria and its continuation the Kum-daria seemed more alluring than any previous river trip.

We lived on the water. The water was our driving power and led us ever nearer our distant goal. The Konche-daria's volume of water slipped away down to the

eastward in its slowly falling, capriciously winding bed.
The waterway we were now navigating was the lowest part
of the whole drainage system which is collected in the main
river, the Tarim.   We were gliding down a river which was
to become smaller and smaller the farther east we went.   A
few days later we should pass the last small tributaries from
the Tarim, and then would begin the string of lakes and
marshes which levy tribute on the river and leave less and
less water in its main bed.

The journey of Nils Hörner and Parker C. Chen in
the winter of 1930–31 had shown the statement that the
river went as far as three days' journey from Tun-hwang
to be false.   We knew, too, where the new Lake Lop-nor
was situated, and where the Kum-daria stopped.   The only
question was whether the river was navigable as far as the
region in which Hörner and Chen had explored the arms of
its delta.   This was the exciting part of the tour of exploration on which we set out on April 5.

The grey-green water through which we were gliding
came from distant regions.   When one filled a cup from the
river, one's thirst was quenched, but the drops of water did
not tell us where they had fallen to earth from the clouds, to
pass through brooks and tributary streams and at last meet
together in the Tarim.   The Kashgar-daria, the Gez-daria
and the Raskan-daria carried water that came from the
eternal snowfields and blue-shimmering glaciers of the
Pamir, the Karakorum and Western Tibet.   The Kun-lun
mountains, through the Kara-kash and Yurun-kash, made
their combination to the Khotan-daria, which during a few
summer months joined the Tarim ; and the Tien-shan and
Khan-tengri paid their tribute to the ruling stream through
the Aksu-daria.   A good deal of the water which babbled
and eddied under our canoes had its home in the parts of the
Tien-shan where lie the head-waters of the Khaidu-gol—
the river we had crossed at the beginning of March at the
town at Kara-shahr.

So, when one drank a cup of water from the river on
which we were now to live for a time, it was not like drink-
ing from a spring, or a beck in the mountains.   There was
something especially wonderful about that water, that

draught which was a mingling of tributes from the whole of innermost Asia, the real Central Asia—that circle of mountain ranges, some of the loftiest and wildest in the world, which lies around the Tarim basin to north, west and south. I soon grew accustomed to it, but at first I could not help feeling a certain awe at the thought of that vast world of mountains, whence flowed the springs which formed that river, slowly diminishing as it moved eastward. We received greetings from, and drank a toast in return to, the distant heights on the edge of the glaciers and the eternal snowfields, where *Ovis Poli*, Marco Polo's wild sheep with the sharply curving horns, lives its free life and jumps lightly from rock to rock. I could almost hear the noise of the torrents formed by the melting snow, on whose banks the orongo antelopes and the wild yaks graze in peace and safety, and thought I could catch a dying echo of the Tibetan hunters' monotonous chants and the shots from their muzzle-loaders. In the regions where this river is still young the wild asses form their squadrons and are attacked by hungry wolves. In the meadows and pastures in the high valleys of the Tien-shan, where Kirgizes and Mongols had pitched their tents, the herds of sheep and their shepherds drank of this water, whose current was bearing us farther and farther eastward along its lowest reaches.

Into all those regions, in which the head-waters of this river sang their unceasing melodious song, I had penetrated with my horse, yak or camel caravans, and forty-four years had passed since I first knew them. This being so, it was not so strange that I felt the trip to be a renewal of acquaintance, and looked on the eddies that played on the surface of the stream as old friends. I felt completely at home among them.

" Aha ! " I greeted them, " you come from the glaciers of the Muz-tagh, from the Taghdumbash-Pamir, from those fearful heights where, in the winter of 1907–08, I began my desperate march through Tibet to Tashi-lunpo, the holy city ! Do you remember how you foamed and roared round my little white *ladaki*, as he bore me through your icy-cold gravel beds ? "

The Tarim in its different stages, like most desert rivers,

resembles human life. First an infant streamlet, babbling among the mountain mosses and lichens; but this grows into a youth, a rushing, roaring torrent, which breaks its way with irresistible force through the hardest rocks. Then, in the prime of life, it leaves the great mountain barriers behind it, and flows out over more level regions a more sober, placid stream. The river ages; its course grows ever slower and quieter. The strength it has developed is no longer increased, it diminishes. The river has passed the noon of life, as man does. Now it struggles no longer, it has become passive, begun to vegetate; it gradually decreases in size, and at last it dies and falls for ever into its grave, Lop-nor, " the wandering lake ".

But the lowest stretch of the Tarim, we were to find in a few days, was not so enfeebled by age and hardships as not to be capable of one more great achievement. It had demonstrated its power in 1921, and in this way, despite its air of feeble senility and its tranquil peace, it had been strong enough to burst the fetters of centuries and break itself a new road.

And now we were travelling down this river, following slight bends whose general tendency was to carry us to the ESE. The concave banks were sharply eroded by the water and were generally perpendicular, from 3 to 6 feet high, while on the opposite side the banks were convex and fell gradually, usually with a narrow strip of mud close to the water. Poplars grew on the banks, in small groves or solitary; not the tall Lombardy poplar, but the *Populus diversifolia* with its low, round top, which is the prevalent variety throughout Eastern Turkistan. Between the trees prickly bushes, tamarisks and reeds grew thick, and there from time to time we caught sight of a herdsman, with his flock of sheep and goats.

On the left bank we saw a hut (*satma*) of the simplest kind, built of poles, boughs, brushwood and bundles of reeds. A herdsman spent his nights there, while the sheep were protected in a fold. Opposite, a narrow channel led to a lake close by, one of those parasites which, all along our route, sap the strength of the river. When the river is full, a little current runs into the shallow lake, and the ceaseless evaporation from its surface sucks up the river water through the channel.

We glided quietly and pleasantly downstream. There was no wind ; the surface of the water was often as smooth as a canal, and sharply reflected the picturesque canoes. Some of the boats were ahead of us, some behind, but the grouping was continually changing ; sometimes I was ahead, sometimes last of all. The boatmen's song rang out from every boat. The rhythm of the monotonous, melancholy songs made the paddling easier. A paddler who sings does not get tired ; at any rate, he does not notice that he is tired until he has stopped singing. The singing starts at the first stroke, accompanied by the plash of the blades. Sometimes, when our boats were keeping quite close together, the men sang in unison, or in a kind of catch, with several boats' crews joining in the chorus. Their repertory was not large ; the same songs recurred every day and echoed across the river from morning till night. We soon knew them by heart, but we did not get tired of them, and we understood that paddling without singing was unthinkable.

I sat on a plank laid across my two canoes, leaning forward against the packing-case which served as my writing-table, and on which map-sheet no. 1 was spread out. Compass, watch and pencil were the instruments I used most. Just now and again I could take a bearing for five minutes ; as a rule our course changed every minute or two. I was, therefore, continually occupied, and was able to make an entry in my diary only when we did not change our direction for several minutes on end.

Chen was equally busy ; he was continually gauging the swiftness of the current, and the speed we could attain with the help of the paddles. The paddles counted for more than the current ; and the two added together gave the distance we had covered. It was also part of Chen's duty frequently to measure the depth of the river and here and there its breadth also.

Hummel had his laboratory on board his boat, made of three canoes made fast together. He was always busy with his plants, insects and birds, and we soon lost sight of him.

Now the sun stood just on the horizon, and suffused bushes, tree-trunks and banks with a red glow. It was six o'clock when my forward paddler, Sadik, suddenly called out " *Ördek keldi !* "

Ördek means in East Turki " wild duck ", *keldi* " has come ". Busy as I was with my map, my first hurried thought was just that Sadik wished to call my attention to the first wild duck we had seen since we had left Konche a few hours before. But when at the same time he pointed to two horsemen who were riding along the left bank in the same direction as ourselves, I realized that one of the horsemen, an old man with a white beard, was my old body servant Ördek, " Wild Duck ", who had come to see his old master once again in this life after more than thirty years.

I therefore ordered my rowers to make for the shore. We steered diagonally across the river and landed at the point where the two horsemen had dismounted. The whitebeard slithered down the bank, there hardly 6 feet high, and came on board. He approached me with tears in his eyes and held out his hands to me, hard and horny from time and toil. And it was really Ördek himself. The many years had ravaged him mercilessly. He was thin, shrunken and withered ; his forehead was deeply wrinkled, his beard and moustaches hung down to his chest in straggling tufts. He wore on his head a shabby fur cap, and was dressed in a *chapan* or East Turki coat of the usual kind, bleached and ragged, and secured about the waist by a cloth girdle. His tattered boots had evidently been worn for decades on countless toilsome journeys through desert, steppe and brushwood.

" Well, Ördek, how have you been getting on since we last met thirty-two years ago ? "

" God has protected me, sir, ever since I was in your service. I have been comfortable enough, but I gave up hope of ever seeing you again a long time ago."

" How could you know that I should be rowing down the river on this particular day ? "

" Well, it's nearly a month since someone told me, in my hut at Yangi-köl, that you were back at Korla at last, and since then I have never rested till I found you. When we parted at Kashgar thirty-two years ago, you promised to come back to us again some day. We waited and waited, and you never came. Many of your servants of those days are dead, but some are still alive. And now I am glad that my wish has been fulfilled at last."

This Ördek had entered my service in November, 1899, when I was coming down the great Tarim river by boat and, soon after, stuck fast in the winter ice. He was also one of the four men who took part in the crossing of the Taklamakan desert between Yangi-köl and Tatran, on the Charchan-daria. On the night of New Year's Eve, December 31, 1899, he sat with me and his three comrades round our little camp-fire in the heart of the great desert.

He took part likewise—in March, 1900—in our great march along the bed of the Kum-daria, then dry for 1,600 years. He played an honourable part in the discovery of the ruins of Lou-lan on March 28 in the same year. For he and one of the Cossacks went ahead to pilot the camels through the easiest passages, and was of the two harbingers who first discovered ancient wooden houses built by men's hands.

In the preliminary excavations he left behind our only spade, and was obliged to return alone from our next camp to fetch it. A sandstorm came on during the night, and Ördek lost our tracks, but pushed on courageously and was brought by a lucky chance to a ruined temple, whence he brought some beautiful wooden carvings, now preserved in the Museum of Far Eastern Antiquities in Stockholm. He did not give up until he had found the spade, and reached the caravan two days later to the great delight of myself and the others, who had almost given up hope of ever seeing him again.

Ördek's discovery of the ruined temple upset my whole programme. I realized at once that these discoveries were of the very greatest historical importance, and decided to return to the ancient city in the desert early in the next spring.

When, in the summer of 1901, I pushed forward from Northern Tibet towards Lhasa, disguised as a Mongol and accompanied by the Burjat Cossack Shagdur and the Mongolian monk Shereb Lama from Kara-shahr, we took Ördek with us so that we ourselves might be able to sleep quietly for a few nights longer in an uninhabited country, and entrust him with the care of our horses and mules by night.

We had travelled for two days without seeing a trace of a human being, and lay down to rest on the second night with minds at peace. But at midnight Ördek thrust his head in through the tent opening, frightened out of his senses, and hissed : " *Bir adam keldi !* "—" A man has come ! " We rushed out with rifles and revolvers and fired a few shots at a couple of thieves who had stolen our two best horses. Next morning Ördek had to return to our base camp alone and on foot, and arrived there quite worn out and still half-crazy after all the nocturnal shadows he had seen and taken for robbers seeking his life.

On December 29, 1901, I had seen Ördek for the last time—the faithful " Wild Duck " who had played so important a part in my life many years ago.

When I had realized that my rower, Sadik, by his " *Ördek keldi* ", meant not an ordinary wild duck, but my old travelling companion and body servant, I was struck by the similarity between the curt phrase " *Ördek keldi* " and Ördek's own ominous tidings " *bir adam keldi* ", that inclement night in Tibet when the wind wailed round the tent and tattered storm-clouds swept by like menacing dragons under the moon. The words would have been just as apt now. Then " a man " (*bir adam*) meant the scout whom a robber band sends ahead up a ravine to scare the horses into flight in the right direction. Now, after thirty-three years, the man who had come was only my harmless Ördek. As so many years had passed over his head, we could not expect too much of this renewal of our acquaintance late in life.

The other horseman who had come with Ördek to meet us on the Konche-daria was his son, also named Sadik. Ördek had married a few years after we had last met. Both he and his son had reed-built cottages at Chara, near Yangi-köl, and lived on fish, duck and wild geese, and their eggs. Several times during the war then in progress their region had been looted by Tungans, who had taken from them a few horses and some sheep.

I had had my base camp at Yangi-köl in the winter of

1899–1900. The Tarim, in whose covering of ice the boat
lay frozen in, had then been a big river formed of many
tributaries ; it collected all the streams of the whole of
Eastern Turkistan except the Konche-daria, which went its
own way and did not join the main river until lower down.
Now there was only an insignificant trickle of water left in
the old bed, and not a drop got as far as Lake Kara-koshun,
on which I had made long boat trips in the years 1896, 1900
and 1901. Where this lake, discovered by Prjevalsky in
1876–77, had been, the country was now being turned into
sheer desert. The lake itself had moved to the northward
in 1921, and it was for this new lake, the historic Lake
Lop-nor, come to life again after 1,600 years, that we were
now bound ! A safer guide could not be imagined than
the watercourse along which we were moving farther and
farther eastward.

But now we could not tarry longer. The sun was setting
in the west between the poplar trunks, and the dusk would
soon spread its veil over the river and make it harder to
take bearings along the new bends ahead of us. Ördek
clambered up the bank, got into his worn saddle and
galloped ahead with his son. He was to choose a suitable
camping-ground for us, where fuel was to be had, and
make a level surface for our tents among the trees.

The river was here flowing south-east in an almost
straight line, and before the last gleam of daylight had died
away we reached the place where the two riders had tethered
their horses and, using a couple of boughs as rakes, were
clearing away twigs and brushwood to make a camping-
ground right on the edge of the river. Counting from
Kwei-hwa, via the Etsin-gol, Hami, Turfan, Kara-shahr,
Korla and Yü-li-hsien (Konche), this camp bore the number
54. The wooded region hereabouts was called Uzun-
bulung, " Long Bend ".

Our boats' crews landed side by side in a row along the
shore, amid shouting and plashing of paddles. It was the
first time on the long boat journey that we were camping in
the wilds, but the crew were at home in their parts at once
and quickly brought tents, boxes and cooker ashore.
While the cook, Chia Kwei, was setting up his simple cook-

ing apparatus in the open air, Ördek and his son collected fuel and a few of the boatmen fetched water from the river in pails and cans.

The furniture of the tent in which Hummel, Chen, Kung and I were to spend the night consisted of our four sleeping-bags and the small boxes we required for daily use. The tent opening allowed us a view of the river through a light screen of poplars, tamarisks and undergrowth, but the shades of twilight, and then darkness, quickly fell on it. It was not long before a fire was crackling under the cooker and the water for our tea was boiling. Chia Kwei and the Cossacks had their own tent, while the crew prepared to sleep round their fire in the open air.

After the month of tension we had spent at Korla, guarded by soldiers, it was a delightful feeling to be out in God's air again and see the fires blazing in the darkness. My first map-sheet looked promising, and I rejoiced in the thought that we were now at last on the way to that capriciously wandering lake, which only one European had seen till now. That was Nils Hörner, who, with Parker C. Chen, had visited it through the desert from the eastward in the winter of 1930–31, and had made a detailed map of it.

We had no need to complain of oppressive spring heat that first day ; light, refreshing breezes blew from time to time over the river and the woods that flanked it. In the evening, sitting still and writing had become a rather chilly occupation, and at night the temperature fell to 30·6 degrees.[1] Our sheepskin sleeping-bags were splendid things to have, and when the first iron brazier of glowing coal was brought in the tent grew comfortably warm and our stiff limbs thawed.

After supper, which consisted of vegetable soup with bread and butter and cheese, rissoles, potatoes and coffee with cake, Ördek came to see me and told me stories of his life for hours. We recalled in memory the exciting days in the desert when we discovered Lou-lan, and Ördek recollected every detail of his search for the forgotten spade.

At last the embers grew pale, and the silence of the night fell upon our airy dwellings at Uzun-bulung.

[1] Fahrenheit, and in subsequent passages.

III

THE WHOLE EXPEDITION AT SAI-CHEKE

THE camp was alive at sunrise. We heard the Cossacks ordering the boats' crews to collect fresh fuel from the fallen boughs and debris, and fetch water for making tea and cooking. A pan of burning embers was brought in to keep the tent warm while we crept out of our sleeping-bags into the fresh morning air. I myself slept as unclad as I do at home, and had a big tin basin filled with hot water for washing. We were not so particular about shaving, but even that luxury was indulged in at least every third day.

We were hardly dressed when breakfast was laid on a low packing-case in the middle of the tent—tea, a hot dish, bread and butter. Rice, cooked in Chinese fashion, was a standing dish.

But our most important article of food was mutton. All the way down the Konche-daria we passed flocks every day and were able to buy sheep. Chia Kwei was skilled in preparing it according to all the rules of Swedish cookery, and also in its Turkish form of *shislik*, roasted in small pieces on spits over embers, with thin slices of fat in between.

Striking camp is much simpler on a river trip than in the desert, where everything is loaded on camels. Boxes are packed, sleeping-bags and tents rolled up, and all the baggage is stowed away in its usual places on board. Before one has time to turn round everything is ready, the paddles are thrust against the bank, the canoes glide out into the current and are carried down by the ceaseless moving stream.

A new day had begun. The peculiar landscape, silent and impressive, spread its contours and colours in the morning light. The sky was brilliantly clear. On the banks

were patches of woodland—scanty, wild, uncared for—
amid a dry undergrowth of bushes and reeds.   The sky
alone was as blue as its reflection in the river ; all else was
grey with dashes of brown and yellow.   The trees were still
leafless, but buds had begun to appear.   The sand and dust
and the sharp-cut river terraces were grey ; only the tamarisks shone out green.   The canoes themselves, and the
men's bleached, shabby *chapans* were grey, but the scattered
flotilla was nevertheless a picturesque sight, and the singing
rang out clearly in the cool air.

An arm of the Tarim ran into the river on its right bank.
It looked much larger than it was ; no current was visible
on its surface, and its tribute to the Konche-daria was
negligible.   There was not a breath of wind, and long
stretches of the river lay as clear as a mirror, reflecting the
banks and their trees.   Only the canoes, driven ceaselessly
onward by the boatmen, shattered the mirror for a time.
We often heard duck and other waterfowl rise with a beat
and rustle of wings, and sometimes a fish jumped on the
surface.

The bank terraces were 4 feet, sometimes 6 feet high.
They were perpendicular and not seldom overhanging,
thanks to the undermining power of the water.   On their
edges last year's yellowed reeds shook in the wind, and their
roots hung down like draperies trailing in the water, which
murmured cheerfully round them and made them twist and
writhe like so many snakes.

The river was more capricious now than it had been the
first day.   After one or two semicircular bends it took a
course due south, then turned again to the north, then SSE,
NNW, SSE, and NNW again, and went on to cut the
most fantastic figures, as though seeking its way towards a
distant, unknown goal.

It was enough to make one giddy.   As long as we were
going east and ESE we had the blazing sunshine right in
our eyes, and its reflection in the shining water helped to
blind us.   But then the river made a sharp turn, and before
we realized it we had the sun at our backs and all the light
effects changed.   So the sun seemed to swing to and fro all
day, first on the horizon, then higher and higher up the sky

as the hours passed. While the needle of the compass pointed north all the time, its brass case swung this way and that with my craft at the constantly recurring bends.

About noon we went ashore for half an hour or less, to give the boatmen a little rest and have some tea and cakes. This was our lunch-time rest, which we observed for the greater part of the trip. Chia Kwei was a past-master at getting a fire to burn and water to boil in a few minutes.

Along some of the bends the wood stood fairly thick along the banks and made a charming picture. Late in the afternoon five horsemen appeared on the edge of the wood on the left bank, and rode swiftly downstream as though their object had been to cut us off. A month had not passed since our motor convoy had been cut off by Tungan cavalry, who had fired on it with their carbines. Were we now to be stopped and fired at on the river too ? They might be marauders from Big Horse's broken army, out looting, and meaning to bring off a good haul in the shape of our provisions and other belongings.

" Rifles ready ! " I shouted to the two Cossacks. But this time there was no danger. Ördek's son, Sadik, who had stopped a little farther down, told us that the horsemen were peaceful merchants from Turfan who were encamped in the neighbourhood with their families and possessions, and meant to go on from Yar-cheke to Kucha.

It was beginning to get dark when we reached the camping-ground for the day, Yar-cheke. Here the caravan road from Korla to Charkhlik crosses the Konche-daria, and travellers and merchants with animals are conveyed across the river on a ferry composed of five canoes, with planks laid across them to form a deck. The ferry is drawn along a rope stretched across the river, and the ferryman has his clay hut on the right bank, where we too pitched our tents.

Meanwhile we went up to the ferryman's abode, where a carpet was spread out on the ground in the open air and tea was served in china bowls. Our host was most astonished at so unusual a visit, and did not at first know what to make of us. But he was gradually reassured and presented us with two sheep, some fresh fish and new bread, for which

Camp no. 56, April 8.

he was amply compensated in the not very reliable local paper currency. While waiting for Hummel and a few transport boats which had been left behind, we sat by a blazing camp-fire and thoroughly cross-examined the ferryman about his district, traffic, the effect of the war on trade, and the seasonal rises and falls of the river.

Our hopes of an early start next morning were dashed. In the middle of the night a violent storm set in. Hummel woke and hurried down to the boats to wake our boatmen, who were sleeping on the beach. In rough water the canoes fill by degrees, and the cargo may be destroyed or lost altogether. Now all the baggage was carried ashore, out of reach of the waves. Our tents, which were threatening to fly away, were made fast with the help of boxes and sacks, and we crept back to bed, while the waves thundered on the beach.

The next morning did not encourage us to make a start. Sand and dust filled the air, we could hardly see the river close by ; the whole country was shrouded in an impenetrable fog ; it was out of the question to defy such weather. We stayed comfortably inside our tents. The boatmen sat in the ferryman's hut playing dice with sheep's bones ; the

Cossacks kept the cook company in his temporary kitchen, and we worked up our notes, read, and took life easily.

After a temperature of 31·1 in the night the morning of April 8 was chilly, and I sat wrapped in my fur coat, drawing my map with stiff fingers. But now the weather was quiet, and we navigated new windings of the river.

Little shining yellow islands, long-shaped and covered with reeds, cropped up along the banks ; others were lumpier and suggested saffron buns. As we were passing a promontory we saw an old woman standing there with a basket, waving to us. One of our boats stopped. Her basket was full of fresh goose's eggs, which we bought with pleasure. Camp no. 56 bore the significant name Churul-mech, " the winding (river) ".

On the night of April 8–9 the thermometer fell still lower, to 28·8 degrees. While we were waiting for the camp to be struck and the boats loaded, Kung went for a ramble in the woods and calculated that there were about 21,000 trees to a square mile. Most were of moderate age, but there were some old trunks too, twisted into fantastic shapes and resembling dragons with outstretched legs and claws.

We made a short trip to the little village of Ak-supe, to which we had ordered some new canoes, oars and ropes, as well as flour, to be sent from Konche and Tikenlik. There were about seventy families living in Ak-supe ; they were mostly immigrants from Chara and grew wheat. They had moved to these parts for the sake of the water when the Tarim dried up in their neighbourhood. The bottom of the irrigation canal was now 3 feet above the surface of the river, but in September and October the water streamed into it and was spread over the fields. This afforded us valuable proof that irrigation was a practical possibility lower down the river.

The little community at Ak-supe even had its school-house, which was more like a *satma*, as they call the draughty huts built by the herdsmen. Sali Bek, the head-man of the village, a big, burly, dignified Turki, came to call on us with presents in kind. He told us that the Tarim now joined the Inchike-daria at Eshek-öldi and that the water then came to the Konche-daria from the Chong-köl in three arms. The river was at its highest in September and October and at its lowest at the end of the summer.

On April 10 we woke to find a *sarik-buran* or " yellow storm "—in other words, a pretty high wind, though not to be compared with a *kara-buran* or " black storm ". That day, too, the swift wind came from the eastward. We defied it and set out. It was a rather rough, noisy and exciting trip. The waves thumped against the boats' sides and came on board, and I was soon sitting in a foot-bath. Everything was drenched with spray. Under the lee of the shore it was beautifully quiet, as the perpendicular erosion terrace and its reeds gave us shelter, but when the river made a bend to the eastward, and we passed a last cape and came out into water where we were at the mercy of the wind, the waves began their dance again, and the paddlers exerted themselves to the uttermost so as to get into shelter again as soon as possible.

We sat wrapped in furs, and yet we were cold. We must get warm for a little while. On the left bank were dead, dry poplars and tamarisks. Why should we not land, make a fire, and have some tea and bread and goose's eggs with salt ? These daily rests for lunch were pleasant breaks in the journey and the rather exacting map-making work. But we could only allow ourselves forty minutes. When we had warmed ourselves up well both inside and outside, we hurried back to the boats and pushed off. Our paddlers were clever in avoiding the treacherous sandbanks which lay in ambush below the surface and betrayed their presence by a yellowish tinge in the water. Just now and again we went aground, but quickly got off again. Sometimes we glided past whole poplar trunks which had been plunged into the river by the undermining power of erosion and had stuck in some shallow in midstream. Other debris, such as dry reeds and tamarisk boughs, had clung to the stranded poplar and its branches, and gradually a little island had been formed, beside which the stream babbled melodiously. Wild geese flew proudly past above our heads. The sun set in a mist looking like an uncut ruby. At our camping-ground, Aghzi-tar-tokai, " the woodland at the narrow mouth ", Kung counted 27,000 trees to a square mile, and

found that their diameter just above the ground averaged
9 inches.

The minimum temperature on the night of April 10–11
sank to 27 degrees—surprisingly cold for so late in the
spring. It was more like the approach of autumn. But
the day was fine and clear ; it brought, too, an enlivening
break in our otherwise rather monotonous voyage.

We had negotiated a few bends when the river suddenly
seemed to make an effort and extend itself in an almost
straight line for a good way to the ENE. On the left bank,
a considerable distance ahead, we sighted several white
tents among tamarisks on sand dunes and also a number of
men, mounted and on foot, and horses.

" That's Sai-cheke ! " my boatmen Sadik and Hajit explained. It was there, at " the river bend in the gravel
desert ", that we had fixed our rendezvous with the rest of
the expedition.

Now Sadik and Hajit paddled as never before. The
paddles were like bows at full stretch, the water foamed
about the canoe's stem, and our craft sped forward along
the stream like a duck scared into flight. The details of the
crowded canvas in the background stood out clearer and
clearer. Some of the men were standing in a group on the
top of the bank, others were hurrying down to the landing-
place. There they all were, all our fellows—Bergman, a
manly, erect, bearded figure ; Yew with his American
spectacles ; Georg, tall and smiling ; the fair, sun-burnt
Effe ; Serat and Jomcha and a few Chinese boys.

As I stepped ashore, Effe and the others joined in a
resounding " hurrah ! " and the gramophone played a
march. There were many handshakes, and we filed up to
the camp among the dunes, watched by merchants travelling
from or to Turfan. We were invited into Bergman's tent,
placed in a well-chosen spot on an eminence, with a magnificent view upstream—the way we had come. Coffee and
bread and butter were served, over which we spoke of our
voyage and they of their laborious journey over desert and
sand. We saw the cars, and in the evening Georg held a
reception in his tent. In the middle of the tent a fire burned
in a *tolgan*—the double iron ring which holds the cooking-

pot. The orange light fell upon weather-beaten faces, Swedish and Chinese, Russian, Turki and Mongolian. There sat the white-bearded Ördek, with the glow full on his face; Sali Bek was there too. Tea was handed round, and there was lively talk in several languages. It was a picturesque scene, and its vivid colouring was softened by the smoke which all the time rose from the *tolgan*.

When I walked back to my tent, the left bank of the river presented a spectacle unusual in that usually so lifeless region, where, as a rule, the smoke from a shepherd's camp-fire was but rarely seen. Now no fewer than sixteen fires were burning in our immediate neighbourhood, like a string of pearls along the bank upstream. Turki merchants from Kucha and Turfan were encamped there. The brilliant illumination reminded one of the sea-front in a little seaside town. Downstream only five fires were to be seen, round which our servants and boatmen were having their evening meal.

"River bend in the gravel desert"—the very name shows that at this point the desert reaches the river and that the stifling dry wilderness, where the silence of death reigns, stretches out its hands towards the life which is nourished by the waters of the Konche-daria. It was not the first time I had encamped at Sai-cheke. I had been there thirty-eight years earlier, on March 23, 1896, but then I had with me a small caravan of camels and horses.

We remained at Sai-cheke for more than a day to organize the expeditions which had been planned for the immediate future. Only Chen and I were to go to Lop-nor. Hummel was travelling slowly, and wanted to stop at good places for his collections. Kung stayed behind to take part in a motor trip to Bujentu-bulak and Altmish-bulak, and possibly the Su-lo-ho, and back to Lop-nor, whence the motorists were to help Chen and me to return to headquarters.

We had six double boats and ten paddlers. The baggage was packed and stowed away, and the boats prepared for a long voyage. The double canoe on which the bags of flour were loaded was decked in with stakes laid side by side. The two biggest canoes were bound firmly together and in them were placed seven large petrol drums, each containing

150 chin (one chin = 1⅓ lb.) which, in order to reduce the
load of the motor-lorries, we were taking with us downstream to the expedition's future headquarters near the
meridian of the Yardang-bulak spring.

The cooking apparatus, the cook, Chia Kwei, and
Gagarin, occupied the third double canoe ; in the fourth we
had sheep and provisions. The fifth and sixth were Chen's
and mine, and these remained unchanged.

On the morning of April 13 our two provision boats and
the kitchen and petrol boats went off ahead of us downstream. Hummel gave Chen a little travelling medicine-
chest and some medical instructions, and finally we had a
coffee party down by the landing-place, where all eight
members of the expedition assembled to say good-bye.
This was the last time we were all together. After that our
ways parted, and at our final departure from Sinkiang for
China two members were absent, Hummel and Bergman.
Even at the next meeting-place, the headquarters at Yardang-bulak, some were missing. The motor convoy was
to start for that camp on the following day. It consisted of
Bergman, Yew, Kung, Georg and Effe, the Mongols and
the Chinese servants, except Chia Kwei, who was cook to
Chen and myself, and Li, who belonged to Hummel's party.

All aboard ! cast off ! good-bye and good luck ! A last
handshake. We were going to meet the unknown. Would
our boats be caught fast in reed-bound lakes and marshes ?
Would the cars be stopped by impassable sand, ravines or
boulders ? No one knew. The metropolis we had con-
jured up for a few days on the river bank at Sai-cheke was
now to vanish, and the silence of the desert would fall once
more over the dunes and tamarisks.

IV

THE LAST DAY ON THE KONCHE-DARIA

I MAY here say something about the volume of water in the Konche-daria in the spring of 1934. The measurements were very carefully and exactly carried out by Parker C. Chen, who used for the purpose Lyth's hydrometric float with electric transmitter.

The river Khaidu-gol, which comes from the Yuldus valley and falls into Lake Baghrash-köl, carried, on February 28, 1,222 cubic feet of water a second. That the Konche-daria at Korla, on March 5, carried only 695 cubic feet proves that the canals above Korla deprive the river of a very considerable part of its volume. The result of the measurement at Yar-cheke on April 7 is very interesting, for the river was found to be carrying a volume of 2,285 cubic feet ; the size of this figure proves that it receives a handsome contribution from the Tarim. At Sai-cheke on April 12 the volume of water was 2,615½ cubic feet, revealing yet another minor contribution from the Tarim. The river at Sai-cheke was 73 yards wide, the maximum depth was 17 feet 10 inches, and the greatest velocity 3 feet 7 inches per second. This volume of 2,615½ cubic feet per second was the highest we measured. To judge from the high-water marks on the banks and the information we received, the volume of water is much greater in the autumn (September and October) than in the spring, and probably amounts to 5,000 cubic feet or more a second, of which by far the greater part comes from the high water on the Tarim.

Thus all this water, which runs out into the desert below Sai-cheke, is wasted. It was our task to investigate means of controlling it and utilizing it for the benefit of men. The population of the oases of Eastern Turkistan is almost entirely dependent on the water which streams down from the surrounding mountains—the Kun-lun, Pamir and Tien-shan—and is spread over fields and gardens through in-numerable *ariks*, or canals. The volume of water carried through the desert to Lop-nor down the Konche-daria and its continuation the Kum-daria, which has come to life again since 1921, could, if controlled by irrigation, provide many thousands of people with their daily bread.

We started on April 13 from Sai-cheke, that picturesque metropolis which our visit had caused to spring up among the dunes on the bank of the Konche-daria, and voyaged downstream into the unknown as along the most perfect high road. Long-shaped reed-clad islands lay in a string along the banks, where the reeds also formed wide yellow fields. Wild geese, duck and other waterfowl often rose with a rustling of wings and shrill cries of warning. As we passed a little overgrown islet one of the boatmen sprang ashore and came back with half a dozen duck's eggs. When a hen bird rises from a patch of reeds in the river, it is always likely that she comes from a nest containing eggs.

We heard a couple of shots from Erashin's gun among the thick brushwood. He had wounded a wild boar, but it got away.

Black clouds of smoke rose from a burning bed of rushes a short way ahead. I had a shock ; I wondered if the petrol boats had caught fire. No, that was all right ; they were behind us. I gave strict orders that our two inflammable boats should always be moored at a respectful distance from the camp-fire and to the weather side of it.

At times the air was still and the river as smooth as a mirror. Then the gnats danced round us, and we defended ourselves as best we could with the help of mosquito veils and cigarettes. We pitched our camp on the left bank, among scattered trees and a jungle of fallen trunks and branches, as the dusk was spreading its pall over the river. Chia Kwei set up his cooker in the open air, and soon a fire was crackling under the pots containing our supper. Chen and I had a strong lamp burning in our tent, and by its light we compared notes for the day. The river was unex-pectedly deep that day, as much as 26 feet !

Woodpeckers were tapping busily at the tree-trunks

when we cast off on the morning of April 14. We slipped along at a good pace through the clear, greenish water between wooded banks, and again we passed close to a string of little islands, thickly covered with reeds. At Sepe Niasigi, where we encamped on the right bank, we had a visit next morning from Ala Kulu, the *bek* or headman from Chara. He brought with him 260 chin of wheat flour, five new paddles and 27 fathoms of fishing-net. He entertained us to tea, bread and eggs in a *satma*, or shepherd's hut, on the river bank, and presented us with a sheep. One or two of his companions were from Yangi-köl and still remembered my visit to their home; thirty-four years' poverty and struggle for life had not obliterated it from their memory. Among the visitors were also Ördek's wife and daughter-in-law.

A little farther on, at a place called Kuyush, we were met by another village headman, Yusup Bek, who regaled us with *shislik*.[1] Among those who accompanied him were old Khodai Kulu, who took part in my march along the dry river-bed in the spring of 1900. I recognized him easily, although he had become wrinkled and bent. It was always a pleasure both to my old servants and to myself to meet after so many years and to recall our adventures in old times.

Still farther down we halted again at the point where the Dilpar arm pays the Konche-daria a tribute of scarcely 27 cubic feet a second. But the Konche-daria, here 65 yards wide, still carried a volume of water of 2,563 cubic feet a second, its depth was 23 feet and the speed of the current 3 feet 11 inches.

At that day's camp, Dutte, we numbered no less than thirty, including crew, visiting *beks*, herdsmen and Ördek's womenfolk.

On April 16 we measured two more tributaries, the Gurgur and Ak-bash, carrying respectively 54 and 13½ cubic feet of water; they came from the Inchike-daria, whose water originates in the Tien-shan and runs past Shah-yar and south of Kucha. The Gurgur arm forms a roaring waterfall 2 feet 5 inches high. Below it a pictur-

[1] See page 22.

Waterfall on the Gurgur.

esque wooden bridge crosses the tributary, which is a good
3 feet higher in autumn. All these little arms are said to
come, in their last stage, from a lake or marsh, the Chong-
köl. The Yarkend-daria, or Tarim proper, runs to Yangi-
köl and almost dries up there during the summer.

Close to our camping-ground for the day lived an old
man of seventy-six named Islam, who had spent sixty years
there, as his father had done before him. He owned forty
sheep, twenty cows, three horses and some donkeys, but
lived mainly on fish and eggs. He was handsomely paid,
like everyone else, for the fish he presented to us.

A fresh breeze was whistling through the reeds as we
went on downstream between scanty, ill-nourished poplars.
The river made the wildest bends. Sometimes we were
not far from completing a circle when the river swung off
again at the last moment in the opposite direction, away
from the loop in which it had been wasting so much time.
Again herdsmen and other wanderers came down to the
river and gave us eggs and fish. But these well-intentioned
visits took up time, and we longed to get away to regions
where no human beings could any longer disturb us.

We had just passed a patch of wood called " the seven
poplars " when we heard a dull thundering noise ahead, the
river narrowed to a width of only 20 yards, and the current
grew swifter. We landed to make a reconnaissance, and to
avoid being shipwrecked in what might be furious rapids.
This done, I ordered full speed ahead and led our fleet to the

critical point. The roaring grew louder, the tension increased; our paddlers yelled and uttered shrill cries of warning. But my double canoe was amid the rapids already, and
white-crested waves were dancing round us. My paddlers
understood that it was neck or nothing now ! They
kept the boats' course parallel with the banks and guided
us forward between treacherous shallows and rocks, know-
ing that if we got broadside on to the stream the canoes
would fill in a moment and inevitably be wrecked.

Just there the river executed a very sharp S-shaped
double bend, and great care was necessary. The waves
swept into the canoes, there was a splashing and hissing all
round us ; each moment we expected to run aground and
capsize. The roaring of the torrent drowned the cries
behind us. But we were nearly through now. The white
crested waves grew smaller, the river grew wider again and
the water quieter. The whole thing had happened in a
minute. Next moment my boat was safe and alongside the
bank. There we saw the others struggling with their
paddles, seeking a way through between the insidious rocks
and shallows. Only the petrol boat went aground. When
the others had got clear of the rapids they returned along
the bank to the stranded craft, unloaded a few petrol drums,
got the boat off, and reloaded it in calmer water.

The Ak-bash, a tributary from the Inchike-daria, entering the Konche-daria.

My canoe in the rapids, April 17.

We pitched camp at Kalpuk-ochogu, on the left bank. All the men were still shaken up by the exciting voyage down the rapids, and wondered if we should encounter more places like it. The canoes could hardly weather swifter rapids than those at " the seven poplars ". Shepherds came and gave us a sheep. Now we had seven. One was slaughtered in the evening, and we celebrated our successful passage of the rapids.

A cool east wind was blowing in our faces as we pushed off on the morning of April 18. When gliding along in the shade of terraces from 6 to 9 feet high, one felt downright cold, and was glad to have a light sheepskin coat at hand. But as the day advanced it grew hot—as much as 77 degrees. Isolated, sickly poplars grew here and there, and where the terraced banks overhung the stream, their roots trailed in the water. We had cackling fowls and bleating sheep on board some of our boats, and the flotilla suggested a farm gone adrift. The boatmen sang, often in catches. The rhythmical song helped the paddling. From north to north-east we could see the Kuruk-tagh in faint outline, but distinctly.

It was nearly five when we landed at Tömenpu, a very interesting place on the right bank of the Konche-daria. There a terrace 12 feet high runs right along the edge of the bank; it presents a curious appearance because it has been excavated in four parallel passages which resemble yawning gateways. Below this rampart a dam was built across the river four years ago at the orders of the *amban*, for it was just at this point that the Konche-daria, in 1921, left its old bed and opened a new way for itself along the dry bed of the Kuruk- or Kum-daria, the bed which I had followed and mapped in 1900. In the course of a few years practically the whole river had gone over to the bed of the Kum-daria, and the Kona-daria, " old river ", which had previously run to Tikenlik, had almost dried up. Only in the autumn did some water still come this way to Tikenlik, and this was not nearly enough for agriculture.

The vain idea was cherished that men's hands could conquer one of nature's caprices, and compel the Konche-daria to return to its old bed and, as before, water the fields around Tikenlik. Four hundred men were called up from Charkhlik, Tikenlik, Yangi-köl, Konche and Ullug-köl, and in the summer, when the river was at its lowest, 500 stout poplar stakes were driven into the bed of the river, forming two lines across the stream. The river at this point, on April 19, 1934, was 75 yards wide; its maximum depth was 11 feet 7 inches, the maximum velocity of the current 2 feet 2 inches, and the volume of water 2,165 cubic feet a second. The stakes in each line stood closely packed, but there was an interval of a few yards between the lines, and the 400 workmen had, with feverish haste, to fill the gap with earth, reeds, roots, boughs and debris. When the work was completed, the river would meet this imposing barrier and be compelled to turn away to the right and seek an outlet through the four passages which had been dug in the high bank—in short, return obediently to its old bed.

With clatter and noise, yells and shouts the 400 hurried to the dam to fill the gap between the rows of stakes, their barrows fully loaded with earth and rubble. The swarms of men suggested a great battle-field; they raced and tumbled, rose, emptied their loads and hurried back for new. But all was in vain. The water trickled between the stakes and washed away the filling; and when the high

View NE from the easternmost passage at Tömenpu, April 17.

water came in autumn, the whole dam was swept away and the massive stakes hurled on one side like matches.

The attempt had been repeated since then, the desperate struggle with the river, but with no greater success.   Only on the left bank are 10 yards of shattered fragments of the dam still to be seen, and on the top of the block of clay between the dug passages on the right bank there still stand ten huts, in which workmen used to live.   The bottoms of the four passages are about 6 feet above the surface of the river in spring, and in the autumn some water goes through them to the old bed and Tikenlik.

This attempt, made only a few years ago, to harness the river, and compel its masses of water to follow the laws of man and not those of nature, was not the first in the history of our stream.   An old Chinese document called " The Classic of the Waters ", dealing with rivers and water-courses, tells of a hard fight on the lower course of the Kum-daria—evidently an attempt to force the river water into an irrigation canal by means of a dam and so utilize it for the field crops.

This work tells of a Chinese general called So Mai, hailing from Tun-hwang, who became instructor to the people

of Lou-lan in the art of irrigation—in that very region to
which we were now on our way. About A.D. 260 he
entered the town of Lou-lan at the head of a thousand men
from Suchow and Tun-hwang, with the intention of estab-
lishing a Chinese military colony there.

So Mai enlisted men even from neighbouring countries
to build a dam across the bed of the Chu-pin river, the
estuary of the so-called Southern River—i.e. the lower
Tarim. But on the day when the river was to be dammed,
the water hurled itself against the obstruction with such
violence that the waves overthrew the dam.

Then So Mai spoke sternly : " When Wang Tsun raised
his sign of office, the dams of the Hwang-ho sank not under
the water ; when Wang Pau gave proof of his complete
sincerity, the river Huto stayed its course. The divinities,
which are stronger than the power of water, are the same
to-day as of old."

Then So Mai in person said prayers and offered sacri-
fices. But the water did not fall. Then he drew up his
soldiers in order of battle and armed them. They beat
drums and uttered fierce war-cries, brandished their swords
and discharged their arrows. So they fought a great battle
with the river for three days. Then the water drew back
and sank. After that the river served for irrigation and
produced fertility. The inhabitants regarded this as a
miracle. So Mai sowed wide fields and in three years'
time harvested a million bushels of wheat. His prestige
made him revered in foreign lands.

So the old story runs. The kingdom of Lou-lan had
existed long before So Mai's time. But the manuscripts I
found in the years 1900 and 1901 dated from just that time
(265–310) when the energetic Chinese general was estab-
lishing his military and agricultural colony and stimulating
the fertility of the soil—certainly by more effective means
than the beating of drums and the clash of arms.

Tömenpu was an extremely interesting place. It was
our last camp on the Konche-daria, and there we saw the
last groves of living poplars. Next day we were to set off
down the Kum-daria, the Sand River, the new river. The

View SE from Tömenpu, April 19. Pool in foreground.

whole of our voyage right down to Lop-nor was to be through desert, with no living trees and almost empty of herds and huts. We were to be the first to navigate the Kum-daria and map it in the minutest detail; and I was to see again, with an emotion tinged with melancholy, a region through which I had travelled with camels thirty-four years earlier. We eagerly awaited the coming day and the abrupt transformation of the scenery caused by the river's change of course.

V

THE FIRST DAYS ON THE KUM-DARIA

A T Tömenpu, then, we left the point where the river, newly formed since 1921, breaks out of the Konche-daria's old bed to seek a new route into the desert—or, more accurately, to return to its ancient bed, the classic channel down which water flowed in the Christian era and as late as the beginning of the fourth century A.D.

At Tömenpu, where the river forks, and where the vain effort was made to force the water back into the bed of the Konche-daria so that it might continue to water the Tiken-lik fields, I closely questioned our boatmen and the *beks* who came to meet us about the characteristics of the river and to what extent it was navigable. No one knew any-thing about it; no one had been on it in a canoe. One prophet of evil thought that we should meet with dangerous rapids, in which we should be wrecked, and lakes and marshes overgrown and choked with new reeds in which we should be caught fast and be unable to escape.

On the morning of April 20 we took leave of Isa, Habdul and Emin Bek, the three chiefs—who had secured us four new boatmen—and of the Konche-daria, and pushed off from the bank on one of the most interesting and, in its geographical results, the most valuable expeditions it has ever been granted me to carry out in Eastern Turkistan.

The chieftains and their people stood on the bank and followed our vanishing flotilla with wondering, anxious looks. They probably thought that we were doomed to destruction. But their hopes followed us too, for they had implored me to lay before the Nanking Government their prayers for help in mastering the capricious river and radic-ally improving the local irrigation.

Hardly had we pushed off when we saw the most striking

change in the river landscape! We were gliding between
the last living poplar groves, which raised their crowns of
spring greenery high over the treacherous stream. But to
the south-east, along the route we were to follow, not
another single green poplar was to be seen. The change
from woodland river to desert river was effected in just one
bend. When we had left that behind, we were surrounded
by bare desolate country; the river was entering the flat,
yellow Lop desert. It grew wider, some 160 yards, and
shallower. The greatest depth we noted on that day's
voyage was 13 feet. The banks were sharply defined and
fell perpendicularly to the river. Sand dunes and tamarisk
mounds were cleft by erosion, and the roots of tamarisks
and reeds hung down like curtains into the gently murmuring water. A grave-like silence surrounded us. It was
disturbed only by the scuffling noise when whole blocks of
sand and clay fell down from the top of the bank. The
water, which in the Konche-daria was clear and light-green,
now became turgid and assumed a grey-green hue, caused
by the continuous landslip from the banks. A little grove
of moribund poplars was drawing new life from the stream's
return. Here and there we saw dead trunks, grey and dried
up, and in midstream branches and twigs, stranded on
hidden sandbanks, stuck up out of the river. About half
the bed of the river was occupied by sandbanks, exposed
when the stream, as at that time, was low.

On the banks were wide yellow beds of rushes, now to
our left, now to our right. Late in the afternoon the river
cut through a belt of bare sand dunes, about 20 feet high.
The stream washed their feet, and the sand slipped down to
be carried away by the current and form new sandbanks.
On the top of a dune three graceful antelopes were sil-
houetted against the sky. They stood still for a few
seconds, paralysed with astonishment; then they made off
with elastic bounds, as swift as the wind, and disappeared.
Our dog, Tagil, who followed us on the right bank, soon
gave up trying to catch an antelope. Apart from them not
a sign of life was seen all day; not a bird, not a fish. In
places there was no vegetation either for some distance, and
then we were surrounded by sheer desert on all sides.

Sand dunes on the right bank, April 20.

The river had a tendency to expand into wide, lake-like stretches, in which it was hard to follow the channel, and to find one's way at all.   The banks ahead of us seemed to form solid land; but the boatmen had a flair for keeping their course, and I would find myself quite unexpectedly gliding round a promontory, beyond which a new reach opened.   The river ran straight for some distance.   The air was hazy.   Sky and river seemed to melt into one.   One could imagine that one was rowing down a gulf towards the boundless ocean.   I continually had to use my glasses.   Twilight was falling, misty and murky.   The sun was sinking in a fog.   Before it grew dark we landed on the right bank, pitched our tents and lighted our evening fires.

I casually mentioned just now a passenger who has not yet been introduced to the reader.   The dog Tagil was an Asiatic wild dog of no particular breed, such as the shepherds use to watch over their sheep.   I remembered the river trip on the Tarim when we had dogs on board, and it occurred to me that we ought to take a four-legged companion with us this time, too.   How well I remembered my two dogs on the boat on the Tarim, Dovlet and Yoldash, those comrades who cheered my solitude and gave me so much pleasure.   During the heat of the day they lay panting in the cool shade below deck, but when the sun sank towards the horizon, they came up and put some life into the proceedings in the tent which was set up forward.   If they caught sight of hares, antelopes, or sheep with their shepherds and watch-dogs, they jumped into the river and swam ashore to give chase or offer battle.   Then they would

follow the boat, running along the bank till they were tired
out and swam back to us, and were grateful when someone
took them by the scruff of the neck and hauled them on
board. I remember, too, my sorrow that autumn morning
when Dovlet died and was buried on the banks of the
Tarim. I felt that I had lost a good and faithful friend.

So now I was seeking another Yoldash or " comrade ".
But at Korla we sought in vain. The dogs in the war zone
were as starved as everyone else. Not till we reached
Yü-li-hsien (Konche) did we succeed in getting hold of two
sheep-dogs. Hummel took over one of them, yellowish-
white in colour; the other, tawny or, in Turkish, *tagil*,
came with us to Lop-nor. And he was called Tagil as long
as he remained with us.

Tagil was a most intelligent dog. He knew his part from
the very beginning, and understood that it was his duty to
keep guard round the tent and by the boats. He had a keen
discrimination and could distinguish between friends and
enemies. Unlike my Tibetan dog, Takkar—a savage, dangerous brute who, after he had become my companion,
showed an implacable hatred of his own two-legged coun-
trymen—Tagil was always friendly towards the shepherds
we met from time to time, and understood that they wished
us no harm. Although I was as unlike an East Turki
shepherd as anyone could be, he treated me with the greatest
amiability from the first moment, and we soon became very
good friends.

He was big, with hairy, clipped ears, a bushy, turned-up
tail and a coat which became less and less necessary to him
as the hot and sunny summer days approached. Then he
used to leave his place on board one of the luggage
boats, jump into the water for a refreshing cold bath, and
follow us along the bank. I shall tell in a later chapter of
the great presence of mind he showed in a—for a dog—
rather complicated affair.

Meanwhile our first day on the newly risen historic river
had come to an end. I was happy and grateful to feel that
after Norin's valuable reconnaissance on the left bank and
Ambolt's precise astronomical and geodetic observations, I
was the first to map the whole course of the river and see

with my own eyes that my predictions of 1901 had really proved correct. This gave me a feeling that the Kum-daria, dry and wet, was *my* river. It was almost awe-inspiring to follow its turbid waters into the heart of that desert which I had been fortunate enough to conquer thirty-four years earlier. Our boats were gliding over my own camels' tracks in the now pathless river-bed. These had indeed been obliterated by thirty-four years of hard easterly storms, but yet it was here, just here, that my caravan had gone in March, 1900. Now every day would bring its new excitement. Should we succeed in pushing forward with our boats to the river's end, or would the pessimists prove right?

The sky cleared up towards nightfall, and the eternal stars shone out over our camp. The smoke rose up towards them from the cook's and boatmen's fires, and the mysterious infinity of the silent desert encompassed us about.

A new day dawned with a piercing wind. We pushed off, and missed the woods of the Konche-daria, which had sheltered us from the blast. Now the country was bare and fearfully desolate. The banks were as much as 6 feet high, and we sought shelter beneath them as far as we could.

In a few hours we reached the point where the caravan route from Turfan to Tikenlik crosses the river, and there we were near Ying-p'an, where the Chinese had a fort and a temple on the old " Silk Road " a few thousand years ago. On February 20, 1928, at Turfan, I had heard for the first time that the road from that town to Tikenlik crossed, near Ying-p'an, a river so large that a ferry-boat had to be used. And then I knew that the waters of the Tarim system had returned to their old bed, the bed which farther eastward is split up into a delta north of the ancient city of Lou-lan.

As it was blowing pretty hard it suited us excellently to land at the Turfan road ferry station, on the left bank. A few canoes lay on the shore, and the ferryman, Osman, came and bowed to us as we landed. He told us that our motor convoy had lain at the entrance to the Shindi valley for three days, and had thence sent letters to the *beks* of Tikenlik and to me. He had left the letter from Bergman to me on the right bank, so he crossed the river in a canoe in the bitter wind to fetch it. He was soon back again, and looked for the letter inside his *chapan* and his belt, but could not find it. The wind and stream had evidently carried it away !

Chen wrote to the *beks* of Tikenlik in Chinese, asking them to send to us at Yardang-bulak 900 chin of flour and thirteen sheep.

The wind increased to half a gale. I put on my fur coat as I sat at my writing-table on board the boat. White horses chased one another across the river and threatened to swamp our boats. It was not worth while to travel in such weather ; the boats would fill and sink. We decided to camp.

A few riders with a small caravan loomed up through the dust on the top of the right bank, evidently merchants bound for Turfan. They made signs to Osman that they wanted to cross. He went out in his canoe and tacked about a bit, but returned immediately. The waves were washing over the bulwarks. He went out again and wrestled with the white horses which the boat's stem split in two. At last he succeeded in getting over with the boat half filled with water.

At dusk a man named Rozi Ahun arrived with a quantity of flour for us from Tikenlik. He told us that the village had been almost without food since a hundred Turki soldiers, and later 500 White Russians, had been there, bound from Turfan to Korla. We had witnessed the Russians' arrival at Korla. The Turkis had not paid for what they had taken, but the Russians had given 260 *liang* for 100 chin. The price had now fallen to 250. At Bugur we had given 45 *liang* for the same weight of flour. In June and July, at Urumchi, the price rose to 14,000 *liang* ! But then the paper value of the *liang* had fallen from 30 to a silver dollar to 400.

Rozi brought a bushel of flour from Yssyp Ahun, son of the old Kirguj Pavan who had been my guide in this region thirty-eight years before. Another greeting and remembrance from old times !

April 22 was calm and clear after a stormy night. The river widened to 200 yards, and the maximum depth for the day was only 9 feet 9 inches. But the stream was as a rule very shallow. The double canoe which carried our store of flour, and had only one paddler, grounded on a bank. The paddler pushed with his blade with all his might ; the boat slid off, but the paddle stuck, the man lost his balance and fell, and there he stood on the sandbank, solitary and abandoned, while his boat continued its voyage downstream on its own account. We roared with laughter at his misadventure, while one of the others came gliding by and saved him. My boat too went aground, and Chen's bore down on us swiftly and ran into us. We swung round in a circle and got off. The carcass of a black cow was stranded in the middle of the river.

The banks were desolate, but in a little while dried-up tamarisk mounds and still living bushes reappeared among yellow reed-beds. Three shepherds were resting there with their flock. They were frightened and tried to make off, but we reassured them and bought two fat sheep. I asked a young shepherd what the name of the river was, and he replied clearly and distinctly Kum-daria, " Sand River ", not Kuruk-daria or " Dry River ", as it was generally called on my previous visit, when there was not a drop of water in its bed. But he could not tell us where it went.

A few dead, withered poplars still stood on the bank like crosses on graves. A high terrace on the left side almost overhung the stream. My boat went by its foot all right, but just as the next boat was passing a huge block broke loose and plunged into the river with a thud and a splash. The boat and its two paddlers had a regular drenching. There were yells, shouts of warning and excitement, but still more amusement and laughter.

The river ran straight for long stretches to the SE and ESE. The sun was setting behind us, before us reed-beds appeared as yellow streaks, and above them sand dunes reared their heads like giant dolphins.

In the evening we had a quite adventurous landing. Ahead of us the river divided and went on each side of an island. My boat went badly aground. Two of the others passed us and landed out of sight on the northern shore of the island. Three boats had stopped on the right bank a good way above us. When we had got off we paddled to them against a rather strong current and reached them as dark was falling. It grew pitch dark, and the kitchen boat, with Chia Kwei, the Cossack Erashin and two paddlers, was still missing. They signalled to us with gun-shots from a long way upstream. We replied by lighting a fire on the bank. Evidently they were aground and could not get off in the dark. They stayed there all night and slept on board. The worst part of it was that the whole kitchen section was on board their boat. But Chen, ever provident, had a supply of grape nuts, cocoa and marmalade in his boat, so that we fared excellently without our admirable cook.

Next morning we assembled our scattered flotilla, and the kitchen boat turned up along with the others. We chose the left arm of the river, which follows the gravel plain, which the Turkis call *sai*, at the southern foot of the Kuruk-tagh. The arm was narrow—only 30 yards across—and ran straight and deep as a canal between tamarisk mounds, blocks of clay and reeds. On the right bank we saw a *satma* or shepherd's hut, and a sheepfold.

Four wild pigs, and soon after five more, dashed away as we came spinning past the reed-bed in which they had been grubbing for roots in undisturbed peace. There was a creaking and crashing of dry reed-stems as they set off in wild flight and disappeared out of range of Erashin's gun.

The terraces along the banks were 10 feet high. For several yards debris was sliding down into the water and causing quite a sea, rather disagreeable for the nearest boats.

We passed a sharp-cut promontory where an arm joined the stream from the right. An eddying whirlpool was formed at its base, and the boatmen had to be careful, but we got safely past and glided into another arm scarcely 40 yards wide, and here we pitched camp at twilight—as usual, at a place where dry timber was to be had.

April 24 was an exciting day. In the morning our boat-men had discovered the tracks of motor wheels not far from the left bank, and the footprints of five men who had been out scouting. So the motor convoy had passed, and it was not far to the neighbourhood of my old spring Yardang-bulak, which was our rendezvous.

About four o'clock the flotilla was gliding quite peacefully down the river, there a hundred yards wide, when the
continuous singing was suddenly interrupted by a lively
discussion among the men. Chia Kwei and Erashin were
standing up and looking north-eastward over the grey *sai*,
the edge of which we could see about 500 yards from the
clay mounds of the yellow alluvial plain.

" What is it ? " I asked.

" We can see cars, two tents and several men," they
answered.

They wanted to land and reconnoitre, but Sadik declared
that it was only tamarisk mounds they saw. But through
my glasses I could make out a camp, and a little later the men
in the other boats shouted that there was a group of men on
the left bank. There was no longer any doubt now ; this
was the new headquarters not far from Yardang-bulak.

My two boatmen planted their legs wide apart, plunged
their blades perpendicularly into the water and pushed with
all their might. The double canoe flew forward like a wild
duck, the foam hissing about its bows ; I expected to hear
a paddle snap at any moment. The river at this point runs
straight NNE for a long way, and our fellows could be seen
more and more plainly, waiting for us to arrive. Cheers
were raised and caps waved. We glided quickly forward to
the bank, where the river was deep, and ran against a little
promontory with such violence that Sadik, who was the
forward paddler, lost his balance and fell head-first into the
river. He disappeared under water, but came up in a
second and crawled up on to the bank, where he shook
himself like a wet dog. There were cheers and humorous
questions : had he found anything, had he seen any fish,
and had he got wet ?

I jumped ashore and shook hands with Bergman, Yew,
Kung, Georg and Effe, Serat, Jomcha, the Cossacks
Gagarin and Nikolai, and our servants. The small car
came and drove Chen and me and our things to camp
no. 70, about a quarter of a mile from the shore.

We had a big coffee party in the three Swedes' tent, over
which the Swedish flag flew. They told us of their toilsome
journey along the foot of the Kuruk-tagh, whose ridge was

E

Various styles of paddling and punting.

faintly visible to the northward. Then I had a long talk
with Yew, Kung and Effe about a plan we had already
discussed at Korla, and of which Bergman and I had often
spoken in Peking. Chen and I were to go on down the
Kum-daria to Lop-nor, while Hummel completed his zoological and botanical collections along the river. But what
should the others do in the meantime? Well, I had proposed to our road experts, the engineers Yew and Kung,
that they should use the two months we had been permitted
to spend in the Lop country for a tour of exploration from
our headquarters, via Altmish-bulak, to the Su-lo-ho and
Tun-hwang in Kansu. Two thousand years ago there had
been a road from Tun-hwang to Korla via Lop-nor, Lou-
lan and the Kum-daria. Hundreds of thousands of camels
and ox-carts had gone that way for nearly five centuries, till
about A.D. 330, when the river and lake moved to the southward, Lou-lan was abandoned and this part of the old Silk
Road fell into disuse.

Now both lake and river had returned to their old historic

beds, and now the time had come to revive the old Silk Road. In my first memorandum to the Nanking Government I had pointed out the importance of strengthening the links between China proper and Sinkiang, the largest and most remote of the Republic's possessions, by creating a new traffic artery from Kansu to Eastern Turkistan.

Hörner and Chen, on their daring advance from Tun-hwang to Lop-nor, Lou-lan and the delta of the Kum-daria in the winter of 1930–31, had found that the road they had followed through the desert—previously mapped by Sir Aurel Stein—was not suitable for motor traffic. My intention now was to find a parallel road to the north, within the mountain regions of the Pei-shan and Kuruk-tagh, or at their foot.

And now the search for the old road was to begin! The men were ready to start on April 27. Effe's truck stood loaded; the small car was to be driven by Serat and used for reconnaissance work. Yew and Kung were in charge of the expedition. They took with them the Cossack Nikolai and my old guide the camel-hunter Abdu Rehim, who had turned up at our headquarters. With the two servants, San Wa-tse and Liu Chia, the exploring party was eight men strong. They had enough petrol to take them to Tun-hwang and back, and eleven gallons of lubricating oil.

Their experiences form a separate chapter of our story. But perhaps I ought to say here at once that the enterprise was only half successful. The attempt to advance eastward along the southern foot of the Kuruk-tagh was quickly proved to be impracticable, so the party made a detour into the mountains. After driving 150 miles from the base camp they reached the desolate salt spring of Altmish-bulak. They could not proceed farther eastward because the difficult country had made too severe inroads into their supply of lubricating oil.

My desire to find a new Silk Road had thus been frustrated. But I did not in any way give up hope of being able to carry out the plan later. Six months were to pass before it was executed. But I shall tell the story in later chapters of this book.

It was not only the plans for the discovery of the 2,000

years' old Silk Road, or some other practicable route between Korla and Tun-hwang, which occupied our thoughts
and our time during the three days Chen and I spent with
the other sections of the expedition at our headquarters near
Yardang-bulak.   We had other plans too—and the question
was how to utilize to the best possible advantage the short
two months which General Sheng Shih-tsai had allowed us.

The most important of these plans had been stimulated
by the strange and exciting accounts Ördek had given us of
the curious discoveries he had made in the desert to the
southward, many years after my first expedition in 1900. He
confessed that the finds we had made at Lou-lan had tempted
him to try his luck again.   The depths of the desert probably
concealed archæological remains—graves containing gold
and all manner of precious things—in comparison with
which our discoveries at Lou-lan were quite insignificant.

Ördek's last expedition—about ten years earlier, say in
1924—had led him eastward from my old lake Avullu-köl,
discovered in 1896, but now dry. He had, he assured us,
found wonderful things a day's journey into the desert.   In
one place he had seen a burial-place in which innumerable
coffins of solid wood stood stacked one on top of the other,
in two layers. He had opened several of the coffins, the
interiors of which were richly carved and painted. In
addition to the well-preserved corpses, clad in fine silk
robes, the coffins contained a quantity of papers with
writing in some curious character and gaily ornamented.

A little way off he had seen a house whose door stood
open. He had seen a blinding light through a narrow
window and had been so terrified that he had not dared to
approach the house ; for it was undoubtedly haunted by
ghosts and goblins which would strike him dead if he went
near the place.   Farther east, in the direction of Lou-lan, he
had discovered two fairly high watch-towers, which made
us wonder if the old Silk Road had not hereabouts run south
of the Kum-daria.   Still farther east, and at a still greater
distance from the burial-place, there was a *budkhaneh* or
house of Buddha, a temple, possibly belonging to Lou-lan.

Ördek's imagination had free play at this time, and he
often came and sat down at my tent-door to tell me some

new detail he had just thought of. Bergman and I could not help thinking that these strange and seductive descriptions must have *some* foundation in fact. We hoped that the watch-towers might help us to locate an old road, and we wondered whether the great burial-place did not betray the proximity of one of the places named in the manuscripts from Lou-lan that I myself had found. It was therefore decided that, while Chen and I went to Lop-nor, Folke Bergman and Georg Söderbom should set off through the desert towards the region where the Avullu-köl had formerly been. They would take a couple of servants and Ördek as guide, and put their baggage on to the few draught animals that could be raised in those parts, which the war had sucked dry.

Ördek's alluring descriptions were soon shown to be exaggerated. Perhaps he still recollected the keen interest I took in the discovery of the ruins of Lou-lan, and now, after thirty-four years, was erecting on their foundation fantastic houses and magnificent burial-places. Ördek had grown old; the strength and endurance which had been so conspicuous in 1900 had waned; his memory failed him, and he could no longer distinguish between dreams, hopes and realities.

I will take leave of him here. I did not see him again. His end was tragic, so far as we were able to trace him. The summer was over when the motor convoy, as I have already narrated in my book *The Silk Road*, rejoined me at Urumchi. I then heard from our fellows that Ördek and other servants had been dismissed after Bergman's return from the desert.

Then he had presented himself one fine day to the *beks* at Tikenlik and delivered an entirely fictitious message from our expedition to the effect that we required a further supply of flour and rice, which would be paid for when we left. The *beks* had supplied us on several previous occasions and had no reason to suspect this time that anything was wrong. Ördek got what he asked for. But instead of going to our headquarters by the river, he had gone by a roundabout route to his own home, Chara, near Yangi-köl. When the *beks*, later on, presented the bill to Georg and Effe, the latter replied that no goods had been ordered at the date mentioned, and that Ördek had left our service long before. Then the *beks*, as the representatives of authority, had instituted an inquiry ; Ördek had confessed and had been arrested.

Poor Ördek ! it would have been better for him if he had not met me again. For him—if he is still alive—the recollection of our second meeting must be very different from the recollection of the first. So it is for me ; but I regard his exit from our stage just as an episode, only too common among the East Turkis, and the happy memories of 1900 are not dimmed by it in the slightest degree.

Colonel Salomakhin had promised us at Korla that he would have 100 poods of petrol and 6 poods of oil sent to that place for us within six weeks. I now wrote to the commandant at Korla, Captain Deviashin, and reminded him of this, asking at the same time that, to begin with, 4 poods of oil should be kept in readiness for us. The letter was carried by Ibrahim, who had been in Bergman's service in 1928.

Before the Silk Road people went off there were no fewer than forty-three of us at camp no. 70. Some Turkis came to the camp from Tikenlik with a horse, nine donkeys, a quantity of flour and 400 eggs. And two shepherds arrived with eighteen sheep which we had ordered.

It was pathetic to see my old friend and guide, Abdu Rehim, again. In 1900 he was young and active, and swung himself up on to his bounding riding-camel with the ease of an acrobat. Now he was old and shrunken and complained of many pains. It was doubtless risky to take him on the proposed journey to Tun-hwang, but he himself was keen on going, and he was the only man who knew the country. He fell ill on the journey and had to be taken to Singer in the small car.

We had some long conversations during the three days we were together. It was cheering to hear Abdu Rehim explain the causes of the wanderings of the Kum-daria and Lop-nor—they agreed in all essentials with the theory I had formed in 1901. He told me that the river was now getting lower daily, but would rise again in July and reach its

Paddlers in single canoes.

maximum height late in the autumn. Then it would freeze and fall again under the ice. The river had begun to send water into the bed of the Kum-daria thirteen years before, and the volume of water in the latter had increased since then each year, till in 1926 or 1927 the whole river had changed its bed.

"Here is the water," he said. "Why not grow wheat? There is plenty of good soil along the Kum-daria."

At camp no. 70 we got rid of the petrol boat and a quantity of flour which we had bought for the others. We thus left behind four canoes and three paddlers, and would proceed with a reduced flotilla of only five double canoes and ten paddlers.

On April 26 we had a little "yellow storm", with a gale of 37 miles an hour. Everything was wrapped in fog; neither the Kuruk-tagh nor the Kum-daria could be seen. We were able to study the formation of sediment in our teacups.

A new night fell over our wandering city, and next morning we were to be parted from our comrades again.

VI

TOWARDS THE MYSTERIOUS DESERT

APRIL 28 was a new day of separation. The engineers,
Yew and Kung, had already started on their tour via
Altmish-bulak through unknown desert regions in the
direction of Tun-hwang, in search of a new Silk Road.
They took with them the ever-cheerful Effe and the Mongol
Serat as mechanics and drivers, the old camel-hunter Abdu
Rehim as guide, the Cossack Nikolai by way of escort,
and a couple of Chinese servants. We were to hear nothing
of them for a long time. It was a risky enterprise to ven-
ture into a waterless desert over difficult ground with only
two cars. If the cars broke down, or the petrol supply gave
out, they would be lost, for they had little chance of finding
their way to water on foot in the approaching summer heat.
But the Central Government at Nanking had commissioned
us to locate the course of the old Silk Road from Tun-
hwang to Eastern Turkistan, so we must do everything
possible to carry out our mission, even at the risk of our
lives.

When the motor convoy set off eastward I had given
Yew and Kung, as its responsible leaders, the following
orders. When, on their way back from Tun-hwang, they
reached a point due south of Altmish-bulak, they were to
send a reconnoitring party to the northern shore of Lop-nor
to see if Chen and I were still in the neighbourhood with
our flotilla.

The whole plan was adventurous and, I freely admit,
rather rash. It was easy enough for Chen and me, as long
as we had flowing water under our canoes and the river
continued eastward, to go on in this direction—i.e. as far
as the region where the Kum-daria runs into Lake Lop-nor
—but what was going to happen to us if the motor convoy

never came back? According to our calculations, and under normal conditions, the petrol supply ought to last as far as the lake into which the Su-lo-ho runs, not far from Tun-hwang, and back to base camp no. 70 near Yardang-bulak. But who could know whether the ground would not be so soft and sandy that twice the normal amount of petrol would be consumed? In that case the cars would be able to get to Tun-hwang but not to return, and it would be impossible for Yew and Kung to let us know. Further, General Sheng Shih-tsai would have thought it extremely suspicious—and with justification—if half the expedition made a bolt out of Sinkiang and went off eastward to Kansu, after it had been agreed that the whole party should be at Urumchi at the end of two months.

If Chen and I, on the completion of our work at Lop-nor, failed to make contact with the motor convoy, we could not expect much help from the other groups. All we knew of Hummel was that he was concentrating on the region about the Konche-daria. Folke Bergman and Georg Söderbom were to march southwards into the desert to look for a burial-ground, with Ördek as guide. Base camp no. 70 would meanwhile be guarded by three or four men.

The prospects for both the motor convoy and the flotilla of canoes were, therefore, very uncertain. It would have been much easier for the former to travel in winter, when a large supply of ice could have been taken on the cars. But the cold season, when the river is ice-bound, was of no use to Chen and me, who had to map it.

But the alluring prospect of being the first to map every bend of my own old Kum-daria overcame all other considerations. "How shall we get back?" was a question to which I did not give a thought at the moment of our departure or throughout the journey, when each day was taking us farther and farther from our one firm support, base camp no. 70. No obstacles might now arise in our path. What efforts and what patience it had cost me to return once more to that region, to which I had given so much attention a generation earlier, and where the theories I had formed had become reality before my very eyes!

If anyone asked how we were to get back with our baggage and food supply, I simply replied:

"If we succeed in reaching our goal, the wandering lake, we shall find some means of getting back again. Single canoes are easily managed, but paddling against the stream would be too hard work. If the cars don't turn up, we shall have to send our boatmen up the river on foot to collect some donkeys and horses at Tikenlik. Worst come to the worst, we must walk it, in short day's marches."

Parker C. Chen, who had received his baptism of fire under Nils Hörner's command, and who had walked all round Lop-nor in his company three years earlier, took the situation as calmly as I did, and looked forward to the new journey, which was to take him back to the " wandering lake " and perhaps to the ruins of the ancient city of Lou-lan, as a marvellous adventure.

The " flagship " of our squadron remained unaltered. I sat as usual on a plank placed crosswise, with a leg in each canoe, and had an empty packing-case as writing-table. Its bottom was cut out so as to make room for my knees under the table and also for my map-case, glasses and various other trifles. My rolled-up sleeping-bag served as a support for my back, but I made very little use of it, as I always sat leaning forward with my elbows resting on the table, a pen in my right hand and a cigarette in my left, and compass and watch lying before me.

On board the other double canoe Chen continued his observations of the river's depth and the velocity of the current, and also the extent to which we increased our speed by using paddles. On board the third double canoe was our trusty cook, Chia Kwei, in company with the Russian Cossack, Gagarin; we took the latter with us at his own request instead of young Erashin Sokolenko, who became a guard at the base camp.

The fourth and fifth vessels were used to carry our supplies—1,300 chin of flour, a bag of rice, six sheep and, to give a farmyard touch, a cock and a few hens.

It took some time to get all this stowed away, and the sun was at its noonday height before " all clear " was reported. We marched down to the " harbour " on the northern bank of the Kum-daria, took leave of Bergman, Georg, Erashin, Ördek and the East Turkis who belonged to the camp, got on board and pushed off, and the current bore us eastward towards the lake of our dreams.

We had not gone many boat's lengths before one of the hens flew ashore with a shrill cackling and laborious flapping of its wings. At the same time one of the sheep jumped overboard, swam across to the right bank, and disappeared at once among the broken ground. The creatures evidently scented evil to come and thought it wisest to make a bolt for it while yet they could.

Once more we were surrounded by the great desert, which had lain silent and dead for many centuries, since the river had left its old bed about A.D. 330 and gone south. But now the water had come back and filled the old dry bed, and seeds of reeds, tamarisks, poplars and other vegetation were being carried down by the current, coming to shore, sprouting, taking root and growing up to new life. In the region we were now traversing even dead trees and floating timber were absent, but reeds stood fairly thick along the banks here and there. They were last year's plants, all yellow and dry, but it could not be long now before the fresh green reeds shot up and brought a touch of life and colour into the desolate grey landscape. Dead tamarisk mounds stood at frequent intervals along the banks, resembling Mongolian *yurts* in shape and concealing in their heart a skeleton of roots.

The river-bed was wide and shallow ; the depth was not more than 8 feet 8 inches.

We caught sight of our escaped sheep grazing in a reed-bed on the right bank. We landed, and the men started a hunt ; but the fugitive was swifter than they and escaped from its pursuers. At last Gagarin took the gun and fired four shots—all misses ! One can imagine that the wild antelopes were pretty safe from this crack shot, who could not even hit a tame sheep !

The moon shone down silver-white on our camp that evening, and the countryside was as silent as the grave.

That night (April 28–29) the temperature fell to 33·3 degrees, unusually low for so late in the year.

We glided past an occasional tamarisk bush with pretty violet clusters of flowers, and saw a single living poplar on a mound, surrounded by dead trees. Water-birds of different kinds, especially ducks and gulls, were sometimes seen, and small birds as well. Dr. Hummel, whom we had left behind us a few weeks earlier, was to make a fine collection of birds' skins during the spring and summer.

The Kuruk-tagh was plainly visible to the northward, and this side of the mountains a strongly marked bank terrace, which had long ago been formed by the erosion of the river. On a cape on the left bank were tamarisks seated on their throne-like mounds ; they had been dead for many centuries, but still preserved a spark of latent vitality, and so were reviving now that the river was coming back. A falcon flew over our heads, and four antelopes dashed away.

The river made the weirdest bends. Our goal lay to the east, but at times we were moving westward and the evening sun shone in our faces. In nine hours we covered just under 20 miles. The velocity of the current was only 1 foot 6 inches a second, but we paddled 2 feet 1 inch a second ; so that our average speed was rather more than a yard a second. The maximum depth was again about 18 feet.

We pitched camp at the foot of a sand dune, where there was an ample supply of dry wood. We found fragments of black clay pots or dishes round the camp.

When we pushed off next morning the river was like a sheet of glass. It ran ENE for a few hours below sharp-cut terraces and a fairly thick growth of dead trees, some still standing, some fallen. The Kum-daria is often a broad and imposing stream. I landed for a short time on a mound on the left bank. The other four craft were in midstream, presenting a gay and lively picture, made all the more impressive by the boatmen's singing.

The river swung northward. Here it was 76 yards wide, and the bank terraces from 9 to 12 feet high. An awning about 4 square yards in size was stretched between four poles over my writing-table. A violent gust from the SW came and carried it away, and the boat drifted towards the left bank.

To the north the yellow desert extended, with death written on its face. It consisted of long undulating ridges and a mass of *yardangs*, those lumps of clay modelled in curious shapes by the wind, with deep corridors between them, which I remembered so well from earlier journeys. They ran down to the bank, looking like long rows of huge coffins and catafalques, the mortuary of a vanished splendour, destroyed by storms and drought. But now the song of life is heard again through that vast cemetery, sung by the water as it murmurs round its driftwood and its promontories, and plant and animal life can spring up anew.

The bank terraces were now 16 feet high and perpendicular. Solid roofs of light-coloured clay projected over grottoes formed by the looser material being washed away by the river. The roots of tamarisks and reeds often hung down like a drapery over their mouths. Again and again we heard the splashing of lumps of clay as they fell into the water. The bank terraces gave birth like the glaciers of Spitzbergen and Greenland.

When we pitched camp in the evening we had covered 20 miles and Chen had sounded a maximum depth of 14 feet 7 inches.

The 1st of May! We might have been in the country. The cock crew and the hens cackled in their prison under the deck planks, and the sheep, which were tied up among the flour-sacks, bleated their longing for the next camp. Our pleasant farmyard glided on eastward.

We heard the noise of rapids ahead; we reached them. The boatmen kept their craft straight with the current, and we surged forward through waves that leapt playfully about us.

In a little while we passed two small poplars, three or four years old, and soon two more. These were the pioneers of the woodland, harbingers of the forests through which the easterly storms would roar in time to come as they did thousands of years ago in the days of Lou-lan. A little farther on, on the left bank, a patch of spring green appeared—another living poplar. We landed. It had been dead for hundreds of years, but had been restored to life since the river returned in 1921. It was thickly covered

View towards S 75 degrees W from the left bank, May 1.   Deformed *yardang* in foreground.

with heart-shaped, serrated leaves.   A sapling which had taken root by its side had long-shaped, narrow leaves; when the trees reach a certain age the leaves become heart-shaped.   That is why this kind of poplar bears the Latin name *Populus diversifolia*.   It was delightful to sit for a while in the scented green shade and dream of the return of life to the desert.   Chia Kwei offered me a bunch of green twigs in honour of the 1st of May.   He and Gagarin took with them a whole arbour of boughs to give them shade on board their boat.

Sharp bends, stranded driftwood, babbling water, live tamarisks and reeds.   The river was 50 yards wide between perpendicular terraces.   The speed of the current was increasing.

Sand was slipping down from a dune over the edge of a high terrace and plunging into the river like a cascade. We could hear a deafening splashing noise quite a long way off.   Clouds of dust were formed, as after the explosion of a bomb.   The wash ran across the river, which was a hundred yards wide at that point, and we rolled merrily in the swell.

Then all was quiet for a time.   Chia Kwei, who is a Christian, sang a hymn which he had learnt at a Swedish mission station.   Its notes rang out solemnly over the river, which had never before heard Christian or Mohammedan hymns.

Again we heard a roaring noise ahead of us.   Was a

Sharply-cut and eroded deposits on the right bank, May 1.

storm coming up? It grew louder. Evidently more rapids. We landed to reconnoitre; then we defied the rapids and whizzed down over their boiling, rushing water. "We'll upset in a minute," Sadik said. Not a bit of it; we got through all right and were soon in calm water again.

It was getting dark. We must pitch camp, when we had first found a suitable place with level ground for the tent. But such places were rare in country so broken up by *yardang* formations. The camping-ground we finally chose was an original one—the top of a *yardang* ridge, 23 feet high, whose surface was as smooth as a floor. There the tent was pitched and the cooker set up. The boatmen preferred the depression below. The ridge ran from NNE to SSW. From its summit there was a splendid view over a labyrinth of *yardangs* as far as the eye could see. The river at this point was only 50 yards wide, and from our eminence looked like a narrow little canal. "If it blows to-night," I thought, "the tent'll go."

But when I woke it was still there, and below lay the stream, as smooth as a mirror.

The river soon widened to 80 or 90 yards, and there was a good current. Small sandbanks gave rise to funnel-shaped eddies. Fresh landslips were continually heard—the river at work, carving out its bed. Sadik sang for nine hours without a break, and the others joined in. The songs were always the same—love, adventures, war, or the lives of holy men. This music was rather trying to the listeners, but it was no use complaining—one might as well get tired of the chugging of a motor-boat. It was a necessary part of the business.

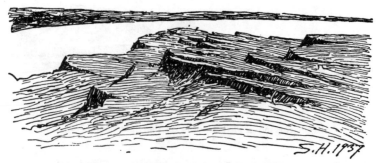

View eastward, looking downstream, May 2.

The banks were only 3 feet high.   There was an antelope, grazing.   Earth was slipping away from both sides at once. The two washes met in midstream and caused a little sea. We struck ground—it was a *yardang* whose top lay just under the surface.

We spied out the land from a fairly high *yardang*.   The river, confined between its terraces, suggested a canyon. How desolate and dead this country had been when I traversed its deserts thirty-four years before !   How splendid it was now, when life was suffusing it with a new dawn ! No music in the world could charm my ears more than the soft triumphant melody played by the water as it babbled round a stranded tree-trunk.

The landscape changed its character and became more and more confused.   It was as though the flowing water could not make up its mind what course it should take. Chen, who, as I mentioned before, had been to Lop-nor and the Kum-daria in the winter of 1930–31, declared that we were just at the beginning of the delta.   We wondered rather anxiously if we should succeed in finding the main arm which would take us straight to Lop-nor, or if we should go astray in a labyrinth of lakes and little waterways.

The *yardangs* grew higher.   They assumed more and more fantastic shapes, resembling tables, projecting roofs and mouldings with deep shadows underneath.   Sometimes they had a deceptive resemblance to towers, walls, old houses and fortifications built by men's hands.   They assumed the shapes of lions in ambush, recumbent dragons,

inscrutable sphinxes and sleeping dogs. We drifted
through a fairy country, bewitched and mysterious, light
grey, yellowish, rose-coloured, yet bearing the stamp of
death and dissolution, and without one single trunk of
dry timber or ancient woodland.

After a time this strange *yardang* sculpture disappeared;
we saw no more sleeping giants and dreaming guards.
The banks became high, flat and monotonous. The river
was 80 yards wide and was still imposing. Reeds and
tamarisks grew rare; the latter became so uncommon that
I could mark on my map each bush that we passed.

An arm of the delta broke away to the right and entered
a lake of clear, still water, but returned to the main stream
lower down. To the south the sunshine glittered on fairly
wide spaces of water. Most of the riverside lakes are on
the south bank. They were all mapped during the summer
by Chen, who displayed a phenomenal energy and completed my river map in a manner that compelled admiration.
The country on the north, or left bank of the Kum-daria had,
as I mentioned before, been mapped by Norin and Ambolt.

Sar is the Turkish name—a name with an imperial ring
about it—for a kite. One of these birds sat in solitary
state on a riverside hillock, and followed us as we glided
past with a gaze of mingled severity and astonishment.
A pair of swans had settled on a quiet strip of beach; their
nest was probably close by. Newly hatched, straw-
coloured chicks were swimming round their mother. The
paddlers in one of our boats caught two of these bewitching
creatures, which I caused to be released at once at the spot
where they had been taken. Farther on we surprised a flock
of snow-white swans, which rose in majestic flight and
vanished southward.

We had seen no swans west of this point, and throughout
his trip along the Konche-daria, as far as base camp no. 70,
Hummel did not observe a single representative of this
tribe, the most beautiful of earth's winged creatures. Only
here, close to the delta of the Kum-daria, where there are
fair-sized reedy lakes, and where the swan has freedom of
movement and a view over open water-spaces, does it
occur now and again in pairs.

F

I had often seen swans in 1896, 1900 and 1901 on the open spaces of the Kara-koshun, which were flanked with impenetrable jungles of thick reeds. The local fishermen used to catch the birds cunningly with their hands. If a couple of fishermen, out in their boat setting or taking up their nets, surprised a swan swimming unsuspiciously just outside a reed-bed, they urged their craft to top speed and steered straight for their victim with lightning rapidity. The swan, seeing danger approaching too swiftly, it seemed, for it to rise from the water, sought safety in the reeds and swam in to hide among the dense mass of stems. But the Lop-men followed it with the greatest ease, and even among the reeds paddled more quickly than the bird swam. The reed-stems stood high and dense everywhere. The white swimmer had no chance of escape. It had no room to spread its wings, much less rise out of that confined space. The canoe overtook it; it flapped and beat its wings in desperation; but a Lop-man jumped into the water, put his arm round the swan's neck and killed it instantaneously by wringing its neck.

The lakes on the lower Kum-daria do not yet contain such thick masses of reeds, and such a high growth, as the Kara-koshun. I have there measured stems about 25 feet high, round which one could only just get one's hand at water-level. But the waterways on which we now were were only thirteen years old, and were still carving out their beds. The reeds which had taken root along their banks and in the lakes close by were new-comers, which did not yet feel themselves at home and had not had time to develop to the same extent as the reeds in the southern lake, now dry. That would require centuries, and stable conditions. In the region of the lower Kum-daria and its delta everything was still moving in—water, plants and animals. That was one of the chief reasons why our trip was so intensely interesting. We had come just at the right moment to see with our own eyes a radical and seemingly capricious transformation of the earth's surface in the very heart of Asia. We had already observed that the fish and all the water insects spread as quickly as the river itself, and that among the plants the reed was the first to set foot, like a herald, in the new land. In the Lop country Nature was fighting a life-and-death battle. To the south the desert, drought, death had conquered. Here, round the Kum-daria, the desert was being beaten and life was emerging victorious in the shape of the irresistibly advancing river, and its army of animals and plants.

But we had still much to see before the whole wonderful drama was unrolled before our eyes, and before we could say that we had definitely solved the whole of the Lop-nor problem. Let us return, therefore, to our voyage down the Kum-daria.

We came to a place where the river broadened out like a lake, and the channel was hard to follow—a labyrinth of stretches of water, arms of the stream and islands! The air was dim, and we were surrounded by a dirty grey mist out of which the other boats loomed up like spectres. The flotilla had to keep together to prevent any of the boats getting lost in some byway of the river. We stopped now and again and peered about us. That watery labyrinth was unfathomable. I noticed a deformed *yardang* with a remarkable likeness to one of the old graves on the west coast of Sweden—a huge horizontal slab on the top of a truncated cone.

When we had searched for the right course for a long time we were forced to encamp by dusk and a rising wind. We picked our way among islands, peninsulas and creeks out on to a broader stretch of water, where we landed on a small island. We found fuel there, and went to sleep to the pleasant sound of rippling water.

We woke on May 3 to find a regular north-easter blowing —20 miles an hour. Furious foam-crested waves were breaking on the northern and eastern shores of our island. We could see how the lumps of *yardang* were undermined by the washing of the waves. So the face of the country is modelled, levelled and transformed as time passes, now by storms, now by water. The ceaseless roar of wind and waves filled the air—bewitching classical music, recalling memories of the old Lou-lan days.

Our island was 270 yards long and 88 yards across, and its direction was NE–SW, as is usual with *yardang* forma-

Yardangs resembling sarcophagi on right bank, May 2.

tions.   To the south was a fairly wide sheet of water, filled
with *yardang* ridges and islands.   A flock of white gulls sat
chattering in the lee of a *yardang* at the north-eastern point
of the island.   Chia Kwei collected soft sappy stems, the
tips of the fresh spring shoots, and they tasted excellent—
a sort of desert asparagus.

Our boats were moored on the western shore of the
island, the lee side, so that they should not be carried away.
In the evening the weather was so horrible that Gagarin
and Chia Kwei had to move in and spend the night with us.
The evening was long.   Chen was always busy working
out the day's observations, and I with my notes.

I filled up some of the time in hearing Gagarin's life-story.

He was born at Archangel and lived as a peasant near
that place until 1928, when he and twenty-five other
peasants were transferred to Alma Ata (Verny) and put on
to building work.   After a while he ran away to Pishpek
and home to Archangel, but was captured and again
deported to Alma Ata.   He got 15 ounces of flour or bread
daily.   He ran away again, this time to Bakhty and Chugu-
chak.   When the disturbances broke out in Sinkiang he
was taken for the army and placed in the 1st Regiment.
There were then four regiments ; the fourth was afterwards divided up among the first three.   He was transferred
to Urumchi, under Colonel Nikolaieff, and took part in
the march of the 500 over the mountains to Korla via
Shindi, Ying-p'an and Tikenlik.   Gagarin was now thirty-
one.   His father was dead, but his mother was alive in
Archangel.

The spirits of the air were in a noisy mood on May 4

also. We could see nothing for flying sand and dust. We expected the tent to fly away at any moment. Foaming waves rolled towards the little island on which we were prisoners, and every now and then we heard strips of *yardang* tumble into the water. One of our double canoes broke loose during the night and was cast up full of water on the shore of a neighbouring island. Luckily its cargo of sacks of flour had been brought ashore in the evening.

Sky, earth and water formed one uniform grey fog. The lake, whose water had been crystal-clear a few days earlier, was now as turbid as pea soup from the eating away of the shore by the waves and the flinging up of mud from the bottom. A sheep was slaughtered, and our faithful dog Tagil had a good meal of " innards ". Our three boatmen ate up their share at once, and had therefore to live exclusively on bread during the next three days. They found on the island fragments of pottery, some pieces of the mechanism of an old Chinese crossbow, and a pearl.

When we went to bed on the evening of May 4 the storm had been raging for nearly fifty hours, and we longed to be able to cross the treacherous water. But as we crept into our sleeping-bags the storm showed no signs of abating, and we lay down to sleep and dream to the roaring of the wind and the splashing of the waves.

VII

TO AN UNKNOWN PRINCESS'S GRAVE

MAY 5 ! an anniversary. Thirty-nine years ago I found water in the bed of the Khotan-daria in the nick of time and was saved as by a miracle.

The storm had raged for a good fifty hours, and this morning too was unpleasant, with an overcast, lowering sky. But we packed, went on board and steered out across a broad lake to the north-east. It was shallow; the paddles touched bottom everywhere; the average depth was less than 2 feet. We ascended a *yardang* hillock and discovered an arm of the river to the southward. In a couple of hours' time we glided into an arm running eastward; this led to a lake with dense reed-beds which rose from its surface like yellow islands.

We took another observation from a *yardang* island. Sheets of water of no great size lay both north and north-east of us. We kept a north-easterly course, but got into a blind alley, so we sent Sadik and Hajit to reconnoitre to the eastward. They saw a big lake to the south-west, to the northward nothing but *yardangs*. We steered into a little canal, in places only 5 or 6 yards wide, which ran between solid clay banks and islands of thick reeds. At 12.30 we emerged on to a fairly broad sheet of water, and hoped that this was the main arm of the delta. We followed its left bank. We caught sight of some grey tree-trunks some way off inland. Two of them formed an X. We must find out whether this mark—symbolizing the unknown—was a freak of nature or the work of man.

We landed, therefore, at 1 o'clock, walked about 200 yards north-west, and found the remains of a house, obviously dating from the Lou-lan era—i.e. at least 1,600 years old. On the way we passed quantities of red and black fragments of clay pots and bowls.

Looking N 35 degrees W from shore near old house, May 5.

Eighteen vertical posts still stood upright, and the walls were made of reeds and tamarisk boughs plaited together, in which the vertical work predominated. The material and method of building were thus the same as at Lou-lan. The house was about 45 feet long by 26 feet wide and was divided into four rooms. It ran from north-east to south-west. The house stood on a hillock about 6 feet above the surrounding land. Round about it lay a number of smallish beams and pieces of wood, none of them carved. There were doorways between the rooms. In one case the two door-posts had come loose and were leaning over, forming the cross we had seen. One of the doors had a threshold.

There was a fireplace in one corner with traces of coal in it. In one of the rooms, which may have been an outhouse, there was a quantity of sheep's dung. We found in the house fragments of clay utensils, cattle's horns, fish-bones, a wooden card, a knife-blade, the bottom of a cooking-pot, scraps of close-woven cloth, the bottom of a wicker basket, and other things. South-west of the house there had been a walled-in yard; the greater part of the wall had disappeared. We found in the yard fragments of large wooden drinking-troughs for horses.

We wondered what purpose this house had served in its time. It did not contain a trace of anything valuable, or of manuscripts, but only the very simplest utensils. Had it been an ordinary poor farm, or a small post on the old Silk Road? Perhaps an inn for travellers to and from Lou-lan?

Door-posts in SW wall of old house, fallen together so as to form an X.

We stayed there just an hour and then continued our journey in a fairly strong north-east wind. About five we took another observation from a hillock and found that we had the choice of two arms, running ENE and south. We took the former, and soon found ourselves on a north-easterly course. By a small reed-bed we found that what current there was was against us, and turned back. But it was growing dark, so we landed on the right bank and pitched camp in a place where fuel was to be had. Our camp was at the south-eastern foot of a *yardang*, or fragment of a *mesa*,[1] about 13 feet high, on the top of which was a cairn to mark the route. It resembled a bundle of small logs, so cunningly joined together that it had resisted the storms of centuries. The bundle was 9 feet 9 inches high. The marks of axes were plainly visible on the logs, and one of them, which was round, had been hewn at both ends. The cairn had without doubt marked a fair-sized road, the course of which was presumably indicated by other similar sign-posts to east and west of it. Perhaps the Silk Road had passed just here and gone by the house we had seen the same day.

[1] *Mesas* are blocks of clay, the remains of deposits left by erosion.

View WSW from the old house.

Chen placed a Swedish flag on top of the cairn to cele-
brate the thirty-ninth anniversary of my escape on the
Khotan-daria.

The temperature fell, as it usually does after a storm.   At
eight that evening it was only 57 degrees, and we tucked
ourselves up in our sleeping-bags as if we were in the Gobi
desert in winter.   The minimum temperature during the
night sank as low as 45·9, and the morning of May 6, with
a biting ENE wind blowing, was distinctly uninviting.
We went on board wrapped in furs, and had no need of our
awnings.

We went on down the river, whose course here was plain
but irregular—a labyrinth of islands, peninsulas, creeks,
capes and *yardangs*.   The current was visible at every reed-
bed, where the yellow stems with their seed-tufts stood
nodding like plumes.   We spied out the land from a *yardang*, and were soon slipping across a wide open water-space.

The river showed a pronounced tendency to run NE and
ENE, i.e. right against the prevailing winds and parallel to
the direction of the *yardangs*.   The water naturally found its
way into the channels between the *yardang* ridges, which lay
open to carry it off.   We had noticed this tendency ever
since camp no. 73.

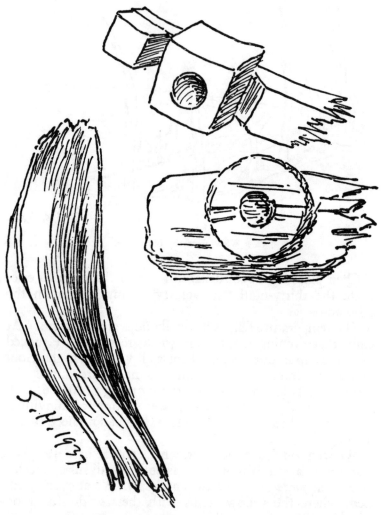

Door-latches ; wooden trough warped by drought.

We went between *yardangs* for long spells, and when our
course was north-easterly we had them broadside on to
right and left of us.   They were generally short, resembling
sarcophagi, but seen end-on, either from north-east or
south-west, they were quite narrow, often only a few yards
wide, with vertical sides and flat tops.   Then they looked

like cubes, ends of walls or towers. Their contours were
sometimes so regular that we could not help stopping and
making sure that we were not looking at an old watch-tower
marking an ancient road, which it might be worth our while
to investigate.

We landed again on a small island, to which we had been
attracted by two curiously formed, tall, narrow pillars—all
that erosion had left of a *yardang*. At a distance one could
not believe that they were not the work of men's hands.
To the north we saw a landscape of *yardangs* and mounds,
and farther off the grey *sai*—the completely flat stretch of
gravel at the foot of the Kuruk-tagh, whose lower ranges
stood up like a threatening wall of cloud.

Sea-birds flew round us screaming, as if warning one
another of our arrival. We glided past a monumental
mesa, one of those huge reddish-yellow remains of erosion,
dating from an old, late tertiary sedimentation. We left it
on our right and proceeded north-east. But in a time we
again perceived that the weak current was against us; and
turned back south-west. When we approached the monumental *mesa* for the second time, Sadik, my senior boatman,
suggested that he should get up on top of the *mesa* and look
out for what seemed the best channel. After some time he
came back with the information that the view was extraordinarily wide, but the channel so confusing that he could
not decide which direction we ought to take. He asked me,
therefore, to come up on to the *mesa* myself and determine
our course.

Meanwhile several of the other boatmen had jumped
ashore and disappeared among the reeds on the bank and
the rough ground. As Sadik led me up a fairly precipitous
slope, on which I often needed his strong arm to ascend a
perpendicular ledge, we met one or two of the others, who
reported that they had found an old grave.

" Go and fetch the spade ! " I replied.

We had actually one spade ; I say this in order to show
that archæological excavations were not the object of our
journey. One spade among fourteen men does not suggest
any great interest in excavations. We had the spade with
us to level the ground for the tent, improve landing-places,

Undermined *yardang* with overhanging summit on right bank, May 5.

carry glowing coal from the camp-fire, cut a path through reeds, and so on.

All these apparent trifles have a certain importance because they are closely connected with one of the clauses in the instructions we had received from Nanking. The instigator of this clause was the Minister for Education, who, in turn, had been urged by certain learned men in Peking to forbid our expedition to carry on any kind of archæological work or do any digging. That was why one spade was enough for the Lop-nor expedition, and why I now gave the order, " Go and fetch *the spade* ! " During the hours that followed I would have given a great deal, notwithstanding Peking's ill-will, to have ten spades at our disposal.

Meanwhile the discoverers of the grave conducted Sadik and me to the interesting spot on the western slope of the *mesa*. It was situated 57 feet above the surface of the water, and the top of the *mesa* was 80 feet above our landing-place.

Some of our boatmen were already busy excavating the shallow grave, using their bare hands or tree-stumps which lay scattered about on the ground. The grave, which was on a little balcony, or smooth terrace-like surface, was evidently a mass grave, for when I arrived the men had already laid out on its edge three skulls and numerous other parts of skeletons, and various rags of clothing.

Camp no. 76, looking NW.   Swedish flag hoisted on ancient cairn, May 5.

Now that they had the spade the work went more quickly. I remained for a time and watched the digging, which was intelligently and carefully directed by Chen, and went on from 1.10 to 3.30.   The grave was covered with flat boards ; a few upright posts marked its edge.

While the work was going on I went right up to the top of the *mesa* alone.   There was an astonishingly fine view all round the horizon.   To the north the Kuruk-tagh loomed up, with the grey *sai* at its foot.   Apart from this I was surrounded by the usual fantastic landscape, a maze, a jig-saw puzzle of blue-green, winding channels and lakes, with greyish-yellow *yardangs* and strips of yellow reed-bed.   It would be impossible to get it all clear on a map, except by a photograph from the air.   I had to content myself, as hitherto, with mapping our route through this labyrinth of newly arrived water, which in its advance had filled the gullies and depressions between the *yardangs*.   These stood out in the view as yellow strips, always running from north-east to south-west.   Here and there the beautiful, pictur-esque *mesas*—resembling castles, fortresses and towers— rose above the surface of the ground, which taken as a whole was absolutely flat.   There was more red in their colouring than in that of the lower *yardangs*.

Mesa on right bank, May 6.

Tamarisk and *yardangs* shaped like tables, May 6.

Objects found in mass grave (no. 1), May 6.

I took out my sketch-book and drew a complete panorama all round the horizon, with the points of the compass
marked. When this was done, I went down to the mass
grave again at 3 o'clock. The men had now laid out on the
edge of the grave fifteen skulls, four little food tables each
with four short legs, two bows, three wooden combs, eight
round or oval wooden bowls, and two light-grey clay
vessels. There were a few hair-pins, made of bamboo and
lacquered ; a crushed wooden jar, cylindrical in shape,
showed signs of pretty lacquering. There was a small
covered basket and four wooden spindle whorls ; also a pair
of small leather slippers and several pieces of silk of different
colours, some with beautiful patterns. A few small silk
purses, with delicate chain-stitch embroidery, were especially pretty. Chen was taking photographs all the time, and
I made a sketch.

The bodies did not seem to have lain in coffins. We
found the fragments lying all anyhow under their protection
of boards. Possibly the grave had been robbed in ancient
times, though the boarding suggested that this was not so.
We left behind a number of fragmentary skulls in bad condition, but took away everything else, besides three of the
skulls.

Two of our hawk-eyed boatmen discovered another grave
from the top of the *mesa*. This one was on the eastern side
of the *mesa*, on the top of a quite small *mesa* at the foot of the
big one.

Leaving the mass grave to the peace we had so heartlessly
and violently disturbed, we went down to the solitary resting-place, and as I saw that there would be no more paddling
that day, I ordered camp to be pitched just to the south-west
of grave no. 2. But all the men begged to be allowed to
stay with us till the investigation was over, and I could not
refuse them that ghoulish pleasure.

The small *mesa* with the single grave ran from north-east
to south-west. It was only 41 feet long by 12 feet wide.
Its summit was 29 feet above the surface of the water and
24 feet above the surrounding earth. From the top of the
big *mesa* one could see that the hillock contained a grave,
for a post of tamarisk wood stood on it, which could

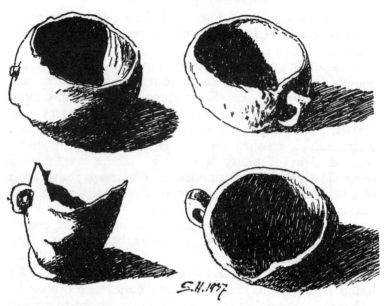

S.H.1937

Wooden bowls from mass grave (no. 1) ; originals 3·5, 4, 3·9 and 3·3 times as large as drawings.

not be natural, as the tops of *mesas* are always bare and sterile.

The isolated post invited digging, and the men got to work. But the clay of this *mesa* was almost as hard as brick, and in the process of transformation into clay-slate. So an axe was fetched up from the landing-place and the men cut their way through the hard material. The grave was rectangular. It was quite close to the north-western flank of the *mesa*, and the clay wall was only a foot thick on the top, lower down 2 feet. At a depth of 2 feet 3 inches the diggers struck a wooden lid, which was exposed first with the axe and then with the spade. It consisted of two very well-preserved boards 5 feet 11 inches long. The breadth of the lid was 1 foot 8 inches at the head and 1 foot 5½ inches at the foot, and the thickness of the boards was 1½ inches. The head lay towards the north-east.

As soon as the lid had been cleaned, and we had found that the coffin exactly fitted its clay case and that it was impossible to lift it out without enlarging the hole that had

The young woman's grave (no. 2), May 6.

been dug, we decided to clear away the clay wall on the north-western side, which cost us both time and labour. But at length the last obstacle was removed, and the coffin could be carefully coaxed out and lifted up on to the top of the *mesa*.

The shape of the coffin was characteristic of that watery region. It was just like an ordinary canoe, with the bow and stern sawn off and replaced by vertical cross-boards.

The two boards which formed the lid had been lifted even before the outer wall of the *mesa* was broken through. We eagerly awaited the sight of the unknown dead who had slept so long undisturbed. But instead we found only a blanket in which the corpse had been shrouded and which hid it completely from head to foot. The shroud was so brittle that it broke up into dust at a touch. We removed the part which concealed the head—and now we saw her in all her beauty, mistress of the desert, queen of Lou-lan and Lop-nor.

Death had surprised her young, and loving hands had enshrouded her and borne her to the peaceful mound within which she was to rest for nearly 2,000 years, till the children

G

of an age then far distant should wake her from her long sleep.

The skin of her face was like hard parchment, but its shape and features were not changed by time. She lay with eyelids closed over eye-balls that had fallen in hardly at all. About her lips a smile still played that the centuries had not extinguished, and which rendered the mysterious being still more appealing and attractive. But she did not betray the secrets of her past, and her memories of the variegated life of Lou-lan, the spring green about the lakes, river-trips by boat and canoe, she had taken with her to the grave.

She had seen the garrison of Lou-lan march out to battle against Huns and other barbarians ; the war chariots with their archers and spearmen ; the great trade caravans which had passed through Lou-lan and rested in its inns, and innumerable camels carrying bales of China's precious silk westward along the Silk Road. And surely she had loved, too, and had been loved. Perhaps she had died of grief. But of all that we could know nothing.

The length of the coffin inside was 5 feet 7 inches, and the unknown princess had been a little woman, about 5 feet 2 inches.

In the afternoon sunshine Chen and I began a fairly minute examination of the clothing in which she had been committed to the earth. She wore on her head a turban-like cap, and round it a simple band. Her body was covered with a linen cloth (possibly of hemp), and under this were two similar coverings of yellow silk. The breast was covered by a square red piece of embroidered silk, with, under it, yet another short linen garment. The lower part of the body was wrapped in a double silk covering, a kind of skirt, which formed the continuation of the yellow silk and the linen. In the same way a white cloth skirt was the continuation of the short linen garment. Under this again she wore a thin skirt, drawers and woven silk slippers. Her waist was encircled nearest the body by a kind of girdle.

We took away samples of all these garments, some—the headdress and slippers, for example—entire, and a purse of beautifully patterned silk in many colours. Outside the coffin, at its head, we found a rectangular four-legged food

Fleet of canoes on the Konche-daria

The flotilla on the Konche-daria

Author in his double canoe

Ördek

Rest for lunch on the Konche-daria : Author, Chen and Kung

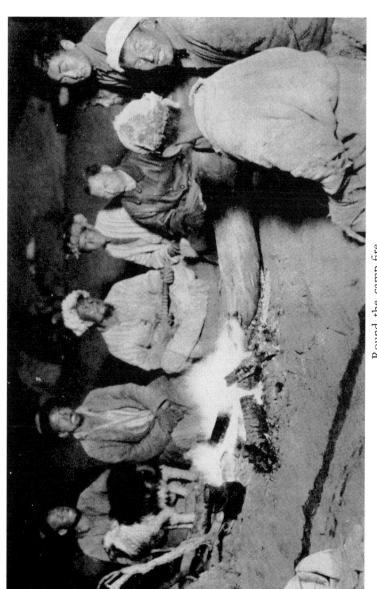

Round the camp-fire

Author talking to *beks* at Tömenpu

The faithful Tagil

Kitchen department on the Konche-daria : Li, Chia Kwei, Gagarin and two boatmen

Landing-place at base camp no. 70, Kum-daria

Abdu Rehim from Shindi

The Kum-daria

Yardangs south of the Kum-daria

" The unknown princess " lying beside her coffin

Author studying finds from first mass grave, May 7, 1934

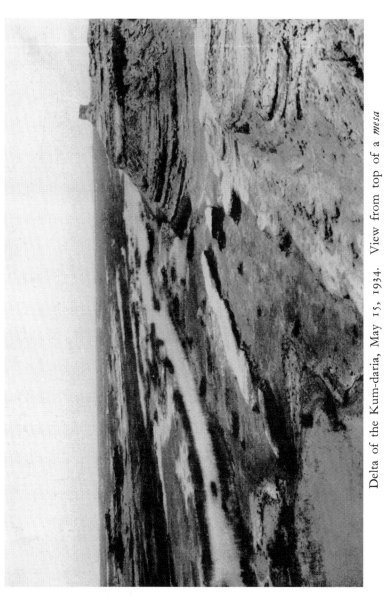

Delta of the Kum-daria, May 15, 1934. View from top of a *mesa*

table with a low rim ; a red-painted wooden bowl and the skeleton of a whole sheep—provisions for the traveller on her journey to another world.

But now it was growing dark again and we went to our camp, no. 77, where we were in danger of being eaten up by mosquitoes and gnats. The unknown young lady was left in her coffin in the starlight just for one night, and the breezes caressed her pale, somewhat yellowing cheeks, and her long hair. For one single night in nearly 2,000 years she had risen up out of her grave and returned to the world. But now she was only a dried-up mummy ; the land where she had spent her short life lay around her yellowish-grey and desolate, and the returning water had not yet recalled to life the woods, gardens, meadows and fields she had seen long ago.

Chen photographed " the Lady of the Desert " in the morning light of May 7. Then she was carefully placed in her coffin ; the coffin was let down again into the grave, and this was filled in as well as possible. Having taken a last farewell of the unknown one, and of our strangely realistic contact with antiquity, we returned to the landing-place, where the five double canoes lay loaded, and the river which had come back and given new life to that haunt of peace where the young woman had slept through the centuries.

VIII

IN THE MAZES OF THE DELTA

ON the morning of May 7 we again left the solitary grave on whose edge the " queen of Lou-lan " had slept in the starlight for one single night in 2,000 years.

We went on board and glided on down the capricious river-arm which by pure chance had elected to run past the foot of that interesting *mesa*, and into which equally pure chance had led us in the course of our trip to Lop-nor.

At a quarter to eleven the sun was darkened for a minute, and a few drops of rain fell—extremely unusual in that dry region. The mosquitoes, our tormentors, were driven away by a violent gust of wind and sought shelter in the thick reed-beds which raised their feathery heads over lakes and water-courses.

While resting again on a clay mound and taking observations our attention was drawn to a *mesa* situated 270 yards to the south-east. In the middle of its summit we perceived a depression resembling a saddle, and in its immediate neighbourhood some posts, obviously placed there by man's hand, stuck up out of the back of the *mesa*.

We went there, crossing a couple of small canals and a reedy marsh. The quite short upright posts, which were about 54 feet above the water, were the last remains of a little house. A few blows of the spade on the surface exposed fragments of shoes, a basket and pieces of ox-hide. Immediately to the south-west of it was a grave containing skeletons, which we left in peace, for this time at any rate.

It was impossible to follow the channel of the river. At 4 o'clock we again ascended a high *mesa* in order to discover our way. To the north-east fairly wide sheets of water appeared, fitted in among innumerable *yardang* ridges. The

Our boatmen assembled round grave (no. 3), May 7.

mesa rose to a height of 82 feet above the nearest bank. From this height the view was very different from that obtained from the surface of the water. The chief difference was that, from the boats, we saw the country horizontally. If we went out on to a lake, it seemed colossal, and the shores looked like a fine yellow ring at a considerable distance. But if we ascended a *mesa* 80 feet high, we saw the landscape more as a map unrolled at our feet. The yellow clay sediment predominated, with its *yardang* formation, and the fresh grey-green water-spaces shrank into mere nothings.

Here, too, the view was so fascinating and instructive that I could not resist drawing a new panorama. I had almost finished it when one of the boatmen came up and reported that they had found another grave—on the eastern slope of the *mesa*.

We went to it. The grave was situated on a small terrace, and was vigorously attacked with spade and axe. Three feet down we came upon a square piece of hardened ox-hide, which was carefully lifted out and placed on the edge of the grave. Then we saw at once an extremely shrivelled and mummified corpse, which, unlike the

The old woman in her coffin.

woman's body described in the last chapter, was not protected by any wooden lid or shroud, though, like the other,
it lay in a canoe-shaped coffin.

The face was uncovered and well preserved, and the
features, with their powerful nose and quiet assured smile,
made a noble, dignified impression. The coffin was 5 feet
5 inches long, and its breadth at the head was 15 inches, at
the feet 13 inches. The corpse was only 4 feet 9½ inches
tall.

This body, too, was that of a woman. She wore on her
head a cap with two upright pins in it, tipped with tufts of
feathers ; it had red strings and a split weasel-skin, whose
head hung down in front. This had doubtless a special
symbolic meaning. Her hair was fairly long and grey, and
was parted down the middle.

For the rest, the whole body was shrouded in a dark brown finely woven mantle, rectangular, with a lighter strip, about an inch wide, at the edges. It measured 6 feet by 5½ feet. The right-hand edge of the cloak was gathered into three round bags, with string tied round them and containing small Ephedra twigs, probably of symbolic meaning.

We lifted the body out of the coffin and spread out the cloak on the ground. Under it the dead woman wore round her body a thin girdle, with long fringes hanging down. On her feet she had boots of rough ox-hide with an inner sole of lambskin.

She was little and weak, the skeleton fine and thin, with the brown skin, as hard as parchment, stretched tightly over it. The colour of the face too was dark brown, in contrast to that of the first female corpse, which had a light skin. On the side of the head were a few locks of brown hair. On top of the ox-hide were some provisions in a basket. We took with us everything which could serve for identification purposes, including the right-hand side of the mantle with the three bags.

Who had she been, this solitary old lady with the dis-

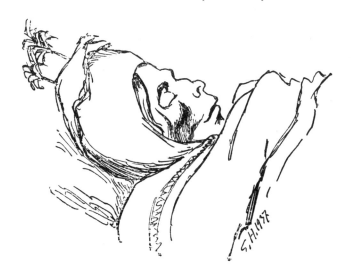

The old woman in profile.

tinguished profile ?   Probably one of the actual inhabitants
of the kingdom of Lou-lan.

The grave was 73 feet above the surface of the water, and
so not quite 10 feet below the top of the *mesa*.   We had now
found four graves, all situated high above the water.   They
had probably been placed there intentionally, so as to be out
of range of even the highest flood.   Although the young
woman's grave lay comparatively low, the water had clearly
never reached it.

From the top of the *mesa* we sighted a good-sized lake to
the southward, blue-green in colour, with yellow strips that
were last year's reeds.   This lake was full of islands, capes
and creeks between the *yardangs*.   To the eastward we could
see small scattered pieces of water and arms of the river
joining them.

We lay down to rest quite near the mysterious woman's
grave.   We felt cold, for the minimum temperature dropped
to 37 degrees.

About midnight we heard, once a minute, a piercing cry
which we had never heard before.   Was it the old lady
expressing her anger at being so brutally disturbed in her
thousand years' dream, or simply an owl, or some unhappy
water-bird crying for its mate ?

We steered south-west, west, north and north-east along
a curiously winding arm with a good current.   For long
stretches we felt that we were on one single uninterrupted
arm, but in reality a number of small canals ran out of it,
well-concealed in the reeds and giving access to other arms
of the delta and lakes.   Only from the tops of *yardangs* and
mounds could we make anything of that involved labyrinth
of water-ways.

But at last our channel narrowed, the current disappeared,
and we found a way out into another, which led to a fair-
sized open sheet of water.   We had a choice of two routes,
and took one which ran N 25 degrees E.   The water was
quite clear, of a green colour, and quite fresh to the taste.
A slight current was perceptible.   We were often surrounded on all sides by thick reeds, above which solitary
yardangs stuck up here and there.

We went on searching and searching in every direction,

With headdress removed.

A fresh blind alley forced us back a good way to the south-west, where a channel led us to another large broad, bordered at some distance by reed-beds. A few flocks of wild geese rose and disappeared to the south-west.

"What grazing grounds for sheep and cattle!" Sadik exclaimed. He was right. The reeds grew and withered there each year to no one's profit, and masses of valuable water were lost instead of being used for irrigation, which could give bread and prosperity.

It was half-past seven when we encamped on a bank where there was no fuel. We sacrificed two deck planks to the camp-fire.

A little while before we pitched camp we had passed a graceful clay obelisk and several splendid *mesas*, like royal palaces and fairy castles. The boatmen received orders in the evening to go out early next morning and look for a more promising arm of the river.

There was a minimum temperature of 42·4 degrees on the night of May 8–9, strangely cold for so late in the year! The scouts had been out, and when we got up in the morning they reported that they had not been able to find an arm of the river with any current, but that they had found the ruins of a fair-sized house on the mainland to the

Yardangs with tops like tables, on left bank, May 8.

north-west.   Chen suspected at once that this was the fort
T'u-ken, discovered by the archæologist Hwang Wen-pi
during our expedition in 1930.   Just on nine we got into a
double canoe and rowed to the place over open water free
of reeds.   It took scarcely half an hour to reach the place.

The posts of the house rose from a low mound situated
on a peninsula, which had water on three sides—west, south
and east.   Chen had been there in the early spring of 1931
during Hörner's expedition to Lop-nor, and recognized
the place at once.

Some of our boatmen had dug a hole in the middle of the
house without finding anything.   I immediately forbade all
further digging.   Nothing might be touched ; not even the
smallest log might be taken away for fuel.   We stayed for
about an hour, which I needed to make a sketch of the place
with all its details.   Chen took some photographs and
measurements.

We had now an interesting link-up with Chen's earlier
map and knew that Altmish-bulak was 17 miles away to
the NNW.

We pushed off again at 11.15 and returned to camp no. 79,
where our things were embarked ; then we set a course
to the south-west.   One thing was evident—that the ruin
lay on slack water which did not continue to the north-east.
The arms of the delta which conveyed the waters of the
Kum-daria to Lop-nor must be found farther to the southward.

We glided once more past the curiously formed obelisk or
column we had seen the day before—this time at a greater
distance.   Seen sideways on it resembled one of the superb
propylæa at the entrance to the palace of Xerxes at Per-
sepolis.

Looking S and SW, May 8.

We were out in the open again, but often passed yellow reedy islands rising out of the clear, grey-green water. Our direction was north-west and north. We entered a labyrinth of islets and reeds. At 2 p.m. the temperature of the air was 71·8 and of the water 59. We sighted to port an island with fuel on it; we steered to it and collected a fair store of dry tamarisk boughs and stems. Then we went northward and landed at dusk. We found a *yardang* with a flat surface just wide enough for the tent. On every side except the south-west it was bounded by a perpendicular drop of from 6 to 10 feet, so that one had to be careful if one went out star-gazing in the dark.

When we were settled down in this camp, no. 80, I sent for the boatmen.

They had seen Yew, Kung and Effe go off eastward on April 27 with the small car and a lorry on their attempt to reach Tun-hwang via Altmish-bulak. What we now wanted to know was whether the motor expedition had passed eastward and come back in the direction of the cars' base camp, no. 70. The instructions, therefore, which I gave to three boatmen, Apak, Hajit and Ismail, was to start at dawn and walk straight NNW to the mountain foot, but to return as soon as they found wheel-tracks. They were, further, to decide whether the tracks showed that the cars had returned or not. They took with them a red and white signal flag, which, if the cars had not come back, was to be set firmly in the track, and an empty jam-tin in which we had placed letters from Chen and myself saying that we were

Mesa island south of T'u-ken.

on the nearest water 6¼ miles east of the meridian of Lou-lan.
We asked our fellows, when they returned to base camp
no. 70, to send the small car to fetch us. The three scouts
had orders to return to us the same evening.

Just as Chia Kwei was about to serve our dinner, a violent
ENE storm burst. We heard the clatter of flying saucepan
lids and plates. The boatmen packed up their things and
took refuge in a deep hollow between two *yardangs*. Our
tent was made fast with a few boxes, flour-sacks and blocks
of clay. The faithful Tagil curled himself up in the shelter
a hollow afforded.

On the morning of May 10 two single canoes were got
ready. The larger, Chen's, had three paddlers ; I took the
smaller one with two paddlers. We steered NNE, with
solid land and *mesas* to our left and a maze of *yardangs* and
reedy islands to our right. Our intention was simply to
make a trip to Chen's camp no. 106 of the Hörner expedition, and so link up with his map yet again.

It was a lovely day ; a light north-easterly breeze lashed
the water into waves that shone in the sun. The water was
green, and made a vivid, colourful contrast to the yellowish-
grey *yardangs* and the pale reddish *mesas*.

We slipped along a channel hardly 20 yards wide, between
the mainland on our left and an island of dense reeds on our
right. With only one boat and two sturdy paddlers we

worked up a good pace, and the water foamed about our bows. My canoe was ahead. Fifteen yards ahead of us appeared a wild hog, swimming from the mainland to the reeds. He was timid, scented danger and swam for dear life. The water foamed round his bows too.

" Paddle your hardest ! " I cried, but the paddlers only pretended to increase their speed.

" He's got knives in his mouth ; he's dangerous," Sadik said.

Anyhow, he had already reached the edge of the reed-bed. The yellow stems were pushed aside like curtains as he advanced ; his feet touched ground, a bound or two and he was on dry land ; we heard the reeds cracking and snapping under his feet, and he disappeared on the eastern side of the island.

An antelope stood at the foot of a *mesa* and stared at us. He was as still as a stuffed museum specimen. But next moment he gave a start and vanished into a gully between the *mesa* and a clay mound.

Tamarisks and reeds looked up out of the water. It was a delicious place ! I sat with my sleeves rolled up and dabbled my hands in the cool rippling water. The channel we had been following for half an hour came to an end ; the mainland bounded it on the north. We landed there, and Chen had no difficulty in finding his camp no. 106, where he had been at the beginning of March, 1931. A *mesa* rose near by, and I ascended to the top of it to draw a panorama.

While I was thus occupied, the boatman Ali rushed up breathless and reported that he had found the fresh tracks of two riders, going north-east on big horses. He was convinced that they were scouts searching for us. A little later Sadik told us that he had seen the tracks of two camels, two horses, three donkeys, seven sheep and a man walking. We decided that it must be the archæologist Hwang, who was also about in those parts, and whom we had not seen since we started from Korla. He was probably now on the way to his old haunt, T'u-ken. It came to light later that he had smelt out a store of flour at a spring called Nan-chan-bulak in the Kuruk-tagh (Tun-hwang group). He had also come across the shepherd whom Bergman had sent to Chen

Mesa columns, looking NE, May 8.

and me with several sheep, and had simply taken two of the
animals without further ado. This way of obtaining provisions on the march is both practical and convenient, but
may be fatal to those who are robbed of their supplies.

We embarked and steered homewards. In the light of
the setting sun the panorama of *mesas* to the south-west was
fantastically splendid, the landscape of a dream. We saw
sleeping dogs, lions and dragons, fairy castles, fortresses,
towers. Just before six we slipped into the deep shadow
flung by a tall *mesa*. We landed and ascended to its summit,
and I made one or two more sketches of that wonderful
mingling of fresh green water and weather-hewn *yardangs*
and *mesas*.

We were home at twilight. At 7 o'clock we heard shouts
to the northward. Gagarin fired one or two shots as a
signal, and a fire was lighted on the top of a *yardang*. Now
and again the boatmen answered the shouts ; but now all
was quiet to the northward. The three scouts did not
appear in the camp till half-past eight, when they were
immediately summoned to my tent.

Apak told their story. When they had gone 80 li, and
were nearer to the mountains than to the lake, they had
come upon the track of a lorry and small car going eastward.

View SW from a *mesa*, May 10.

The tracks of the small car were just to the left of those of the lorry. The ground was so hard that the track was not clear, but they followed it for a short distance eastward, where the ground was softer, and then they could see plainly that the cars had only gone eastward, so that they had not yet returned from Tun-hwang. The *sai* was hard up to a point 15 li from camp no. 80. They had seen the same tracks of a caravan that we had found near Chen's camp no. 106. They had also surprised nine wild camels, one of them a gigantic beast, which had fled towards the mountains. The scouts had planted the flag in the cars' tracks and placed the dispatch-tin securely within a ring of stones.

The whole report, which Apak delivered in a tone of complete assurance, sounded perfectly credible. The two cars, then, had passed eastward on one of the last days of April or at the beginning of May, on their search for a practicable road to Tun-hwang. It had been my dream, as I have said, to revive and open for motor traffic the old Silk Road, abandoned for 1,600 years, which had led from China proper via Tun-hwang, Lop-nor, Lou-lan and the Kum-daria to Kashgar.

It seemed to Chen and me curious that Yew, Kung and Effe had not yet returned. Perhaps they had remained at Tun-hwang for some days trying to get petrol and lubricating oil from Anhsi, where the German-Chinese Eurasia aeroplane company had one of its depots on the Shanghai-Urumchi air route. But the responsibility I bore for the eight travellers' lives made me nervous. If the lorry had suffered any irreparable injury half-way to Tun-hwang, or the water supply had been exhausted, their lives would not have been worth much in that awful desert, where in 1901 I had walked for eleven days without finding a drop of water, and where Hörner and Chen had sought water in vain for a fortnight.

Our anxieties were thus fully justified, but, as we found on our return from Lop-nor, quite unnecessary. The motor convoy under Yew and Kung came upon such terribly difficult country on its way through the mountains to Altmish-bulak that it did not reach that place ("the Sixty Springs") till May 13. It reached Altmish-bulak from the north-west and returned south-west to base camp no. 70 the same day. The retreat of the convoy was due not to difficult country farther to the eastward, in the direction of Tun-hwang, but to the fact that its supply of oil was coming to an end.

As our men were not at, or near, Altmish-bulak before May 13, the three heroes, Apak, Hajit and Ismail, could not possibly have seen any wheel-tracks on May 10! The whole of the story they had dished up for Chen and me was pure invention from beginning to end! Even the picturesque touch of colour provided by the nine wild camels was presumably a lie. The only tiny scrap of truth they had told was about the tracks of camels, donkeys and sheep on the river bank, for those we had seen ourselves. They had evidently been on the river bank, but, I am sure, not a step farther.

One can imagine how their minds worked. They came to the point where the water ended when the sun was already high and the heat of the day was beginning. And they had said to themselves : " What in the name of the eternal Allah is the use of going to and fro through that

awful desert for a whole day ?   We'll stay here on the bank
and drink our fill of the sweet fresh water and have a good
sleep.   We'll tell Tura (the master) that we have seen the
tracks, and throw away the flag and the tin.   Tura can't
know what we've been doing, and we shall get our reward
for the good news that the track has been found.   When
the sun sets we'll go back to Tura's camp and report."

And they acted accordingly.   When I heard, later on,
that the cars had passed three days after the three heroes'
imaginary expedition, I sent for them, called them rogues
and liars, and announced that they were not to receive the
reward that had been intended.   They sat with bowed heads
and did not say a word.   When I had finished my lecture,
they went to their camp-fire and lay down, silent and
ashamed.   That is what the East Turkis are like.   Reliable
men are rare among that people.   Perhaps the war, the
widespread robbery, the bleeding of the people by passing
Tungans, and the general insecurity have demoralized the
country population, formerly so honest and winning.   If so,
it may be hoped that their good qualities will return when
peace and order once more prevail in Eastern Turkistan.

Not counting the different groups of our own expedition
and a very small number of herdsmen on the Kum-daria,
Chen and I, our ten boatmen and Gagarin were alone in the
Lop country.

We calculated that our nearest neighbours were : to the
north-west Singer, where Abdu Rehim's brother lived, 88
miles from our camp ; to the SSW Miran, 120 miles away ;
to the WSW Tikenlik, 133 miles ; to the south-west Charkhlik, 163 miles ; to the north Turfan, 164 miles ; to the
north-east Hami, 235 miles ; to the ESE Tun-hwang,
262 miles ; and to the south-east Bulungir-nor, 276 miles.
If one connects all these places on a map by straight lines,
there is a very considerable slice of Central Asia, or about
78,000 square miles, in which we were practically the only
human beings.   This area is almost equal to that of Eng-
land and Scotland.   Asia covers an area of 17,000,000
square miles, with rather more than 1,000,000,000 inhabitants, or 59 to the square mile.   The belt of desert where
we were constituted $\frac{1}{220}$th of the whole of Asia and was

inhabited by about a hundred persons. If the whole continent were as thinly peopled as our desert, its population would be only 22,000—rather smaller than that of Winchester.

Chen and I were the most easterly group of our expedition. And now we had made camp no. 80 our base camp, from which our advance to Lop-nor, the wandering lake, was to begin.

IX

THE JOURNEY TO LOP-NOR

WE woke on May 11 to find a strong north-easterly wind blowing—27 miles an hour. The minimum night temperature had been higher than before—64·8 degrees. At 2 p.m. the thermometer rose to 91·9, and the water warmed up to a temperature of 64·9. The day was lost. Lakes and creeks were covered with white foaming waves. Our craft lay moored far inside the reeds, where the water was comparatively smooth. Clouds of flying sand rattled against the tent, which threatened to break loose. Chia Kwei and Gagarin established the cooking apparatus, the larder and their own lair in a deep, grotto-like cleft among the *yardangs*. At 8 p.m. the strength of the wind had increased to 39 miles an hour, and the temperature was still 82 degrees. The light was blown out again and again by violent gusts. It was too hot to lie in our sleeping-bags, and we lay on them very comfortably. The whole of the interior of the tent was covered with fine yellow dust.

Next morning too it was blowing hard—nearly 37 miles an hour. We had to arm ourselves with patience. We allotted to the men the different roles they were to play in our forthcoming plans. Apak, Hajit and Hashim were to go to Bergman's camp on May 13 with letters and orders to send us the small car—if it had returned from Tun-hwang. If they met the herdsman we had sent for, Hashim was to come back with him to show him the way to our camp no. 80. Apak was to come back with the car, also to show the way. The three men had baked bread given them for their journey. Musa, Tokhta, Ismail and Gagarin were ordered to remain at camp no. 80. The dog Tagil was left there too. Chen and I and our cook, Chia Kwei, had this time only two double boats with twenty-six deck planks—

Mesas near camp no. 77.

twelve were left behind.   Our boatmen were Sadik, Babeddin, Rozi and Ali.   We had 150 chin of baked and unbaked
flour, and all necessary provisions for a couple of weeks or
so.   We took five petrol tins, cleaned with boiling water,
in which we carried fresh water for use in the event of our
losing our way on the salt lake Lop-nor.   Curiously enough
our men had never heard of Lop-nor, and were somewhat
depressed when they heard that it was two and a half times
as large as the Baghrash-köl, the biggest " sea " they knew.
The storm howled all night.   But on the morning of the
13th we decided to defy the wind and waves, pushed off, and
kept in shelter as much as possible.   But when we had
reached the island where we had collected tamarisk wood a
few days before, we had great open spaces to the east and
south-east, where the sea was too heavy for the canoes.
We landed on the island and found a well-protected harbour
among *yardangs* and reeds.   The four boatmen collected
fuel.   We waited, hoping that the wind would abate.   But
the whole day passed, and it did not.
The storm had lost us three days—May 11, 12 and 13—
and on the 14th the whole country was shrouded in an
impenetrable fog.   It came rolling up from the south, dark
and gloomy, like gigantic mattresses and bolsters, and two

Small lakes in *mesa* landscape. View NNW, May 13.

hours later the wind went round into the south-west. But this did not drive away the mist. Everything was enveloped in a regular London fog. We could see only the nearest hundred yards or so of the lake. It was a weird picture—the lake a dirty grey, with thick mist over it and the reed-beds looming up out of the haze. A few light showers fell, and at 1.30 p.m. harder rain set in and continued for an hour. But it was quiet now, and twilight fell ; we were so near camp no. 80 that, in the evening, we could hear the men we had left behind singing.

Heavy rain fell in the night, but did not last long. The sun rose into a bright blue sky, and we set off again to look for the tortuous waterway to Lop-nor. From a high *mesa* we had another of those phenomenal views over the Lop delta. The lake, on whose north-eastern shore the fort T'u-ken lies, closed like a bag. So all the water which was carried into the delta must find its way out into Lop-nor somewhere else. But where ? We tried an arm which ran south-east, but there was no current in it. The water was crystal-clear ; the *mesas* were reflected in it and a whole row of *yardangs* which, as so often before, reminded us of coffins.

In the afternoon Babeddin went up on to a *yardang* and reported that he had found an arm of the river, largely hidden by reeds. We followed the current among the reeds, and its speed increased. We took another observation from a high *mesa*. Thick reed-beds lay in several directions, and in one of them we saw an open waterway, possibly a continuation of that which we had been following. The new green reed-stems of the spring had shot up as high as 3 feet above the surface of the water, all the more conspicuous among the straw-yellow reeds of last year. The tamarisks were freshly clad in new green. Fish jumped on the surface, and water-birds were commoner than they had been till now.

At 6 o'clock we were paddling through reeds which grew thicker and thicker, and now usually concealed the banks of solid clay; but long jetties of mud, deposited by the high water in autumn, were visible here and there.

The channel grew wider and wider, as much as 130 to 160 yards. Two eagles regarded us with attention; gulls and terns hovered about us, and little birds twittered over the reeds. Flocks of duck rose once or twice. There was more wild life than before; down here the fresh water from the Kum-daria had discharged its life-giving mission with greater vigour.

But in a little while the reeds grew thinner, and at last almost stopped. Now the dark clay banks, quite bare, lay to right and left of us. No more *mesas* were to be seen, hardly even an isolated *yardang* some distance from the water. We were in a transition stage between the *yardangs* and the saliferous clay, or old salt sludge, which the Turks call *shor*. The arm of the river grew wider and shallower. Among the reeds the depth had been 10 feet, and now it was only 3 feet; we were continually touching ground, and the boatmen were toiling and pushing with their paddles to get us off.

The sun was low; evening was approaching. I ordered the party to land and pitch camp. We were in midstream, at an equal distance from both banks. The sun set, and twilight came on. Sadik tried to bring my boat to the left bank. Impossible. He tried the right. Equally shallow

Pillar left by erosion on islet, May 15.

everywhere ! It grew dark. A small crescent moon was
up, but threw only a weak light.

We turned and steered upstream again, but went aground.
A fresh evening breeze sprang up, and the river, lately as
smooth as a mirror, was broken into little waves, which
plashed melodiously against the canoes. We tried westward, southward—one place as shallow as another. And
now it was getting really dark. But as the result of much
shoving and wriggling we reached the right bank at last and
landed on *shor* as hard as a brick, where not a blade of grass
grew and not one stick of drift-wood had come ashore. We
found with difficulty a level surface large enough for the
tent. A deck plank was sacrificed to our evening fire and
supper. This was our camp no. 82, and from here we were
to make our last advance towards the wandering lake.

When we stepped out of the tent on the morning of
May 16, we were at last able to get our bearings in that most
interesting and peculiar landscape. We were quite near
the point where the Kum-daria, or the main arm of its delta,
ran into Lop-nor, and the northernmost part of the famous
lake lay spread out to the south-east like an inlet of the sea.
Gulls flew screaming over the tent and river, frightened or
angered at the arrival of men in their peaceful fishing waters.

5.H. 1937

Chia Kwei and his kitchen; waiting alone while we went by boat to Lop-nor.

They contributed to the seashore illusion. No vegetation in sight—all was dead and desolate.

A fresh breeze was blowing, and again we had to wait. But meanwhile we made all preparations for a start. Chen and I were to travel in the largest canoe with two paddlers; in two of the smaller canoes, each propelled by one paddler, we had provisions, two tins of fresh water, and fur coats. We did not take the tent; it remained at camp no. 82, where Chia Kwei had to await our return all alone. A sheep was slaughtered, and we took the meat with us.

Our plan was to steer out on to the lake, follow its eastern bank to the southward, cross the wide southern basin and row back northward along the west bank. Our men thought they could paddle us 30 miles a day in still weather. If we were caught in a storm in the middle of the lake, we were lost. The investigations of Hörner and Chen had shown that the banks were so shelving and soft that it would probably be impossible to land. At nightfall, therefore, we should fasten the three canoes together and sleep in them. I was anxious to find out whether the new Lop-nor had changed its shape in three years, and if its configuration was now different from when Hörner and

Chen had made their map. Now, when the summer was coming on, and the volume of water which was carried to the lake daily down the Kum-daria was decreasing, it might be supposed that Lop-nor had become smaller ; for Hörner and Chen had been there in winter, after the autumn flood had filled the lake.

About midday the wind dropped ; we took leave of the solitary Chia Kwei and proceeded down the shallow river. As we now had single canoes and a light cargo, we got over the shallows—with a good deal of bottom-scraping—and steered south-east.

At 1.45 we glided out on to the lake, whose shores seemed to retreat before us. We steered SSE for a darkish cape on the eastern shore, but were continually forced off our course by the shallowness of the water.

I felt myself in fairyland out on the waters of that lake sanctuary, on which no boat had ever moved before ! It was dead still now ; the surface of the water was like a mirror. Some way off ducks were swimming ; gulls and other sea-birds uttered their cries of warning. To the south-east we saw a row of black lumps, evidently hillocks on a pier-shaped tongue of land. The mirage made them appear to be hovering above the horizon, a phenomenon we knew so well from the Gobi desert. Due south and south-west the horizon was quite clear ; there sky and water met just as on the open sea. To the SSW was what looked like a string of Zeppelins flying over Lop-nor. Closer, to the south-east, black objects shaped like horsemen stood out ; these were grazing oxen and camels. But their only motion was a quivering vibration caused by the warmed air as it ascended.

The farther south we went the shallower the water became. Babeddin and Ali waded, towing the canoe behind them, while the two other men, who had left their boats stranded, pushed from behind. Black streaks of mud appeared on the surface behind the boats. The sun blazed down hot, and the light was blinding ; the water shone opaline and steel-grey to westward, but a bright sea-blue to the south and east.

We sought in vain for a deeper channel. We made for

Babeddin dragging his canoe; Ali about to get overboard.

the westward. Babeddin " put up " a fish, and ran in pursuit of it with his paddle lifted above his head like a spear.
He struck again and again with the broad sharp blade, and
the fish leapt so that the water spouted round it. Another
blow, and Babeddin bent down and bore his quarry to us in
triumph.

Strange fish ! they must lie asleep in the sunshine. One,
a good 3 feet long, was evidently awakened by my boat, for
it smacked the side with its tail and swam off.

The canoes jumped, caught and bumped against the
unevennesses of the mud bottom ; stuck fast and bumped
again. At times they were dragged through water a few
inches deep. The topmost layer of sediment was yellow,
from 0·08 inch to 0·27 inch in depth, resting on a rather
thicker stratum of black sediment, which must have been
there when the water came back thirteen years before. It
looked, therefore, as if the yellow layer with an average
depth of 0·19 inch had taken thirteen years to settle.

But evening was near ; the sun was setting, and its farewell to earth afforded us a magnificent spectacle, which no
words can describe. The whole south-east was steel-blue ;
one could not tell where sky ended and earth began. The

Camp no. 83, view to westward.

sun rested on a bed of red, yellow, violet and white clouds,
and a warm ruddy glow spread over the lake to westward.

Sweat dripped from the men as they dragged the canoes
over the stiff muddy bottom till they were dead tired.
Under the sediments lay a layer of hard crystallized salt,
which made their feet sore.

We altered course to the north-east, making for the
nearest island, and passed through water a foot deep, in
which the boatmen could get into the canoes again and use
their paddles. We landed at dusk on an unknown coast, a
miniature island of hard salty ground with a rust-brown
crust, on which not a blade of grass grew. Here the canoes
were dragged ashore and we pitched camp.

Six planks were placed on the ground as a foundation for
Chen's and my beds, which were laid on canvas and blankets.
Babeddin cooked the fish he had caught and made *shislik* [1]
over the embers. We had a peaceful night with a minimum
temperature of 53 ; the gulls screamed above us and the
stars shone clear.

The orders for the day on May 17 were that the two small

[1] See page 22.

light canoes should be held in readiness and should be rowed by Babeddin and Ali, with Chen in one and myself in the other, and no other cargo. The object of the trip was a rapid reconnaissance to the westward. Somewhere in the northernmost part of the lake there ought to be a deeper channel, eaten out by the water that streamed in from the Kum-daria.

A light mist hung over Lop-nor; to the south and east no land was visible; only in the south-west, in which direction we were now steering, was a strip of coast to be seen. A light SSE breeze rippled the surface of the lake. At 2 p.m. the temperature of the air had risen to 79·7 degrees and that of the water to 80 degrees.

The lake was just as shallow to the westward as to the eastward. We measured 7·4 inches, 5·4 inches, and 2·7 inches, and at that point we stuck fast. Babeddin and Ali walked gingerly ahead, dragging the canoes behind them. But at last it was impossible to go any farther southward. We halted, and sent the men southward to search for a channel. They looked as if they were walking on the water; the mud was churned up in their tracks as black as ink.

At our halting-place we took some photographs and further examined the mud on the bottom of the lake. The yellow river mud on the top formed a layer o·19 inch deep, which rested on a deposit of black mud o·39 inch thick. Under this was a stratum of rather coarse sand, o·8 inch thick, and beneath this again a 3·1-inch stratum of crystallized salt. In places the salt was even thicker than this.

And yet the northern part of the lake is fresh! At any rate, its salt content of o·3 per cent. was hardly perceptible to the taste. And fish flourished there in multitudes. The two men had become quite expert at stunning them with the blade of the paddle and catching them with their hands. The biggest fish caught was 3 feet 7 inches long and 6·2 inches from dorsal fin to belly. Another was 3 feet 3 inches long and 6 inches from dorsal fin to belly, the rest from 2 feet 11 inches to 3 feet 2½ inches. It is strange that a fish of such dimensions can live in water 8 inches deep. When they were scared into motion at our approach, we sometimes saw the dorsal fin sticking up like a periscope

View across Lop-nor from camp no. 83, May 18. No land visible to southward.

above the surface, which was covered with ripples and eddies by the fish's rapid movements, so that its pursuit was no difficult matter.

In the northern part of Lop-nor, then, we were in no danger of dying of starvation; there were fish and there was water. But on what do the fish live? We saw not a trace of waterweeds or other vegetation, no crustaceans or insects. Perhaps the mud on the bottom contains some organic matter which affords them nourishment. The white flesh of these fish was poor eating, in contrast to the fish that used to be caught at Abdal and on the lower Tarim.[1]

Late in the afternoon we steered back to the camp on the island, where Sadik and Rozi, while awaiting our return, had erected an awning over their resting-place. On the way home we found a channel 90 yards wide and about a foot deep, and decided to follow this next day.

The Kuruk-tagh was clearly visible, but in quiet subdued colouring, from N 45 degrees W to N 16 degrees E.

[1] Hummel's collection of fish and reptiles from the Kum-daria was unfortunately ruined on the journey home by motor-car.

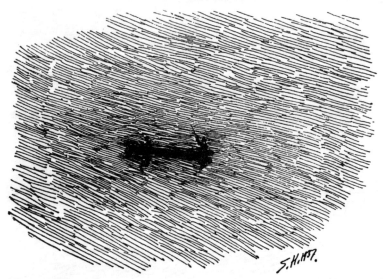

Out on Lop-nor on a misty day. We could not see where sky and earth met.

This evening too there was a magnificent sunset, in shades of umber-brown, violet, pink and blue. The sun itself was orange, and as bright an orange was its reflection in the still shining lake.

A humorous bird was sitting somewhere near by and emitting from time to time loud cries, now suggesting a lowing cow, now a braying donkey, now the short, piercing signals of a steamer or a motor-car. It was presumably a bittern, for this bird (*Botaurus stellaris*) is, Hummel noted, not uncommon on the banks of the Konche-daria in the region where he made his collections. In East Turki the bittern bears the characteristic name of *köl-buka*, or " lake bull yak ". The people along the Konche-daria declare that it has the curious habit of inflating its throat with air and emitting its penetrating cry six or seven times. This effort is said to exhaust it to such a degree that it becomes for a time almost paralysed and can be taken with the hands. They say, too, that a substance which is used as a remedy for consumption can be extracted from some part of its body. We, in our camp on the lonely island in Lop-nor, much enjoyed the bird's far from melodious serenade.

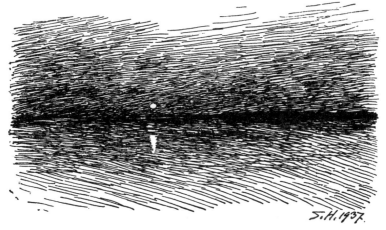

Sunset on shores of Lop-nor.

Next day the sky was turquoise-blue and the lake as smooth as glass. We reconnoitred along the channel we had found, but it grew shallow and disappeared. We had tested the depth of the water in every direction, and everywhere had been stopped by a barrier which in places came right up to the surface of the water. It was clear that a sounding of the whole lake ought to be carried out in late autumn, after the flood has emptied itself into Lop-nor and made its northern half navigable as well as the southern.

My dream that it might once in my life be granted me to navigate by boat the " wandering lake " in its new northern bed had certainly been fulfilled, and I had every reason to be thankful for this. On the other hand, my hope of being able to make a prolonged voyage on Lop-nor had not been realized, though Chen and I had at least the satisfaction of feeling that we had done our uttermost for three days to achieve this object. It was, perhaps, fortunate for us that our four boatmen were not able to drag the two canoes, no longer fastened together and correspondingly lighter, over the wide barrier where the bottom of the lake was practically on the surface, or at any rate not more than 2¾ inches below it. This barrier was probably the boundary between fresh and salt water. The northern basin, in which we sought vainly for a channel of some depth, is continually receiving fresh water from the Kum-daria, and the surplus runs over the barrier into the big southern basin, swollen into the shape of a balloon. This, too, is in all probability very shallow. The greatest depth I ever sounded in Kara-koshun was 14 feet 7 inches, and this was also the maximum depth of Lake Sogho-nor, into which two arms of the Etsin-gol delta run, and which Lieutenant Henning Haslund sounded in the autumn of 1927.

The depth of the new Lop-nor in all probability does not exceed this figure. But that exasperating barrier made it impossible for us to establish this with certainty. But what might not have happened if the barrier had not been in the way ! We had reckoned that it would take us five days' paddling to navigate the whole of Lop-nor as it appeared on Hörner's map. Chen had walked all round the lake with Hörner and knew that it was a good-sized salt pool, 78 miles from north to south and 48 miles across at its widest point. Lake Vänern, in Sweden, is about the same size, 84 by 48. But the whole northern part of Lop-nor is a good deal narrower, and the total area of the lake is not half that of Vänern (2,200 square miles). Vänern has a river running through it, so that it has fresh water and its size remains unchanged, or varies only to an insignificant degree. Lop-nor is a terminal lake, and therefore has salt water and changes its size as the inflow varies with the seasons, and on account of the evaporation, which is very marked in the hot dry air of summer.

We had on board fresh water in petrol tins and provisions for five days, and, as I have already said, our intention was to make a fairly extensive voyage over the thirteen-year-old lake. We took with us also an areometer to investigate the salt content of the water. Fortunately Hörner and Chen had already drawn a complete map of the wandering lake, and it did not matter much whether the maximum depth was 10, 12 or 15 feet, but such a boat trip would have been delightful if only as a piece of sport, an adventure. It would have been daring and risky, and attractive not least for that reason. I for my part should have set out on it with the same feelings as on April 10, 1895, when the camels started on the desert journey through the sand-sea of the Taklamakan. Then, as now, the fascination of the enterprise lay in the pregnant question, " Will it come off or not ? " Neither Chen nor I hesitated for an instant, and our four boatmen, who had never before seen so much water all at once, had no clear idea of the danger. In the early summer of 1900 I had more than once been caught in squalls on the lakes along the Tarim and reached land only in the nick of time before the canoe filled. My boat had sunk on one occasion, but so near land that I and my boatmen were able to wade ashore.

But Lop-nor is a good-sized piece of water, and to cross it for 15 or 20 miles in open canoes would have been a risky undertaking. We had intended to start from the point where the eastern shore projects farthest into the lake, choosing still weather, and paddle hard across to the south-western bank. The squalls nearly always come from the north-east, so if it had begun to blow hard when we were in the middle of the lake we should at least have had a following wind. But there would have been a pretty high sea running, and it would have risen higher every minute.

A cloth boat, such as I had used on the lakes in Tibet, would have been lifted on the crest of each oncoming wave to sink gently into the trough behind and be lifted again by the next wave. But wooden canoes are quite another matter. They are long and straight ; the bulwarks are low and bent inwards in conformity with the shape of the poplar trunk. A wave rolling past a craft so shaped comes on board with the greatest ease. As the sea is rising all the time, more and more water is taken on board. I well remember what it was like. One paddler is in the bows, the other astern. Both kneel, leaning forward ; they make their strokes as long and as swift as possible and put all their strength into them in order to drive the canoe forward and, if possible, so increase its speed that the waves shall not pass it, and that it shall be continually in a trough running in the direction of the wind.

With my experience of stormy boat trips, I have no difficulty in describing what would in all probability have happened to us if we had been in the southern part of the wandering lake and had been caught by one of those furious

I

north-easterly storms which break so suddenly in the spring.
I am now going to paint a fancy picture, and I ask my
readers not to forget that it is imaginary, because the
shallow barrier right across the northern part of the lake
prevented our advancing any farther to the southward.

Here my imaginary experience begins.

" I am kneeling in the middle of the canoe between two
boatmen. I usually sit on the bottom of the canoe with my
legs stretched out. But now it is a matter of life and death,
and it is my task gradually to bale out the canoe as it is filled
by waves which sweep over the bulwarks. I am baling
with an enamel tin bowl which we use for meals, and working like a galley-slave. With my elbows I try to meet the
waves and break their force, at least amidships. The water,
plashing and gurgling, runs up and down the bottom of
the canoe as it rolls. It is an unequal battle ; I cannot keep
pace with the waves. Each new wave brings us more fresh
water than I have been able to bale out with the bowl since
the last wave came. The water is rising alarmingly high
in the canoe. It grows heavier as it fills, and the bulwarks
sink nearer and nearer to the water. This makes it all the
easier for the waves to sweep in, and each flood that comes
on board is bigger than the last, while the boatmen's
strength, and mine, grows correspondingly less. The
nearest shore is still a long way off. It is only a question
of time how long we can keep ourselves afloat, and our
chances of safety are growing less and less."

In such moments of deadly peril I always keep calm ; I
do not know whence I derive this calm, or why. Probably
from the subconscious cold logical instinct that, when death
stares one in the face, the situation is not improved if one
loses one's self-control and the only weapons one has at
hand. Although my servants—four in number then, as
now—fell down and died of thirst in the Taklamakan
desert, my confidence was not shaken. I could do nothing
for them. The only thing that could save them was water.
If I had laid down to die as they did, nothing would have
been gained. My duty was to hold out to the last, without
hurrying unduly or exerting myself at all.

" At last the bulwarks of the canoe are so low in the

water that the next wave fills it to the brim. Its contents, our provisions and camping blankets, are swept away; the tins of fresh water go overboard. We have seen the critical moment coming for a long time, and now that we have lost control of the canoe, the only thing to do is to cling fast to its bulwarks. But the canoe has little supporting power under water, and the paddles still less. Lying on the surface of the water, we do not catch the wind at all, or very little, so that our movement towards the shore is almost imperceptible. If we can only hold out till a lull comes, and till we have drifted into water so shallow that we can touch bottom, we can empty the canoe, clamber into it again, and proceed. The water is not cold, but a good deal cooler than in the northern basin, where it is shallow and quickly warmed by the sun.

" Each new wave washes over us and gives us a fresh mouthful of salt water. But we must hold out. If one of us is exhausted the other two cannot help him. To be able to swim is of little avail in this predicament. The less you exert your body, the longer you are likely to be able to hold fast to the wreck. If you let go, you are bound to be separated from it and carried farther and farther away by the waves.

" The banks of the lake consist of *shor*, as the Turks call the saliferous mud, solidified till it is almost as hard as brick. When flooded it becomes treacherously soft and as slippery as soap. This *shor* stretches far and wide round Lop-nor, to all appearances as smooth as a floor, apart from the little undulating ridges and crests which it forms. We, lying on a level with the water, can see no shore at all. Our situation seems hopeless. We might as well be out on the open sea, awaiting death by drowning.

" We are greatly surprised, therefore, when, in a vertical position, we feel bottom under our feet. It gives way like the softest mud, but still it gives us some hope of safety. No shore is to be seen. We are tossed about by the waves for hours. Sometimes the bottom is firmer; for a fraction of a second one can support oneself against it and have a momentary sense of relief and rest. The water gets shallower by degrees. The storm howls as savagely as ever, but the waves are becoming smaller and less violent as the

result of their friction against the bottom. Our moments
of rest become longer, and sometimes we can walk some
way on fairly solid ground, dragging the canoe with us.
Without it we should be lost.

"The waves get smaller and smaller. The shores of
Lop-nor are extraordinarily shallow and shelving for miles.[1]
Here the sea can no longer rise ; the salt water is whipped
by the storm, but is too shallow to form waves. We stop
for a moment, half dead with weariness. We must take
breath. Then, by the exercise of our combined strength,
we turn the canoe over far enough to empty it of some of
the water. If only we can clear it of water altogether there
is no immediate danger.

"But the enamel bowl which served for baling has gone.
The two boatmen, who have clung fast to their paddles in
the absence of life-belts, scoop out the water with the
blades. It is a slow business, but patience wins, and the
canoe is emptied. While the two men support it, I clamber
in and then help to balance the craft till they, too, have
taken their places.

"Delicious rest after superhuman exertions ! I undress,
wring the water out of my clothes and hold them up in the
wind to dry. This takes no time in the dry, hot wind. My
two boatmen let their clothes dry on them. They have begun
paddling again and go on down wind. The sun is still high.
No shore is to be seen. If we go out into deeper water again
a sea will be running, and there we shall have the same battle
for life that we have just been through all over again.

"But no, the lake gets shallower and shallower. The
south-western horizon has a lumpy appearance. It must
be slabs of *shor* which have risen on end in drying. Now
the canoe touches bottom. The men rise and urge it forward by pushing with their paddles against the bottom.
Soon they have to get out and shove the canoe along. The
water is getting shallower all the time, and at last we cannot
get any further. The depth is 4 inches."

What would Chen and I have done in such a position ?

[1] "How flat the country is is shown by the fact that a fall of less
than 20 inches in the surface of the water uncovers as much as three
miles of ground " (Hörner : *Resa till Lop*, p. 193).

Though saved from the perils of the deep, our position would have been anything but enviable. We should have been on the shore of Lop-nor at its southernmost end—78 miles, or as far as possible, from our camp on the barren mud island at the northern end of the lake. The whole of our supply of fresh water and provisions would have been lost, and the only thing to do would have been to get back as quickly as possible to the camp, our nearest strong point. This we could do in two ways. We could abandon the two canoes, Chen's and mine, and try to find our way back on foot to the camp where we had left Chia Kwei alone with part of the food-supply and the tent. Alternatively, we could have taken the two canoes and paddled northward along the west bank of Lop-nor. A march of a hundred miles or so in the heat of the sun, with no water, would have been no difficult matter for Chen and the young boatmen, but a bit too much for me. And it would have been unthinkable to paddle north with the storm still raging and in a head sea. We should have had no choice but to wait till the storm died down. Nor would such a wait have been pleasant; we had quite recently experienced a storm which lasted for three days. If we had got into a situation like this, we should have had to wait for several days without food or drink.

Fortune might have been kind to us and given us still days and a splendid trip, rich in results, all round the lake. But as it was, neither one thing nor the other happened, for the wretched barrier frustrated our plans and prevented us from entering the salt-water part of the lake at all. The volume of water in the Kum-daria was now diminishing every day, and the surface of Lop-nor was, therefore, gradually sinking. If our plan had succeeded, and we had been able to devote five days to the southern basin, the barrier might have been quite dry when we returned, and our communications with the northern freshwater basin would in that case have been cut off. We should then have had to abandon the canoes and make our way back on foot to camp no. 82, where Chia Kwei was waiting. But this event, with all the complications it would have involved, did not take place either.

When we found that, in the existing conditions, no
further results could be obtained on the wandering lake,
we steered back northwards to the little island where camp
no. 83 was.   Here we packed, loaded the canoes and embarked to return to camp no. 82.   There stood Chia Kwei
on a promontory, waving his hands for sheer joy ; he told us
how delighted he had been when he had heard Sadik's singing in the distance.   He had had a fright in the night, when
he was woken by a heavy splash in the river, and thought it
was some great wild monster making for his lonely camp.
But when he listened and heard nothing more, he had
realized that it was only a piece of the bank that had broken
loose and fallen into the water, and had been reassured.

When we left that camp Chen had set a bowl full of water
out in the open air.   In fifty-one hours 1·1 inch had evaporated.   When the Kum-daria is falling daily in the summer,
the level of Lop-nor must sink too, and the whole of the
northern part must be dry.   Probably an arm of the Kum-
daria winds across the exposed sediment of the lake-
bottom throughout the summer, but it is possible that this
arm, at the height of summer, dries up before it reaches the
southern and deeper salt basin of the lake.   If so, the latter
must be quite cut off, and it still remains to be seen how
much of the salt lake is left after the intense evaporation of
the summer.   The evaporation from the Aral Sea amounts
in summer to some 3 feet a month, and the evaporation
from Lop-nor is probably just as strong, if not stronger.
If the area of the surface of Lop-nor is estimated at 1,200
square miles, the evaporation amounts to 1,539,000,000
cubic feet of water in twenty-four hours.

It was getting late when we landed at Chia Kwei's camp,
but nevertheless I gave orders that we should pack up and
start immediately.   Our route led us back up the delta, and
at sunset we pitched camp among low *yardangs*.

On the morning of May 19 the men brought to my tent
a couple of four-legged food tables, two skulls and a few
oddments which they had found in a grave that had been
opened a good while ago.   The objects were of exactly the
same shape and type as those described in an earlier chapter.

Chen went to the spot and found a dozen graves, all of

which had been opened and plundered. This was evidently the place which Stein called L.F. These graves too were situated on a *mesa*, divided into two blocks by a saddle-like depression. On the north side of the saddle there were traces of fortifications. The graves lay to the south of the saddle.

Six hundred yards from our camp was yet another *mesa*, to which we walked. On the way we had to cross an arm of slack water, which is doubtless flooded in the autumn, when all the riverside lakes and creeks are full.

Near the summit of the *mesa* we found a number of small stakes sticking up out of the ground to form a miniature palisade, 12 feet 8 inches long and from 2 feet to 3 feet 5 inches wide. Close to it were four graves, one of which we opened. It contained eight skulls and a quantity of small objects of the same kind as those we had found before.

A thorough search of the whole country round Lou-lan would doubtless bring to light innumerable graves of this kind, in which Lou-lan's dead were buried during centuries and now sleep their last sleep. In those times, as now, the country round their city and village was menaced by floods, and burial-places out of reach of the water were accordingly chosen. *Mesas*, the fragments left by erosion of an older stratum, raised their tawny pinnacles over the watery region and offered complete protection. No common burial-ground seems to have been used; the graves lay scattered, as they still are in China, and here the dead have slept for 2,000 years, while countless spring storms have raged over their heads.

From the top of this *mesa* we could see Lop-nor plainly from east to S 10 degrees W. One might have been looking at the sharp-cut horizon of a sea.

We felt undeniably warm at 2 p.m., with a temperature of 92·5, but that night (May 19–20) it turned cool again, and the thermometer fell to 61·9 degrees.

When the next morning's sun had once more suffused the wilderness with light and colour, we went on board the two double canoes and steered WNW. The reeds grew thick again, and the fresh spring green became more and more conspicuous. Then we followed for a long time a

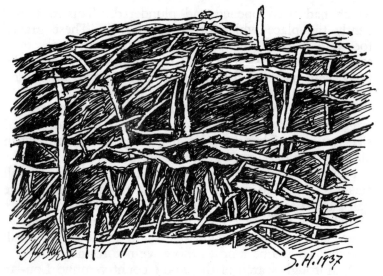

How the wall of the fort was constructed.

sharp-cut channel flanked by *yardangs*. We forced our way through a thick reed-bed, came out into a small lake, and steered south-west. The channel expanded into a good-sized lake, beneath whose clear water we could see the pale-yellow tops of submerged *yardangs*.

In the afternoon we landed on the northern shore of a sharp peninsula on which was an old fortification. The walls consisted of tight-packed earth strengthened with tamarisk boughs and roots. The wall—marvellously strong—formed an irregular rectangle, of which Chen made a plan.[1] We climbed up on to the wall, the top of which was from 3 feet 7 inches to 5 feet across, while the base was 22 feet 9 inches thick. Inside the wall was a kind of separate platform in the shape of an island surrounded by a moat, partly filled in. The surface of the moat was 1 foot 10 inches below that of the lake. The wall rose 21 feet 5 inches above the surface of the lake and the island 10 feet above the water in the moat. The peninsula on which the fort stood was surrounded on the north, east and

[1] This ruin is identical with the fort L.F., where Stein found Chinese manuscripts from the years A.D. 266 and 267.

west by the lake, which in the Lou-lan days must have
formed an excellent natural protection for this fairly strong
defence work. Along the wall facing south, in the middle
of which the entrance gate is still visible, runs a dug moat
which is still full of water to-day and turns the peninsula
into an island.

After a cursory examination of the fort, and the necessary
photographing, drawing and measuring, we re-embarked,
and paddled and punted down a long canal running south-
west and SSW and just wide enough to take a double
canoe. It went almost straight towards Lou-lan, and Chen
and I were tempted to believe that it had been dug by men's
hands and had served in its time as a navigable waterway
between the city of Lou-lan and the fort.

When the sun sank in blazing gold and deep scarlet, and
the full splendour of the afterglow lay over that classic
land, we lay to under a bank on which there was fuel in
abundance, pitched our tent and lighted our camp-fires.
We could not take our eyes from the western horizon until
the colours had died away. And when we had finished
our simple evening meal, put out our lights, and gone to
bed, I began to imagine things. I thought I heard voices
in the night outside, and wondered what they were whis-
pering about among the graves. I heard the plash of
paddles on those old waterways, now recalled to life, which
countless canoes and boats navigated in ancient times, and
whose pure fresh water must have gladdened the hearts of
travellers on the Silk Road, after months of journeying
through the dry, barren deserts.

I listened, and thought I heard the clattering of war
chariots manned with archers and spearmen, the clash of
their shields and swords, and the clang when the bows were
drawn and the arrows sped on their way. How clearly I
heard the countless caravan bells tinkling in time, and how
clearly we saw the endless processions of camels, stepping
silently and gingerly over the desert sands under their loads
of rich, heavy silk, and the joyful gleam of their eyes, and
the widening of their nostrils, when they scented the fertile
grazing-grounds on the banks of Lou-lan's rivers and lakes.

And like an echo that had slumbered for 2,000 years, I

heard the cheerful ringing from the collar of bells round the neck of the mail-courier's horse—the courier who carried letters from China proper along the Silk Road, by Tun-hwang to Lou-lan. I had found a number of the answers to these letters on my second visit to Lou-lan thirty-three years before. A swarming life, an endless multitude of walkers, riders, caravans and carts, an ever-changing, variegated carnival, passed before my inner eye and kept me wakeful, while the eternal stars glittered over the graves.

But there came a day when the life-giving river thought fit to change its course and pour its water into the southern part of the desert and form a lake there. Woods, lawns, avenues, gardens and ploughed fields dried up, withered and died. Then people could no longer live in Lou-lan and the country round ; they abandoned their city and the villages near it and moved off to other oases, which could offer them water and vegetation.

But now the river and its terminal lake had returned to the northern part of the desert and had prepared the ground for new life and new colonization. Now Lou-lan and its villages could blossom anew, and traffic on the Silk Road begin again.

That was why we were there. Was it strange that I lay awake ? The oldest and longest caravan route on earth, which in ancient times linked east and west, was to be raised from the dead. And yet—when our dreams had been transformed into reality, how little the life and movement on the old Silk Road would resemble the variegated scenes of long ago ! No more camels, no tinkling caravans, no mail-courier's horses with collars of bells ! No, the technical apparatus of modern times stifles poetic inspiration. First motor-cars will come, then the railways. Many of us may live to see the day when a new line, in addition to the Siberian Railway, will link the Pacific with the Atlantic. The boat expedition which Chen and I made to the new Lop-nor was only a link in the scheme I submitted to the Chinese Government in the summer of 1933. Was it strange if, with such vast prospects opening before me, I lay awake and listened to the mysterious spirit voices of the night and the silent speech of the desert ?

X

OUR LAST DAYS BY LOP-NOR AND LOU-LAN

HOW strange it felt to wake on the morning of May 21 and know that we were bound straight for my old ruined city Lou-lan, which I had been fortunate enough to discover on March 28, 1900! Would it really be granted me to see this place, so important in history, politics, war and commerce, for the third time—after thirty-four years?

We followed a narrow channel which pointed almost straight to Lou-lan and which might have been dug by men. Tamarisks, solitary or in clumps, lined its banks : it was easy to believe that those desert bushes had been planted to give shade to canoeists of ancient times.

But the channel stopped and turned into a good-sized lake, from whose bottom tamarisks and *yardangs* stuck up. The lake grew narrow and at last stopped altogether, and we had to drag the two double canoes over a small spit of land. On the other side of this we came into another wide open sheet of water, where tamarisks and reeds formed long strips running parallel with *yardangs*, i.e. from NNE to SSW.

There was a fresh north-easterly breeze, and we had a splendid following wind across the lake. The boats rolled, and the water grew turbid. The lake was mainly shallow ; the greatest depth Chen found with the lead was 5 feet 10 inches. The sun shone burning hot ; the temperature was 86·7 in the shade and that of the water 73·6. We scraped along reed-beds which rustled at our touch, and sometimes tamarisks stretched their violet clusters of flowers over us like arms raised in benediction. This voyage was idyllic ; we only hoped that the lake might run far to the south-west, right to Lou-lan. Over our heads gulls uttered their shrill warning cries ; they had never before seen canoes on Lou-lan's sinuous waterways.

Entering the narrow channel.

But we reached the southern shore of this lake as early as 12.30 p.m. and sought in vain for a narrow cut leading towards Lou-lan. We therefore landed, and sent Babeddin south and Sadik south-west to spy out the land. They came back four hours later with not very encouraging reports. To the south they had come upon a fairly high barrier of *yardangs*, which seemed to offer an insuperable obstacle to a further extension of the water in that direction. Where Hörner and Chen, in 1931, had found wide sheets of water there were now only reed-beds. One or two isolated channels had been sighted to the south-east.

Babeddin described a place where there were quantities of fragments of pottery ; this Chen identified with the " ruin of a potter's workshop " on Hörner's map, of which we naturally had a copy with us. Near this Babeddin had found a dry river-bed, with a few smallish pools of water which was drinkable in an extremity. To the SSW he had seen a fort which towered above everything else in the neighbourhood.

So camp no. 86 was to be the final stage of our journey

towards Lou-lan, at any rate for myself, who was not in good enough training for a long march in the summer heat. But Chen was eager to undertake the march, and I was glad to be able—thanks to his youthful energy—to link up with his and Hörner's map of 1931 and my own journeys in 1900 and 1901.   Chen calculated the distance to be 7½ miles, and expected to be back at camp no. 86 early on the afternoon of the next day.   He took with him only bread, soup tablets, sugar, and a large tea-pot in which to carry water—also a compass, watch, measuring-tape and camera.   There was fuel everywhere.   On the banks of the dried-up river in particular—it was probably an arm of the Kum-daria— there were many poplar trunks, erect or fallen.   Sadik, Rozi and Babeddin accompanied Chen at their own request. Their luggage consisted of *chapans* (cloaks), *talkan* (baked flour), and the spade.

They did not start till 5·45, when they went off, walking quickly, and speedily disappeared in the labyrinth of *yardangs*.   The dusk fell at 8 o'clock, and the crescent moon shone bright and sharp over the desert.   After Chia Kwei and Ali had gone to bed I sat up for a long time writing in the pleasant night coolness.   A wonderful silence reigned ; only the cry of a night bird was heard from time to time.

Our expedition was now broken up into seven different sections.   Yew, Kung and Effe were on their way to Tunhwang ; Jomcha, Erashin and a couple of boys were at camp no. 70 ; Dr. Hummel was at work on the upper Kumdaria, Bergman round the riverside lakes south of camp no. 70 ; Gagarin and three boatmen were at camp no. 80 ; Chen was walking to Lou-lan, and I was at camp no. 86.   I inwardly hoped that we should all be reunited without losses or serious mishaps.

I lay on my sleeping-bag completely undressed, with only a sheet over me.   But when the minimum temperature fell to 59 or 60 degrees—after over 85 degrees during the day— I awoke feeling cold and pulled a blanket over myself.   The cup of tea which stood by my pillow had a fresh, cooling effect early in the morning ; apart from that I drank only hot tea and hot water.   But soon the stifling heat came on.

I made Chia Kwei tie up all the edges of the tent so

Pushing a canoe through the reeds.

that the draught could blow right through. The climate
on the lake was quite different from that on the river; there
we never had to complain of the heat.

I shortened the hours of waiting by drawing and painting
the curious landscape which surrounded us. The hours
passed and the sun burned hot; at 7.30 p.m. it was still
76·5 degrees. Chia Kwei and Ali lit a big bonfire on the
top of a *yardang* and kept a steady look-out to south and
south-west. They shouted, but no one answered. The
twilight spread its shadows over the land; the sunset came,
a miracle of colour, and the afterglow died away. Not a
sound was heard. They ought to have been back long ago.
Ali begged me to let him go to meet them before dawn,
following their tracks and taking a few good-sized rolls
with him. As soon as it had grown really dark, after 8 p.m.,
the bonfire was lighted and spread its orange light over the
country round. The *yardang* ridges raised their yellow backs
out of the surrounding darkness, suggesting dragons and
dolphins. Ali called, but the night did not reply; all was
quiet.

And a silence like that of the night prevailed when I woke
next morning. Chia Kwei and I were alone in the camp;

A combined effort.

Ali had gone to meet the missing men. I was growing
more and more anxious about them. Their food-supplies
were inadequate, and they might have found no water on
the way to Lou-lan. Perhaps they had gone astray and had
not been able to find their way back to our camp on the edge
of the lake. I knew from experience that hobnailed boots
left only faint marks on the hard sedimentary clay, uniformly
sculptured by the action of the wind. And what should I
do if nothing was heard of them ? Chia Kwei and I, the
last two left in the camp, could not find their tracks and
carry water to them through the dry burning desert. We
ourselves had more than enough of everything.

The thought of one day after another passing, till at last
we had to start without them, made me shudder. Then
we should have sent a relief expedition with draught animals
in search of them from camp no. 70—a necessary but quite
hopeless enterprise. We could only have found their
mouldering dried bodies.

But it was not to be so bad as all that. At 11 a.m. I went
up on to a high *yardang* again to have a look through my
glasses. I had hardly got to the top when I saw a man
dragging himself wearily towards the camp. Was it Ali ?
No, there came two more, and then another man alone.

They were up to me in a few minutes—Chen and his

three companions.   They were fearfully tired and hungry. To me it was like waking from a nightmare to have them back safe and sound.   I am sure they all felt how glad we were to see them.

I proposed to the weary marchers that they should have a good breakfast and then sleep as long as they liked—we were in no hurry, for Ali was not back yet.   But Chen was so full of what he had seen that he wanted to tell me about it all first.   Then I made him lie down and rest, and he slept like a child.

It had been farther to Lou-lan than we had calculated— 11 miles, not 7½.   After starting on the 21st they had walked hard till 8 p.m., when they had camped by water and dead tamarisks.   They had crossed two channels on the way ; and the next morning they had waded across another, 20 yards wide and 2 feet 7 inches deep, running south-east and possibly connected with Lop-nor.   Then they had crossed a dry arm of the river running SSE, 38 yards wide and about 10 feet deep.   There were sand dunes on its bottom, indicating that no water had flowed along the channel since the Kum-daria was recalled to life thirteen years earlier.   Then followed a belt of *yardangs*, only 8 inches high and obviously of recent formation.   Our men crossed a depression 16 feet deep and 200 yards wide, but it was not formed by running water.   Next, along the route to the SSW and south-west, they came to a 500-yard belt of dead timber and high tamarisk mounds among *yardangs* of varying heights.

From a point where living tamarisks grew they sighted, to the WNW, the high tower at Lou-lan, 4¾ miles away. They passed the last living tamarisk about 2¾ miles from Lou-lan, and 2 miles from that place dead reeds became plentiful.   Fragments of pottery were seen almost everywhere.   They reached Lou-lan at 2·15 p.m., and stayed there two hours.

Chen climbed up on to the tower, where the flagstaff which Hörner and he had planted on the summit still stood upright.   But of the Swedish flag only a small fragment remained.   At the foot of the flagstaff lay the tin case in which three years before they had placed two papers, one describing Dr. Erik Norin's explorations right up to this region in 1928–30 and their own investigations in the winter of 1930–31, and the other bearing the following words in English, so complimentary to myself: " In honour of Dr. Sven Hedin, Lou-lan's discoverer and first explorer, his men hoist his flag here.   Lou-lan, Jan. 19, 1931.   Nils G. Hörner, Parker C. Chen."

Chen now added to these two new papers, one of which recorded our journey to Lop-nor; the other was a poem singing the praises of Lou-lan.

There was no question of excavations or any other kind of research ; they had no water and no provisions and were 11 miles from camp no. 86.   After a rest they began their return journey and marched till they came to an arm of the river whose water was slightly salt.   Chen drank too much of it and was violently sick, but slept well in the night.

They started again before six next morning and came to a channel 15 yards wide and 3 feet deep, where they made tea and at last drank their fill of fresh water.   For the last stretch of their journey they followed their own old tracks. They had found on the way a stone slab, 11 inches by 8 inches in size and 1½ inches thick, without any inscription.

The weary marchers slept deeply nearly all day.   It began to grow dark, and nothing was heard of Ali.   His plan had been to follow their tracks until he found them.   As they had covered the same ground only in the neighbour-hood of our camp no. 86, Ali—if he was able to make out the tracks at all—would be decoyed all the way to Lou-lan.

But he would probably lose the track and wander about vaguely among the *yardangs*, with no compass or matches, and eat up the supply of bread he had taken with him for the others.

" He's gone mad, and won't be able to find us again," Sadik suggested with the utmost placidity.   I could imagine the poor wretch stumbling along with insanely staring eyes fixed on the ground, vainly seeking a lost track.   It is as dangerous to lose one's way in the maze of the Lop country *yardangs* as in the subterranean passages of the Roman cata-combs.   The former cover a wider space, but the sun shines over them by day, and at night the stars twinkle over the lonely wanderer's path.

We could not start without Ali, and I anticipated another trying period of waiting and anxiety. In the evening a huge bonfire was lighted, which must have been visible for miles across the desert.

I had just given orders to Sadik, Babeddin and Rozi to follow the missing man's tracks next morning and find him, when I heard the cry " *Ali keldi* " (Ali's come!); and quite true, there he came staggering to my tent, half-dead, with a distraught look. He had lost the track and wandered this way and that till he had seen our fire.

So now this anxiety too was removed, and next morning we could leave that dangerous shore and restore my old Lou-lan to its majestic solitude.

Our Lop-nor expedition was drawing to an end; of the two months which had been allotted to us by the Urumchi decree, only a week remained. Summer was coming on, but the temperature still fell—on the night of May 23–24 to 60·6 degrees.

In the morning Chen found a scorpion nearly 2 inches long under his bed. This was the first visitor of the kind we had seen. During the summer Chen found a good dozen of these loathsome crawlers at his camping-places.

The day was brilliantly clear; only in the north-west a few light clouds hovered over the earth. There was a faint NNE breeze, which had a pleasant cooling effect. The cloth stretched above my " writing-table " subdued the heat of the sun. Now and then a gadfly came humming like a bomb, but mosquitoes kept away so long as the breeze lasted.

We made our way back to the old fort through the same lakes and canals we had traversed before. On both sides we had yellow strips of last year's reeds; the fresh green stems were now becoming more and more conspicuous. Wide reed-beds lay about us, out of which the *yardang* ridges stuck up, with almost white summits and dark sides.

All these lakes along the riverside and in the delta take their toll of the Kum-daria in autumn before any water gets down to Lop-nor, and the evaporation from them is very great.

Just after 1 p.m. we landed by the southern wall of the fort to inspect its moat, which transforms the peninsula into an island—still, after nearly two thousand years, only some 30 yards of its north-western extremity were dry, and this part had obviously been full of water in the previous autumn.

At 2 p.m. the temperature of the air was 92·8 degrees and that of the lake 78·8 degrees.   The water had fallen since we rowed through this channel for the first time ; so that it was even harder work than before to force, push and drag the canoes forward through the narrow passages, with tamarisk boughs and reed stems creaking, crackling and crashing along their sides.   We moved forward inch by inch.   It was risky to have things lying about in the boats ; they might be swept overboard.   My awning got caught in some tamarisk boughs and torn off.   Spiders and beetles embarked from twigs and rushes.   Once all the baggage had to be carried through a narrow, shallow passage.   The sun sank lower, and its heat was tempered.   To the south-west we saw the curious column formed by erosion that we had passed on the way out.   We encamped on a small island, which had just enough level ground for a tent to be pitched.   There was no fuel at all, and again a deck plank was sacrificed to the flames.

May 25 dawned—the last day of that unforgettable journey to Lop-nor.   We had not far to go to camp no. 80, where we had left the Cossack Gagarin and three boatmen, and where a couple of herdsmen, with sheep for us, ought to have arrived during our absence.   But before we reached the camp we had still one task to fulfil—an exact measurement of the volume of water in the Kum-daria at the lowest point at which the river was still clearly discernible and running in one bed.

We had no difficulty in finding this vital point in a landscape of *mesas* wrought by the wind into splendid and picturesque shapes, resembling camels, lions, fortresses and towers.   Among them the river flowed in a sharply defined bed, and was divided into two arms by a quite narrow oblong island.   I will not give details of our observations here ; it will suffice to say that the river at this point carried

Feeding one of the sheep with reeds.

823 cubic feet a second, a volume of water of which the greater part goes to Lop-nor, but which now, at the beginning of summer, was falling lower day by day.

It was past three when we ceased work, and then we did the last lap to our base camp. We approached the little island by intricate channels. We saw the tent in silhouette against the sky. Our boatmen wanted to play a trick on the campers by creeping upon them stealthily, like pirates. They dipped the paddles in the water noiselessly and did not utter a sound. But it was, in fact, we who were surprised. Not a living soul was to be seen at the camp. Ah, there came Tagil, leaping and twisting and whining with delight. He sprang up and down over the *yardang* ridges and far out into the reeds, unable to restrain his joy. And there were the cock and hens, which did not pay the slightest attention to us. But there was not a sign of a human being. The camp was deserted. Were they asleep, or were they out fishing, or had they found some old graves? Had they been surprised, taken prisoners and carried off by emissaries from Urumchi? Or had they wearied of their long wait, thought us dead, and beat a retreat up the Kum-daria?

We landed. The first thing that struck us was an artificial cave constructed between two perpendicular *yardangs*, with two canoes for a roof, while a pile of flour-sacks formed the back wall. Our four boatmen's baggage was inside, but the equipment of the party was missing. We could see that a sheep had recently been slaughtered. A letter from Bergman lay on an empty box. Gagarin's rifle, sword and fur coat were gone, like himself; a queer sort of guard, we thought—he was supposed to be responsible for the safety of the base camp!

Four canoes were missing. I asked Sadik, Babeddin, Rozi and Ali if they thought that their three comrades, Ismail, Tokhta and Musa, had bolted. They considered it to be out of the question.

"They've no work at Konche. With you they've got pay, bread, meat, tea, everything they need. So why should they bolt? Probably Gagarin has shot an antelope and they've gone to fetch it."

"Most unlikely," I said. "Someone ought to have stayed in camp."

Our boatmen ascended different *mesas* and shouted at the pitch of their lungs—no reply.

"But wait a moment!" someone cried. "There are three donkeys grazing in the reeds, and there are three sheep!"

The more discoveries we made the more mysterious the situation appeared.

"Look here!" Chen called. "Kung has been here!" His footsteps were easily recognizable, for he was the only member of the expedition who was still wearing hob-nailed winter boots.

They must have started that very day, for the coal of their last fire was still glowing under the ashes. But how had Kung got there? With the sheep Bergman had sent under the charge of two herdsmen? These herdsmen too had disappeared.

So, of at least seven men, not a single one remained. Only the dog Tagil had remained faithful to his post. I went out and patted him and played with him, and gave him a whole sheep's thigh-bone.

Chen and I sat up till midnight talking, but long as we

discussed the situation we could not make out what had happened. Kung's footprints made the whole affair more complicated. He could never have paid a flying visit, taken away the men we had left behind and returned westward, as though he considered us irrevocably lost! And if any mysterious reason had compelled him to do so, he would have left a letter behind for us in our tent. No, it was no use puzzling our heads. Our boatmen soon grew tired of shouting. They gathered round their fire and round one of the three sheep, which had been slaughtered as a reward for faithful service.

We went to bed and left the solution of the riddle till next day. In the night we heard the donkeys braying with contentment; they lay down in the reeds in the daytime for shelter against the gadflies, and grazed at night. Tagil barked at them for a time, but then let them bray as much as they liked.

As the minimum temperature remained steady at 69 degrees, we could consider that summer had begun.

We were awakened at 7 a.m. by the cry, " Here comes Musa in a canoe ! " We hurried out. It was blowing hard from the north-east and the waves were plashing on the shore. In a few minutes he came to land and hastened up to us.

He told us that Kung and Serat, while the weather was calm, had had themselves paddled to an island farther east, and that the water had then become so rough that they had not dared to come back.

It was really only Serat, the Mongol from the endless dry deserts and steppes, who had this panic terror of wide water-spaces and rolling waves. They had come in the small car, which had been left about 3 miles from the bank; Tokhta had been sent to watch over it.

Chen and I immediately embarked in our one double canoe, and Musa and Sadik rowed us to the island where Kung and Serat were. We had to worm our way through reeds and channels to a good-sized broad, with a strong wind against us, and reached the island where our men were waiting. They were standing on a *yardang*, on the look-out, and could not believe their eyes when they saw Chen and

me. Our joy at meeting again was mutual. Kung's and
Serat's relief expedition had been most successful. And
now Kung gave us a plain, unvarnished account of their
trip.

The letter I had sent to Bergman had been delivered all
right by Apak. The small car had been got ready at once,
and Kung and Serat had driven to our base camp no. 80
with Apak as guide. They had travelled along the same
" road " through the Kuruk-tagh as on the reconnaissance
towards Tun-hwang. But on that journey they had never
got farther than Altmish-bulak. Now they had steered a
course from the base of the mountains down towards our
region in the Kum-daria delta. A good way from the bank
they had come upon such loose soil that they had to leave
the car ; Serat had remained with it while Kung and Apak
began to search for camp no. 80 on foot. They had walked
and walked, and Apak seemed quite lost. He had ascended
high *mesas* and shouted, but had not seen a trace of our
camp or our men. At last they had reached the bank to
the eastward and had walked more than 6 miles to the
neighbourhood of the T'u-ken fort. Then Apak knew
where he was, and they turned back. They had looked
out from another *mesa*, shouted and been answered, and at
last they had found one or two of our party and reached
camp no. 80.

Ismail and Tokhta were sent to the place where Serat
was waiting with the car, taking water for him. Then he
accompanied Ismail to camp no. 80, while Tokhta stayed
with the car.

All this happened on May 23, i.e. two days before Chen
and I returned to camp no. 80.

Kung, Serat and Apak had spent the night at camp no. 80,
where the two first had made themselves at home in our
tent. On the morning of the 24th Kung had decided to
make a boat trip to the eastward to look for us, and for this
purpose took with him all the men who were at camp no. 80,
eight all told. They had paddled off in single canoes in
good weather, and had landed on an island at a considerable
distance to the eastward. When it had begun to blow and
a sea had got up, they had thought the most prudent course

was to return westward, but the gale increased to such an extent that they had to land on a small island. There they spent the night of May 24–25.

On the morning of May 25 they meant to continue their return journey to the westward, but the water was too rough for the canoes and they stayed where they were, sending Musa to camp no. 80 alone to fetch more provisions and see if we had come or not. As I have related, we had arrived at the base camp the evening before, and had been most astonished at the mysterious situation. But now none of the Lop-nor expedition was missing, nor any of those who had come to take us back to the big base camp no. 70 on the Kum-daria ! We had now to wait for no one ; it had all worked out much better than we had dared hope.

I had often wondered *how* we should be able to get back from Lop-nor. Was the country at all possible for cars ? If not, we should either have to paddle back against the stream in light single canoes, or ride. But the " Tun-hwang expedition ", which admittedly had got no farther than Altmish-bulak, had found a practicable route—just the " road " we needed for the return journey. We had thus every possible reason to be pleased with, and grateful for, the upshot of the Lop-nor expedition.

In the evening Chen, Kung and I sat up discussing new plans. Kung had told us that when he left camp no. 70 on May 21 nothing had then been heard from Colonel Salo-makhin, who had promised to have petrol and lubricating oil brought to Korla for us. It was already clear to me that the next step I must take was a dash to Urumchi to get the oil supplies we required.

Our discussions were interrupted at midnight, when the irrepressible spirits of the air began to fly on swift wings over our tents. The tent-cloth flapped and rattled and threatened to split, and all hands had to get up and make our tent fast with pegs and ropes.

It was a last good-bye fanfare before we left the fairyland by the wandering lake.

XI

BACK TO THE BASE CAMP

MAY 27 was a day of hard work for us all ; we were to leave the delta of the Kum-daria and return to the parched, barren desert. The baggage had to be sorted out. The small car could take only its driver (Serat), Kung, Chen and myself, and as we needed a servant and cook, we took Chia Kwei also. We needed provisions for three days, cooking utensils and a minimum of bedding. So, with petrol and water, the car was heavily laden.

At camp no. 80 we left 600 lb. of flour, which was stowed away in the tent in sacks. Ten canoes were left behind and sunk, so that they might not be injured by wind and weather and sun ; they were made fast to stakes driven into the bottom of the lake. Our intention was to have canoes, tent and flour ready on the spot in case we should return later.

Gagarin, eight boatmen and two herdsmen were ordered to return to base camp no. 70 near Yardang-bulak—five days' journey, we reckoned—with the five donkeys and three sheep and all the rest of our baggage.

All these preparations took time. It was 2.30 p.m. before everything was ready and the caravan set off. The motor party were paddled in single canoes to the point on the bank which was nearest to the car. There we joined the caravan, which intended to spend the night on the bank and was slaughtering one of the sheep. All the baggage which was to be taken by car was loaded on donkeys. It was nearly five before we set out for the place where Tokhta was watching over the car.

In a quarter of an hour we reached a last channel with reedy banks. After we had left it the soil became absolutely dry and barren. We followed a row of picturesque *mesas*. I rode one of the donkeys, which tripped lightly and surely

Mesa column NE of camp no. 89, May 29.

over the irregular clay.   It was past 6.30 when we reached
the last *mesa* and the car at its foot.

Before the four boatmen who had accompanied us to the
car with the donkeys returned to the lake camp and their
comrades, they had to get us a few donkey-loads of fuel.
When this was done they took leave of us.   The sun was on
the horizon and the moon was rising behind the ridge on
which the *mesa* stood.   At 8 p.m. it was still blowing at
26 miles an hour.   The butter, which was usually melted
and was like punch, congealed again in the wind at a temperature of 73 degrees.   We had an excellent dinner of
tongue, bread and butter, cheese and tea.

At dinner Kung told us that he, the last to leave the lakeside camp, had seen the shepherds coming with the three
sheep, but without Tagil.   I could not bear the thought that
the faithful dog had remained at camp no. 80 in the belief
that we should return.   The tent was still there and was full
of provisions.   Tagil presumably thought it was his duty to

Curious *mesa* pillar, May 29.

stay and guard the place during our absence, as he had done a few days before, when they had all left the camp and paddled off eastward. Of course he thought we should come back this time as we had then. I had seen him running about on the bank when we put off in the canoes for the last time, and had given orders that he should be taken on board or accompany the donkey caravan. And now he was not at the new camp by the lake. I could see him in my mind's eye sitting outside the tent, with straining eyes and ears cocked, till the donkeys, the sheep and their drivers had vanished among the *yardang* ridges. And then he would wait in vain day after day, and finally die of starvation. For he would never touch the sacks of flour which lay stacked in the shut-up tent.

Unluckily the donkeys and their drivers had by then left the motor-car camp, and so all communication with the camp by the lake was cut off. We talked long of the dog and his fidelity, and I said I could not sleep peacefully at night so long as I had any reason to think that Tagil had remained to guard the tent alone. Then Chen proposed that he should go back to the lakeside camp next morning

Morning sun behind *mesa* pillar, May 29.

and not leave it till the shepherds had been to the base camp and fetched Tagil. Chen said that he, too, could not sleep at night till the dog had been saved. Kung added that he would accompany Chen on his errand of mercy.

The sun had hardly risen on May 28 when the two good fellows set out on their trip. Meanwhile I drew the remarkably decorative *mesa* block near our camp. I was still thus occupied when Chen and Kung came back. They had been away only three and a half hours. If the caravan had started when they reached the lake camp, they would have gone on to camp no. 80 and the tent, in which case they would have taken longer and would have had the dog with them. But most fortunately the caravan had not yet started ; Tagil was at the lake camp in excellent fettle, and would now accompany the caravan to camp no. 70 near Yardang-bulak. It would have been troublesome to have him in the car, for he was big and heavy.

Meanwhile Serat and Chia Kwei had loaded up the car; we got in and rolled away north-west and north between *yardangs*, passing one last living tamarisk. In a little while we were out in real *gobi*, regular gravel desert, in which Serat looked for his wheel-tracks.

We had been driving an hour when we reached a wide dry stream-bed running down from the mountains, probably from Altmish-bulak. Then we ascended through a valley with solid rock on both sides, running NNW.

At Moholai-bulak, two salt springs surrounded by reed-beds, we found the tracks of the car and thenceforward followed them faithfully. The tracks led us up through a gully which was said to come from Olontementu-bulak, which lies among hills to the NNW. The hills by degrees became considerable mountains, and live tamarisks grew in the gully.

Our course was changed to WSW. Beyond some tamarisks we saw two antelopes in flight. Fair-sized crests towered up on our right; we had mountain landscape on all sides of us. There was no road there, not even a path, but the route we were following in our own wheel-tracks was hard and good.

The highest temperature was only 82·8 degrees; in the delta we had had it 9 degrees higher. But now the gadflies were in full activity and came whizzing in like bullets through the open windows of the car. At 3.30 we had a short rest at Burutu-bulak to fill the petrol tank. Then we left an *obo* on our right and soon after another, indicating that in days of old a road had run among these mountains—unless these cairns were simply guide-marks set up by hunters in more recent times.

At 6 p.m. we left Besh-bulak to the right. The ground then became very wearisome to travel over in consequence of innumerable small gullies which lay from 3 to 6 feet apart and crossed one another. A valley between lofty terraces led us into a country all cut up by erosion. At last we entered new mountains and arrived at Nan-chan-bulak, a spring whose water had a temperature of 54·5 degrees, and none too pleasant a taste. We had covered nearly a hundred miles through wild, roadless regions. The sun went down at 7.25 in strange splendour, amid blue and pink cloudlets whose edges were outlined in shimmering gold.

Reeds and tamarisks and some twenty poplars grew round the evil-smelling spring.   Some distance away there were quite a number of these trees.   Four simple little stone huts had been erected by the spring to shelter wayfarers.   Having no tent, we were pretty defenceless against gnats and mosquitoes, and in the morning against gadflies.

Our course now led WNW, over softish ground which soon gave place to a hard alluvial plain with an excellent motor-road—though ours were certainly the only cars which had ever driven along it.

Conical or hemispherical heaps of earth stuck up out of the ground ; they were covered with dried-up bushes, the most excellent fuel.   These heaps of earth were like negroes' woolly heads.   Tamarisks and tussocks were not uncommon ; one of the former was a regular tree.

The whole sky was clouded over ; a cool breeze got up, and the gadflies disappeared.   We followed another smallish valley between low hills with a luxuriant growth of tamarisks in its gravel and mud bottom.

The aspect of the landscape was continually changing in that patchwork of mountains and hills, steppes and deserts. We drove along a hard level gully through a regular avenue of fine thick tamarisks.   The Azghan-bulak region was visible to the ENE.   We were, therefore, about 4,550 feet up and had risen nearly 2,000 feet above Lake Lop-nor.

We had not far to go now to the Kaksu-dawan pass, which is only 130 feet above the plain to the northward and is immensely steep.   The car took it in jerks, a yard at a time, while we walked and laid stones behind the wheels to prevent the vehicle from running downhill and overturning on the winding ascent.   On the south side of the pass Serat had buried a five-gallon petrol tin ; we now collected this and emptied it into the tank.

We were on a really good road, on which we could see the traces of spades and pickaxes and of innumerable caravans.   But it was the road from Turfan to Ying-p'an, Sai-cheke and Korla, and it was freely used since the road to Toksun had been barred.

We drove south-west along a narrow valley, between pink, black and white mountains resembling tents. The road was marked by cairns on neighbouring hillocks. The country grew open again, and about four we were at the Toghrak-bulak spring, which rises out of the sand of the 8-yard-wide valley bottom and has excellent water. " Poplar Spring " was a delightful place to find among those desolate mountains. On one side rose a lofty cliff, on the other an erosion terrace 6 feet high, and between them grew a few hundred poplars.

We had made a considerable bend to north and west, and now, on leaving the mountains, we came out on to a wide *sai* plain, a funnel for carrying off water between terraces, and steered south-east towards the Kum-daria, which, thanks to its yellow reed-beds, could be seen in the distance.

To our astonishment we passed Effe's lorry. In the driver's cabin we found a letter from Yew saying that the lorry had been going to Ying-p'an and Tikenlik to get provisions, but that the back axle had broken on the way and the passengers had had to proceed on foot. He asked Serat to meet them.

With the mountain ridge of Charchak on our left we proceeded across the barren plain, where the road was good, and stopped at 6.30 p.m. at base camp no. 70, where only the Cossack Nikolai and a couple of Turkis were to be found. Nikolai told us that Bergman and Georg were on the right bank of the Kum-daria with tents, servants, horses and donkeys, ready to start off into the desert next morning. Yew, with Effe and two of our men, had gone off an hour or two earlier to the broken-down lorry, to repair it and bring it back to camp no. 70. The most curious thing about this was that we had not met their lorry; it had evidently taken another route.

The most important thing for me now was to get in touch with Bergman's party before it started. We therefore went to the bank, a quarter of a mile distant, and got ready a couple of canoes. Dusk was already falling when we embarked, and we had to paddle a good way before we saw the outline of Bergman's tent. We landed on the bank close by in pitch darkness, by lantern-light. Georg and the

servants were down on the bank to receive us ; Bergman
had already gone to bed, but dressed hurriedly when he
heard our voices. He did not know till then whether we
were alive or had perished. And now we turned up in
their camp of a sudden at nightfall.

Bergman was, of course, extremely interested in our
discoveries in the graves, and the collections we had made
were handed over to his care.[1] He and Georg confirmed
what we already knew—that nothing whatever had been
heard of the promised oil. They had sent a messenger with
a letter to the commandant of the garrison at Korla asking
for news, but the messenger had not returned. My decision
to go in person to Korla and, if necessary, to Urumchi was
thus the only right one.

We had a lot to talk about, and sat up a good while after
midnight. Bergman entertained us to dinner, at which the
best dish was sour milk, procured from the herdsmen who
graze their sheep on the banks of the lakes along the Kum-
daria.

Bergman's and Georg's little caravan consisted of Ördek,
who had said that he knew of strange burial-places in the
heart of the desert, a Turki from Yangi-su, who knew the
way, a couple of our servants, five horses and three donkeys,
and three weeks' provisions. They were to go west, south
and south-east to the mysterious burial-place, which was
said to be a hard day's march east of Yangi-su and somewhat to the eastward of the lower course of the old Tarim.

As the base camp was short of flour, we decided to send
two of our boatmen and our five donkeys back to camp
no. 80 in the Lop delta to fetch the 500 catties of flour that
Chen and I had left in the tent there.

Our sleeping-bags were sent after us, and we spent the
night in Bergman's camp, where the minimum temperature
did not fall below 72·7 degrees.

Bergman started with his caravan at sunrise. Georg,
who had crossed the river and conferred with Serat, stayed
with us till we were ready to go over to the base camp. We

[1] A description of these collections, as well as those mentioned in
Chapter XIII, has now been published by Bergman (*Archæological
Researches in Sinkiang*, Stockholm, 1939).

said good-bye on the bank, leaving him to follow at once in Bergman's tracks into the mysterious desert.

At camp no. 70 I took out of my suitcases and boxes what I needed for the journey to Korla—or perhaps Urumchi. We had still a fair amount of petrol left, owing to our having eked it out with paraffin, but not enough to take all three motor-lorries as far as Urumchi. What we were short of was lubricating oil. Of this we had just as much as the small car needed to cover the 400 miles which separated us from the capital of Sinkiang. There was not a drop of oil left at camp no. 70 when I set out in the car.

I took with me two changes of clean white summer clothes and three changes of under-clothing, a piece of canvas, a couple of blankets, and two fur coats for night camping. Kung and Chen sought out similar equipment in Yew's luggage. We took a week's provisions for three men, but no tent.

From its very beginning our expedition had been rich in dramatic happenings that might have taken place in a novel. And now, at base camp no. 70, there were further improbable coincidences. Chen and I had been away for a month, and yet we just caught Bergman and Georg on the last night they spent on the Kum-daria. And at half-past one, when I was sitting arranging my belongings for the long and dubious journey, Chen and Kung suddenly shouted in one breath :

" Here comes Dr. Hummel ! "

" What are you talking about ? "

" Well, come and see for yourself ! "

I took the glass. Quite true, there he came walking quickly up from the river-bank, accompanied by two of his men. He was wearing pyjamas and sun helmet in the burning heat, had shaved off his beard, and looked well and strong. We were delighted to meet again ; we embraced, and a torrent of questions and answers broke loose.

All preparations had been made for my departure. Serat stood waiting by the car. The loading up of Yew's and my luggage was all that remained to be done. That might take a quarter of an hour ; and if Hummel had come a quarter

of an hour later I should already have been on my way to
Korla.   So he had come at the last moment.

"But why have you got your right arm in a sling?" I
asked; "and why is your hand bandaged?"

He laughed.

"Oh, rather a nasty business," he said.   "When Constantine and I were out shooting on the Kum-daria we
surprised a family of wild pig and caught three little ones,
and we've had them ever since in a box on board.   One
day when I was feeding them one of them bit my thumb,
and I got a rather nasty bout of blood-poisoning; it kept
me in bed for a fortnight and I couldn't do any work.   I
operated on myself and that made it better, and now I've
almost recovered.   I shall be perfectly well again in a few
days."

He seemed so well and full of life that I never for a
moment thought of any danger, and no one could judge of
his condition better than himself.   How bitterly I regretted,
just a month later, that I had not taken him to Urumchi in
the car and sent him home to be properly treated!   He
suffered no permanent harm, thank Heaven, but if he had
come with us we should have been spared much anxiety
and he himself much suffering and overstrain.   That solution, unhappily, we never even spoke of.

In the meantime we finished my packing, had some tea,
and then accompanied Hummel back to the bank, where
his two double canoes lay moored.

His flotilla was certainly worth seeing!   In an empty
packing-case were those three wretched pigs of his with
striped backs and rooting snouts.   The dog Pelle, from
Konche, kept watch by the tent, and a sheep was grazing
close by, as tame as a dog, and such a nice beast, and so
much of a family pet, that no one would slaughter it.   Between one of the canoes and the bank, inside a fence of
netting, swam five yellow goslings and a mandarin duck,
and a proud heron stood regarding us with a critical gaze.
A young stork also belonged to this delightful menagerie
and was everyone's admitted favourite.   The creatures were
tame and seemed well; but they all came to a more or less
tragic end in the long run.

The doctor's " study " on board bore the stamp of learning and activity, and although his work had been so unfortunately hung up by the pig-bite, he had a fine collection of prepared birds' skins and of plants from the banks of the Kum-daria. He had found both fauna and flora along the river poor.

His servants were now arranging and " furnishing " his tent, while one of them, Kasim, slaughtered a sheep and roasted *shislik* over embers. This Kasim had been a good and faithful servant, but at the beginning of the river trip he had committed a disastrous blunder. When alone on board at a camp, he had unscrewed the lid of a five-gallon petrol tin in which the doctor kept the store of paraffin intended for his lamps. Kasim's brain was not so constructed as to understand paraffin, but only ordinary water. And when he perceived that the liquid had a strange, unpleasant smell, and so might be dangerous to the doctor if he were to drink it, he conscientiously poured away every drop, cleaned out the tin and filled it with pure river water ! Hummel had fearful trouble sending letters and messengers to the main caravan to get more paraffin, and in the meantime he had to get on as best he could with candlelight.

Meantime dinner was ready. Hummel, Kung, Chen and I sat down round the packing-case which served as a table, and had a pleasant, merry time together.

But it was getting late, and I had to drive to the broken-down lorry which we had passed the day before, and at which Yew, Effe and their men now were, repairing the damage. So we walked back to camp no. 70, Hummel accompanying us. The car was loaded, and we had only to get in. Kung and Chen proposed that they should accompany me to Yew's camp, which was only half an hour away. I bade a cordial good-bye to our doctor and the others who were remaining behind, and got in. In a moment they had disappeared, hidden by the clouds of dust which the car threw up.

It was 7.30. Serat drove at a tremendous speed. The dusk was falling deeper and deeper over the earth, and the last reflection of the afterglow died away. I was leaving the whole expedition behind me and setting out on a journey

whose outcome was more than uncertain. I had to obtain
the resources without which our cars were paralysed and
the expedition held captive as rigidly as it had been in
Korla.

Now the powers of darkness had conquered in the west,
too, and " silent as the priests of Egypt, the stars were
beginning their march ".

Our subsequent adventures I have narrated in my book
The Silk Road. Hummel, Bergman and Kung made their
way through the Kuruk-tagh to Urumchi by different routes,
and at long last, in September, Chen, Georg, Effe, our
Mongols and the servants arrived in the capital of Sinkiang.
When the last party arrived, Hummel and Bergman had
already set out on their long journey home to Sweden, as
our doctor's state of health imperatively demanded care and
rest.

Yew and I had reached Urumchi on June 6 in the small
car, driven by Serat, and were detained there for four and a
half months as kind of political prisoners. It was not till
October 21 that we were given our freedom—thanks to the
kindly intervention of the Russian consul-general, M.
Apresoff—and travelled to Anhsi via Turfan and Hami with
the remaining members of the expedition and three cars.
With Anhsi as our base and headquarters we made a fresh
advance, this time in a westerly direction, towards the wide
basin of the wandering lake. I shall tell in later chapters of
this journey through one of the world's most desolate
wildernesses.

XII

WILD LIFE ON THE KUM-DARIA

WILD life on the banks of the lower Tarim—in its present form—is not particularly rich. Generally speaking, it can be said that it is more abundantly represented, as regards both species and numbers, along the old part of the river, from Yü-li-hsien (Konche) to Tömenpu, than from that wooded region to Lop-nor.

The king of Asiatic beasts, the royal Bengal tiger, which formerly inhabited the woods of the middle Tarim, seems to be dying out. As lately as 1899 and 1900 I saw its tracks once or twice on the banks of the river, and there were then tiger-hunters in the Yangi-köl region who had taken several specimens in scissors-traps. From one hunter I bought two tiger-skins, whose wearers had been caught shortly before on the tiger tracks among the thick reeds. On the Kum-daria we never saw a trace of this splendid beast, and there was no reason to expect it to occur in that open, desert-like country.

Of the higher animals, only wild pig and antelope were fairly common. The former find their nourishment in the reeds ; the latter can flee into the desert as swiftly as the wind if danger threatens. It must not be forgotten that it is only thirteen years since the water came back to the desert, and that animal life cannot be fully developed until the vegetation, which nourishes and protects it, has become thoroughly established on the banks.

For a traveller going down the river by boat it is really only bird life that counts. Various representatives of the winged colonists are seen daily from the boats. Dr. Hummel devoted special attention to them on his boat trip from Yü-li-hsien (Konche) to base camp no. 70 near Yardang-bulak, and he brought away a fine collection of the characteristic birds of the river.

His birds' skins, carefully prepared, were successfully brought home to Sweden and entrusted to Professor Einar Lönnberg, who wrote an article on them in the *Zoological Record of the Academy of Science*. Professor Lönnberg states that while the collection contains no new species, it is nevertheless of interest as contributing to the knowledge of the various species' geographical distribution and showing what birds occur on the farthest inland of the world's desert rivers.

Duck and coot live in great numbers on the lower Tarim and its lakes. All the representatives of these families thrive best in the shallow riverside lakes, with their clear water and abundance of food. They are less common on the river, whose water is as turbid as pea-soup. They build their nests in the shelter of the thick reed-beds round the swamps and lakes, and, in the delta, also on islets in the arms of the river. Some of the duck remain throughout the winter, others migrate to warmer climes. A few of the pochards stay during the cold season, the people who live along the river told us, while the greater number migrate.

The mandarin duck plays a curious part in the feathered world of the riverside. It acts as a kind of policeman or watchman; it seems to be always on guard and, if danger threatens, utters shrill cries and makes all the other birds in the neighbourhood take wing. Two hen birds sometimes agree on a common nest and take turns to sit on some twenty eggs.

The mandarin duck builds its nest at some height above the ground in hollow poplar trunks, and makes it soft and comfortable with a lining of down.

The sheld-duck and gadwall are also common.

On this trip, as in old days, the Lop fishermen often astonished me by their extremely intimate knowledge of the habits of the wild duck and geese. They could locate the nest with perfect accuracy from the bird's cries and flight, went straight to it through the thickest reeds, and always came back with eggs in their caps or in a turned-up corner of their coats.

The ordinary wild goose or grey lag goose is called *ghas*, a name which suggests the wild goose's cry and, perhaps just for that reason, is very like the Indo-European names —goose, *gås* (Swedish), *gōs* (Russian), *Gans*, etc. In spring and autumn one often sees the V-shaped flights of migrating wild geese. In my earlier accounts of travel on the Tarim I have spoken of their phenomenal sense of locality, and how unerringly they find their way through the air in any kind of weather. One hears their conversation high above the earth during and after storms which send the dust whirling up in impenetrable clouds, and can understand how they can weather gales and follow their landmarks despite the blinding fog. They fly by day and night, even in what to my eyes has been pitch darkness. One evening, after we had landed on the banks of the Tarim, I observed one flying party after another following exactly the same course and direction. Each new arrow-head appeared between the same poplar-tops as the last one. They have no light-houses, no light signals, and yet they find their way the whole night long. Their sight is probably developed to a degree of acuteness which we cannot conceive. And added to that is their sense of locality, which has been perfected from generation to generation. Their ancient migration routes, which their ancestors have followed for thousands of years, have probably become such a part of their nature that they simply cannot go astray. To them it is the most natural thing in the world to follow their predecessors' invisible tracks across the earth without compass or other aids.

We also observed on the banks of the Konche-daria the very common osprey, which builds its large nests high up in the poplars by the rivers and lakes and lives on fish ; the cormorant, which also lives on fish and smells of carrion—it nests in large colonies in poplars by the river ; and the great crested grebe, with a ring or collar of feathers round its neck, which lives in lakes and rivers. Then there is the black-winged stilt with its long red legs, a pretty, decorative bird, which steps about in the shallows of the riverside lakes and lives on fish. The eastern heron occurs in colonies and builds its nests in the poplars. The great white egret is pure white, has green skin round its eyes and is persecuted for the aigrette on its back, which is sold to Urumchi and thence exported to Europe; the bird lives in the reed-beds of the lakes and feeds on fish, frogs and lizards.

The yellow-legged herring gull is fairly big, quite white with grey wings and orange-red or yellow legs and feet, while the black-headed gull is smallish, white with grey wings, dark head, dark legs and feet and black wing-tips. These species of gull are the same which we saw in such great numbers over the northern part of Lop-nor, in whose fresh water they find an inexhaustible supply of fish.

The graceful little tern catches fish in the marshes. The little crake is grey and brownish. The large-billed reed bunting lives in the reed-beds, where also the little ringed plover is to be found.

The black stork exists in pairs here and there along the Konche-daria.

The bittern is called the *köl-buka*, or "lake bull yak", on account of its curious cry. The Turkis use it as a remedy for consumption.

Birds of prey are numerous and of many different kinds. There are the kite and the long-legged buzzard, and various kinds of eagles are often to be seen—the eastern golden eagle, the sea eagle, and the Asiatic sea eagle. There are also the hobby, the kestrel, and a vulture which lives on the river only in winter.

A number of other birds figured in Hummel's collection.

The woodpecker taps all along the Konche-daria, and is waiting for the poplar groves to move eastward along the banks of the new river; when they do, he will accompany them. At every camping-ground we heard him at work as he sat tapping untiringly at the poplar trunks, seeking insects and caterpillars. We often saw the little red-bellied bird with the dark white-spotted wings so busily engaged that it did not notice a bold spectator.

At night we heard in the woods the characteristic cry of the little horned owl—uh-uh-uh!—a sound which is reproduced in its Turkish name, *ukush*.

The isabelline shrike discharges a medicinal function in Lop-land, for its blood is considered to promote uric acid,

and childless women who eat its flesh have the prospect of
being blessed with offspring.

This shrike is not uncommon in the wooded regions by
the river and round the marshes ; there, too, we met the
starling, which occurs in huge flocks and chatters noisily, by
night as well as day, in the poplars where the birds have
their nests.   The pheasant, the rock-dove, the carrion crow,
the bluethroat with its pretty yellow and blue pattern, and
the cuckoo, are also to be seen regularly in the woods.
Swift, swallow, tree-sparrow, white wagtail, lark and crested
lark live there too ; the last-named remains through the
winter.

XIII

BERGMAN'S DESERT JOURNEY

THE day after Chen and I started down the Kum-daria with our boats, Folke Bergman and his party had left base camp no. 70 to begin their search for the great burial-place and the wonderful remains of which Ördek had given us so splendid and alluring a description.

This search occupied the whole of May without leading to the desired result. When it really came to business, Ördek showed that he did not know his way about the desert as well as we had hoped and expected. First they followed the Kum-daria eastward for two days and roamed through the land south of the river, but no discoveries of importance were made, and Ördek could not find his old landmarks.

They therefore returned to the base camp and succeeded at last in getting hold of a more expert East Turki, who was appointed guide, and then the real expedition into the desert began, which took from May 30 till June 14.

About 14 miles above the base camp, and 47 miles below Tömenpu, there lies on the right, or south, bank of the Kum-daria an often flooded area called the Kum-köl. Its shape is most irregular; it tapers towards the south and a stream here flows through it, with numerous small lakes on both sides and expanses of flat marshy soil.

Bergman followed this stream to a point about 40 miles south of the Kum-daria, or as far as the discovery of old burial-places justified a thorough investigation. This branch of the river is said to continue farther south-east, and finally dries up in the desert about 75 miles from the Kum-daria. It seems, therefore, that it reaches the branch of the river Tarim which is called the Shirge-chapghan, and which at the beginning of the eighteenth century flowed to Lake Uchu-köl.

This branch, a bifurcation of the Kum-daria—or, if you like to call it so, a first arm of the delta of that river—was a quite new and unexpected discovery. At the point where Bergman turned back the little stream was only from 5 to 10 yards wide and still had a perceptible current. Sharply defined marks of erosion revealed that the last flood had been 2 feet 6 inches above the level of the stream in the first half of July. Generally speaking, the stream is irregular, winds about capriciously, and in places forms a labyrinth which reminds one of the Kum-daria delta.

On the banks of the newly discovered waterway Bergman found more or less thick reed-beds and tamarisks, and on both sides sand dunes of varying heights. West of the new arm of the river, continuous sand stretches to the most easterly of the now dried-up arms running southward from the Tarim system, where I had found in 1896 a chain of reedy lakes, the Avullu-köl, Kara-köl, Tayek-köl and Arka-köl. On the eastern shores of these lakes and the short waterways which connected them dunes of a fair height had, in those days, run down steeply to the water's edge.

Now, looking westward from Bergman's route, a serrated line of high tamarisk mounds, the same which I had passed thirty-eight years before, appeared on the horizon. I marked poplar groves and tamarisks on my map. The distance from Bergman's route along the new arm to the Avullu-köl chain of lakes is only 5 or 6 miles.

A few shepherds with their flocks of sheep had settled on the new arm of the river. One of them had come from Charkhlik, others from Yangi-su and Kara-dai or the country between Yangi-su and Arghan.

To judge from the archæological remains which Bergman found on the banks of the little stream, it existed in the days of Lou-lan and had the same bed as now 2,000 years ago. Fragments of clay pots and dishes showed that men had inhabited the region.

About 30 miles south of the Kum-daria and 12 miles from the ruin of the fortress of Merdek—i.e. west of the little arm of the river—Bergman found a watch-tower dating from the time of Lou-lan, which had possibly been a guard-post on a road to Merdek.

The principal burial-place—" Ördek's necropolis ", as we called it—is situated on a low rounded hillock east of the river. It is visible a long way off all round, thanks to a regular copse of upright posts, probably monuments to the dead. A few of the posts bear very primitive sculptures ; all are polygonal in shape. Many have fallen down. Their number is considerably greater than that of the graves, of which 120 have been found.

Greedy " gold-seekers ", so common in Eastern Turki-stan, and centuries of fierce spring gales had devastated this interesting burial-place in lamentable fashion. The coffins lay spread about the hillock and its slopes, shattered and exposed. The fragments, whose timber was still perfectly sound, had laid safely under the earth till they were dug up by looters, perhaps some ten years ago. Other parts were light-grey, bone-dry and brittle like the wood one finds on the surface of the ground round Lou-lan.

Of the 120 graves only *one* had remained absolutely un-touched either by man or by weather. The corpses still lay in five or six coffins which had been looted ; otherwise the remains of the dead were spread about outside the coffins. Some of the bodies were only skeletons, while others were well-preserved mummies.

It is not yet possible to determine to what race the people belonged who had buried their dead on that spot. It seems beyond doubt that they were not Chinese. The bodies were wearing pointed caps of a shape which used to be general among the nomad peoples of Central Asia. The absence of metal, the wooden and bone objects, and the coarse shrouds in which the dead had been wrapped sug-gested that they belonged to a primitive people, perhaps living mainly by hunting and fishing. They were dressed in cloaks of coarse wool, with a girdle round the waist, shoes and felt caps. There was no silk at all in this burial-place.

It is not yet known what purpose was served by some of the smaller objects of wood, bone or stone.

West of the little arm of the river are three smaller

burial-places, one of which was discovered by Bergman, while the two others were already known to the shepherds. They were partly exposed by the wind. There was silk in these graves ; one female corpse was clothed in a peculiarly decorative and extremely interesting silk dress. Bergman made his best and most valuable finds in these three smaller burial-places.

The last discovery was a grave quite close to base camp no. 70, on the south bank of the Kum-daria. It probably dated from a later period than that of Lou-lan, and the corpse probably belonged to a Turkish people, but was not a Mohammedan. It was that of an elderly man, dressed in a long robe of yellow silk and high boots.

In the region of which I speak there are only a few *yardangs* and no *mesas*. The ground is level, and to the eye horizontal. But the country, with its tortuous waterways and shifting dunes, is nevertheless difficult going for horses and donkeys, especially in June, when it is burning hot and the air is full of those bloodthirsty gadflies which are such an unbearable torment to the animals. It was entirely due to the little stream flowing out of the Kum-daria that it was possible to reach the ancient burial-places at all at that time of the year. Georg Söderbom was of invaluable help to the leader in organizing the whole enterprise and in the field work ; and every other man who took part in the desert trip did his duty.

I have already described the dangers which hung, like the sword of Damocles, over our collections from the burial-places in the Kum-daria delta and from the banks of Bergman's river.[1] They were all but confiscated under the law which forbade the export of archæological remains from Sinkiang. And I have described the truly dramatic exhibition in the very *yamên* of the governor-general, Sheng Tupan, in the presence of high Chinese officials and the Soviet Russian consul-general, G. A. Apresoff, and the whole of his staff.

The fate of our collections was to be decided. Sheng Tupan examined every object with eagle eyes. And when he had surveyed all these apparently worthless finds, he

[1] *The Silk Road*, Chapter XVI.

uttered these immortal words, which deserve to be reprinted
here :

" Gentlemen, these things have no value to us and are of
no interest whatever to my province.   You can pack them
all up in your boxes, and you will receive a special pass from
me entitling you to take your discoveries and the rest of the
luggage out over the frontier."

The consul-general, M. Apresoff, deserves my hearty
thanks yet again for having thrown his authority and power
into the scale in our favour at this critical juncture.

After many difficulties raised by members of the " Society
for the Preservation of Antiquities " at Nanking, and two
years' negotiations by the Swedish Minister in China, Baron
Beck-Friis, who gave us vigorous support, I succeeded in
the spring of 1937 in getting the collections transferred to
Stockholm—on loan for two years.   If Nanking had been
as generous as Urumchi, we should have been allowed to
keep them—especially seeing that the greater part consisted
of objects of non-Chinese origin.

But the main consideration to us was that Bergman—
who was himself an expert, had himself dug up more than
half the objects, and had, moreover, worked on my earlier
discoveries from Lou-lan—should have an opportunity of
subjecting our new finds to the scientific examination and
description which would give them their true value to the
historian and ethnologist.   And without doubt his work on
those dumb trophies of our last journeys will help to spread
fresh light over past centuries in that romantically fascinating land, where the holy silence of the graves, and the
solitude of those who sleep in them, is disturbed only by
the lake-birds' cries and the roaring of the spring gales.[1]

[1] Under the title : *Archæological Researches in Sinkiang, especially the
Lop-nor Region*, Folke Bergman published in June, 1939, a detailed
description of all our collections from the Lop-nor region.   His
volume is No. 7 in our *Reports from the Scientific Expedition to the North-
western Provinces of China under leadership of Dr. Sven Hedin—The Sino-
Swedish Expedition*, Stockholm, 1939.

XIV

CHEN'S WORK ON THE KUM-DARIA

AS I said in an earlier chapter, Yew and I, with Serat as driver, started on May 31 in the small car on the long journey via Korla to Urumchi. I described in *The Silk Road* our desperate efforts to get permission to buy petrol and lubricating oil for our lorries, which were drawn up at base camp no. 70, not far from Yardang-bulak.

One month after another passed, and our patience was tried to the uttermost at Urumchi. But it was much worse for all the others, who in the meantime had to wait where the cars were. Yew and I were as good as prisoners at Urumchi, watched, spied on, suspected, and unable to send news to our comrades on the Kum-daria. They could not move without petrol and oil. And the summer came creeping over the desert, with its fearful stifling heat and its burning sun. Their only consolation was the river, in whose cool waters they spent hours, morning, afternoon and evening. For the rest, they lay dozing in their tents or went for short boat trips. They did not revive till after sunset, when the evening had brought a little coolness.

After Hummel, Kung and Bergman had started for Urumchi via the Kuruk-tagh, in June,[1] the loneliness and inactivity became even more oppressive than before for Georg, Effe, our Chinese servants and the Cossacks. No one who has not himself been in such a situation in so desolate a country can have any idea of it. The lorries stood at some distance from the river, where the ground was level and hard, but the tents were pitched by the river. On

---

[1] See *The Silk Road*, Chapter XIII. Dr. Hummel was obliged to leave the Kum-daria on account of his blood-poisoning; there was enough oil to take him by lorry to Singer, whence he proceeded on a horse-drawn stretcher.

every side was the pale yellowish-grey desert, over whose spaces the heated air quivered as if over a boiler. To the north the nearest ridges of the Kuruk-tagh stood out in bluish-grey outline, rather darker than the sky, which was seldom varied by the appearance of clouds. All was silent ; there were no human beings, no roads. The only redeeming feature in that cheerless landscape was the river. But even the Kum-daria was dead. No one ever passed in a boat ; duck and other waterfowl were the only living things to be seen.

Of the members of the expedition engaged in scientific work Chen was the only one who held out all through that oppressive summer.

In the few days of June he measured the volume of water and the evaporation at the base camp and received the little caravan we had sent from camp no. 80 in the delta of the Kum-daria, which included Gagarin and the dog Tagil. He tried in vain to cope with our wireless apparatus, which the Russians had spoilt.

On June 6 a few East Turkis were sent, with four donkeys and two cows, to camp no. 80 in the delta, to fetch the store of flour we had left in the tent there. Draught animals were extremely difficult to obtain in war-time, and one had to be thankful if one could get hold of a cow here and a donkey there.

On the following day there was a violent north-westerly gale and a short but heavy downpour ; 0.3 inch of rain fell in half an hour, and a roaring torrent rushed down from the mountains, forming a shallow lake near the bank. It evaporated in less than a day, and the yellow mud lay smooth and shining like a parquet floor.

After messengers had gone off to Bergman, and Hummel and Kung had started on their journey to the north, Chen set off upstream on the left bank on June 13 with Chia Kwei, a couple of East Turkis, six donkeys and a canoe.

Next day he crossed the river, met shepherds, bought some sheep and retained a guide to take him to the lake which is formed at this point by an arm of the river. Then he spent a few days making a map of this lake, which is called the Yakinlik-köl and is only 3¾ miles long from north to south and 1¼ miles from east to west.

Farther west he found another fair-sized riverside lake, also fed by the stream and abounding in reeds. A further lake was 1⅞ miles long and 1,100 yards wide, cut off from the river and accordingly rather salt. Nevertheless there were duck in the reeds with their newly hatched young.

Chen mapped these lakes, sometimes walking, sometimes (but more rarely) using a canoe, and then went on to the Kum-köl, in whose southern marsh-like basins the arm of the river already mapped by Bergman begins. The Kum-köl was 5 miles long and from 1¼ to 2 miles wide. It is impossible, without Chen's own map before one, to follow his lonely wanderings through those most irregularly and unaccountably shaped lakelets and the channels which join them to one another or to the Kum-daria. Often, when mapping a lake, he was suddenly held up by an arm of water, which he either had to wade across or, if possible, get round.

But nothing in that fantastic maze of lakes, waterways, reed-beds and drifting sand could deter the energetic young Chinese. He mapped the riverside lakes on the southern bank of the river, reached Ying-p'an on July 7, and two days later was at Tömenpu. The ground was difficult for the last 3 miles owing to live tamarisks and dense reeds.

At Tömenpu he drew a sketch-map of the interesting point where the Kum-daria breaks off from the old course of the Konche-daria. When we encamped at Tömenpu for the first time, on April 17, the Konche-daria had been carrying 2,165 cubic feet of water a second. Now, on July 12, Chen found 2,209 cubic feet. The difference is not great. According to the inhabitants the river had already begun to rise.

On July 13 Chen had followed the old bed of the Konche-daria to the south-east and had found it narrower and more winding than the new river, the Kum-daria. The old bed was not entirely dried up; there were so many stagnant pools that they occupied half the area of the bed. Among the pools there were narrow channels with a slow current. Chen's observations show that this part of the Konche-

M

daria had not been entirely abandoned by the water as late as 1934; we had heard, too, that its water rose towards autumn, when the flood came.   But we had also heard from the *beks* at Tikenlik and village headmen that the volume of water which passed through their district down the Konche-daria in the course of the year was quite insufficient for the irrigation of the fields, and that a considerable part of the population had left the place.   As long ago as 1928 Colonel Schomberg had heard that 220 of the 500 families in Tikenlik had gone elsewhere.

Chen then returned to base camp no. 70, partly on foot along the northern bank of the Kum-daria, partly by canoe, and arrived there on July 23.

On July 24 he left the base camp again, now accompanied by San Wa-tse and Chokdung, two East Turkis and five donkeys, and taking a canoe.   They started eastward on the left bank, but soon crossed to the right bank because most of the lakes are south of the river.   These were mapped in turn.   As a rule the men had to remain in their tent during the hottest hours of the day, when the temperature rose to 106 degrees in the shade.

On August 1 an arm broke off from the main stream, but rejoined it next day after following a separate course for a distance of 9½ miles.   On August 2 Chen camped at our old camp no. 75—the head of the delta.

Thence he covered, with two men and three donkeys, the 11 miles which separated him from the ruins of Lou-lan, and arrived there at 7 p.m. after a ten hours' walk.   In the evening and on the following morning they found a quantity of smallish metal objects, such as coins, arrow-heads, strap-fittings, and glass and stone pearls.

After placing another paper in the thermometer-case by Hörner's Swedish flag, now reduced by the winds to a mere rag, on the top of the old city's tallest tower, Chen retreated NNW with his little force to the nearest water, which was in a small lake.   Then, on August 5, they returned to their camp at the beginning of the delta.

Next day the canoe was left on the northern bank of the river, and on its side the words were cut : " Dr. Hedin's expedition, 1934."

Then they made for the *sai* or firm gravel soil north of the river, where progress is not obstructed by *yardangs* and *mesas*, and marched westward as quickly as they could in the evenings and nights; for a messenger had just come from Georg saying that petrol and oil had arrived from Urumchi at last, and that a start would be made for that place as soon as Chen had returned to the base camp. He reached it on August 8, and on the 10th the motor convoy started for Korla and Urumchi.

Our young Chinese comrade, Parker C. Chen, by his exact mapping of all the riverside lakes to the south of the Kum-daria all the way from Tömenpu to Lop-nor, had done a most important piece of work, and contributed greatly to our knowledge of the distribution of the newly arrived water in the desert. As a member of Nils Hörner's expedition he had assisted in the discovery of the new, or rather resurrected, Lop-nor, and had then, in the winter of 1930–31, mapped a large part of the Kum-daria delta quite alone. He had also taken part in my canoe trip from Yü-li-hsien (Konche) right down to the wandering lake, and had carried out all the measurements of the size and volume of the river.

Since, first of all, Erik Norin and Nils Ambolt had mapped as much of the river as they could get at without canoes, and fixed its position astronomically, and Bergman had dealt with the southward-flowing branch on whose banks the burial-places lie, there remained only the mapping of the lakes on the southern bank of the river to afford a complete picture of the Kum-daria's hydrographic system. This work Chen carried out in a manner which did credit to himself and was of advantage to our expedition and its scientific results.

I had never asked him to do it; it would have been cruel to call upon any man to do on foot in the two hottest summer months, amidst clouds of gadflies and mosquitoes, and in constant danger of sunstroke, a job which would be trying enough even at a cooler time of year. Chen had just as much right as we others to retire to more northerly latitudes and rest when the great heat set in. But he did not. He undertook on his own initiative a programme which put the coping-stone on our exploration of the new waterways and lakes, and which justified the assertion that we had left unsolved no problem in connexion with the hydrography of the new river.

XV

TO TUN-HWANG AND THE GROTTOES OF
THE THOUSAND BUDDHAS

THE boat trip Chen and I had made on the Kum-daria
had been in every way successful. The whole of the
new river had been mapped right down to the point where
it ran into the " wandering lake ", whose northern part we
had navigated as far south as possible. We had linked up
admirably with the earlier maps of Norin, Hörner and Chen.
With the help of my astronomical observation at Lou-lan in
1901, and Ambolt's elaborate observations along the
western part of the Kum-daria, the latitude and longitude
of the places we had visited were definitely established.
The levels of the Kuruk-tagh and the country along the new
waterways had been fixed by my series of observations at
Yangi-köl and Ying-p'an in 1899–1900. According to
these the new Lop-nor is about 2,665 feet above sea-level.

Hummel's and Bergman's work had been completed in
an equally satisfactory manner.

The only failure had been the motor trip to the eastward
which Yew, Kung and Effe had made from base camp
no. 70 with the object of finding a route for the new motor
road which was to link Nanking with Central Asia. We
were to have an opportunity of testing this road from Anhsi
to Nanking on our way home in 1935. We knew it already
from Hami to Kucha via Turfan and Korla, and we had
likewise covered the section from Korla to base camp no. 70
on the Kum-daria, or 141 miles. The task of the motor
reconnaissance under Yew and Kung was, therefore, to
push forward to the terminal lake of the Su-lo-ho, a distance
from camp no. 70 of nearly 240 miles as the crow flies.

They were, in fact, unable, for want of lubricating oil, to
get farther than Altmish-bulak; the distance to this place

was 87 miles in a straight line, but for them, with all their twistings and turnings, it was about three times as far. From the terminal lake of the Su-lo-ho to Tun-hwang is another 105 miles, and from Tun-hwang to Anhsi yet another 69 miles.

So what we had missed in our laborious summer was the whole section from Altmish-bulak to Anhsi, or 324 miles.

For cars with adequate supplies of petrol and lubricating oil 324 miles is nothing to speak of—on European or American roads. But in those regions of Central Asia, where there is not a sign of a road, a stretch of 324 miles can be a fearful distance.

The whole expedition—except Hummel and Bergman, who had returned home—had assembled at Urumchi on September 8, 1934; but six weeks more were to pass before we were liberated from that awful town. The governor-general Sheng Shih-tsai insisted on our returning via the Etsin-gol, the same way as we had come. He warned us against the road between Hami and Anhsi, where an organized robber band sixty strong had established itself at Hsing-hsing-hsia, on the frontier between Sinkiang and Kansu, to plunder caravans and travellers. I made no promises, and thought to myself, " If only we get to Hami we'll travel whichever way we like ".

We left Urumchi on October 21 with two motor-lorries and the small car, and reached Anhsi on October 30 without further adventures.

Before we started from Urumchi I had told my three Chinese comrades, Yew, Chen and Kung, that if we could find petrol at Anhsi I meant to make a push to the westward—if possible, as far as Altmish-bulak.

This was only a pious wish, for the supply of petrol we were taking from Urumchi was enough to get us to Anhsi, but hardly any farther. If no petrol was to be found at Anhsi, we should have no choice but to continue along the Silk Road with carts, horses or camels, and an advance towards the Lop-nor depression would be quite out of the question.

But Fortune continually smiled on us, and our desires were fulfilled in a manner which could not have been bettered if the plan had been prepared and organized in advance. We had a friendly reception from the Chinese mayor of Anhsi and from the representative of the Sino-German Eurasia aeroplane company in that town, Herr Pauck. The latter told us that 3,000 gallons of petrol were stored in the place. This large supply, intended for the Berlin–Shanghai air line, was not needed for the present, because the air traffic had never got under way, the Russians having refused to allow Germans to fly over Asiatic Russia.

An exchange of wireless messages between myself and the heads of the Eurasia in Shanghai, Messrs. Walter and Li, resulted in a practically unlimited supply of petrol being placed at our disposal.

All that then remained to be done was to obtain permission from the Nanking Government, in whose service we were, to undertake the proposed motor trip westward. This permission, too, was given us at once, although petrol prices in the heart of Asia are very high, and this new journey of exploration would cost several thousand dollars.

If the motor reconnaissance was to be successfully carried out, it was of the utmost importance that not a living soul in Anhsi should have an idea of our real intentions. Neither the mayor, in whose *yamên* we were staying, nor Herr Pauck, who supplied us with the petrol, was initiated into our secrets. Nor did we let Georg Söderbom or Herr Manfred Bökenkamp, who had been a member of our great expedition for four years and was now at Anhsi on another mission, know anything about it. Our two drivers, Effe and Serat, were simply told how much petrol and oil they should take with them.

All this secrecy was a simple precautionary measure. Altmish-bulak, like the whole Lop-nor area, is in the province of Sinkiang. We had had more than enough of captivity in that province, in the hands of Tungans, Russians and Chinese. If our real intention had become generally known in Anhsi, the report of it would without the least doubt have spread to Sinkiang and reached the ears of the authorities. The mayor of Anhsi was a friend of the lord of Hami, the old fox Yolbars Khan, and talked to him on the telephone every day. If the mayor had found out

what we had in mind, he would have told Yolbars, and
Yolbars would have told Urumchi.   And the ruler of the
province would have been justified in suspecting us if, after
vainly asking permission to make a journey by motor to
Kashgar, we had returned to the province by a more
southerly route outside his sphere of control.   He might
have sent mounted patrols to the Altmish-bulak springs to
search for us, and if we had been captured in such circumstances, he would have had good reason to regard us, and
treat us, as spies.

To conceal our intentions, therefore, we spread abroad
the rumour—only partially true—that we intended to visit
the famous cliff grottoes near Tun-hwang—Ch'ien-fo-tung,
" the grottoes of the thousand Buddhas ".

On November 2 all preparations were made for our
departure, but as usual on the first day, it was a long time
before we were ready.   Although the mayor in his own
exalted person accompanied us for some way outside Anhsi,
we were stopped at the town gate by sentries, who cross-
examined us about our aims and objects.   Our explanations
were evidently found plausible, for we were allowed to pass
without delay.

Our route led southward through an avenue of willows
and over canals crossed by short narrow bridges.   The
ground was soft and sandy.   A stream flowing westward
had, at that season, little water between the belts of ice on
its banks.   We were not far from the low hills to the southward when we pitched camp on the banks of the Nan-chi,
or Southern Canal, with its little bridge and solitary poplar.

On the night of November 2–3 the temperature fell to
8·6 degrees, and the morning was brilliantly fine and clear.
A couple of extra passengers had appeared on the lorry—
the chief of police of Anhsi and a gendarme.   When I asked
what they wanted, they replied that the mayor had ordered
them to accompany us as a guard of honour and be at our
service during our stay at Tun-hwang.   Their real task was
probably to spy upon our proceedings.

The road, full of small knolls of earth, tussocks of grass,
holes and deep wheel-tracks, ran steadily southward, crossing a series of canals with rickety little wooden bridges.

But just beyond the hamlet of Hsi-kung, where a few poor peasants lived in their grey-walled farms, we reached at last the high road between Tun-hwang and Suchow, and here we swung off to WSW towards the first-named town.

Here, too, ended the soft cultivable earth which formed the Anhsi oasis, a criss-cross of irrigation canals ; and to the south, right to the foot of the hills, we traversed sheer *gobi*—a hard, barren desert of close-packed gravel. The road ran through the desert, so suited to motor traffic, and we had the oasis immediately on our right.

An antelope sprang up in the wilderness and disappeared along the track ahead of us before Effe could get his gun ready. Ahead of us were a couple of horsemen, going in the same direction as ourselves. When they heard the noise of the cars, they turned quickly in their saddles, applied their heels to their horses' sides and fled towards the hills to southward. Effe thought they were robbers with a bad conscience.

A little temple rose among the hills, and farther on another, in ruins. Remains of houses and walls bore witness to habitation at an earlier date. We were astonished at not crossing pronounced gullies running down from the mountains ; those we did cross were so shallow that they would not have been noticeable but for a slight jolting of the car.

Now *yardangs*, that curious and characteristic landscape, appeared to the right of our road—long ridges and strips about 3 feet high, shaped by the action of the wind on the clay sediment and alluvium. During our boat trip on the Kum-daria we had seen them in all their glory.

At last a sign of life appeared. A high-wheeled cart came along, drawn by a pair of oxen and accompanied by three men and a donkey. It was loaded with cotton and pears. We heard that the latter fetched a copper coin each at Tun-hwang and three coppers at Anhsi. Of these coins with a square hole in the middle 400 went to a silver dollar at Tun-hwang, but 550 at Anhsi.

At Lu-ts'ao-ko, or " Reed Valley ", we came upon yet another smallish temple in ruins. The hills to the southward grew smaller and moved farther away from us. The country was fearfully desolate ; utterly barren desert now extended on every side. But there was rather more traffic. Time after time we met ox-carts loaded with pears, country-men with donkeys or, once or twice, Chinese riding on camels. At the little inn of T'ien-shui-ch'üan, or " Fresh Water Spring "—the water is bitter despite the name—a few wayfarers were resting with their draught animals and carts. K'ung-hsin-tung was a village in ruins, with a newly built hexagonal watch-tower and five miniature towers in front of it. We sometimes passed road-marks which reminded us of the Mongolian *obos*. Several times we sighted herds of antelope in the distance.

When we had rested for the night, having travelled 54 miles, we thought it could not be much farther to Tun-hwang. Nor was the distance great, but the road was shocking. It led through a string of small villages, over many canals with rickety bridges, past walls, farms and watch-towers, gardens and travellers' shelters—at which neither East Turkis nor Tungans were to be seen, but only Chinese—between troublesome *yardangs* and belts of heavy sand in which we got stuck several times. In places the road was sunk deep in the ground, at others we had to cross high canal dykes, in which the car got hung up and had to be dug free. Gardens and copses became more and more frequent, and in places we drove through avenues. Around An-ting-hsien, " Peaceful Town ", we strayed into a laby-rinth of canals and bridges, and then came into a sunk road from 6 to 10 feet deep. The water often boiled in the radiator, and had to be cooled from a pail filled at a canal. In such circumstances progress was slow, the more so as we were taking bearings all the time for the map of our route.

Mo-chia-p'u, " Mo's Fort ", was built at the end of the fifties. After passing it the road ran over a big canal on a solid bridge of seven beams with flat stones over them. The canal, like the rest, drew its water from the Tang-ho.

The god of literature, Wen-ch'ang, has a temple built in his honour just outside the eastern gate of Tun-hwang. Here we were stopped by soldiers, but they let us through without any further objection. We left our Chinese visiting-cards at the outer gate of the mayor's *yamên*. The supreme authority came to receive us in person, and begged us to stay the night as his guests. We declined, but could not refuse to share his dinner, consisting of minced boiled meat, fried calf's liver and scrambled eggs. The host was a very courteous and hospitable man, who gladly replied to all our questions. He told us that 3,500 families lived at Tun-hwang, while there were only 500 at Anhsi. The inhabitants were Chinese, but a few East Turki merchants from Charkhlik, Hami and Turfan also lived at Tun-hwang. The latter had then not much to do, since the war had paralysed all trade ; but we heard later that the exchange of goods had recommenced in modest forms, and that small caravans were cautiously making their way to the three towns in question.

There are, for that matter, not many towns on earth which lie farther from the beaten track than Tun-hwang. And yet, 2,000 years ago, this town was an important junction. The great caravan road, which was the most important artery of the silk trade, forked at the old fort of Yü-men-kwan (Stein's ruin T XIV), about 50 miles WNW of Tun-hwang. A northerly branch passed through Turfan, Kara-shahr and Kucha, a southerly through Charkhlik, Cherchen and Khotan, and between these roads ran a third, via Lou-lan and Korla, which went north of Lop-nor and followed the course of the river Kum-daria, mapped by ourselves. It was this last road which was of special interest to us. Its course was fairly well known after the journeys of Sir Aurel Stein and those of Hörner and Chen. Our task was to find out whether it was practicable for cars. If the ground was impossibly bad, we would make a new search among the Pei-shan mountains, north of the old desert road. Luckily for us, the mayor was an amenable and tactful man, who did not even ask what we meant to do.

But now we were off to the " grottoes of the thousand Buddhas ", and after dinner we took leave. The whole of the outer courtyard of the authorities' *yamên* was packed with inquisitive spectators, and there was much more life in the streets than at Anhsi. Customers thronged round the open booths in the bazaars, and goods were being carried to and from the shops in carts and on donkeys and camels.

We drove out of the town and were soon out in the country, that confusing maze of grey houses and walls, gardens and avenues, and canals with ramparts and bridges. But the short distance from the *yamên* to our camping-ground no. 116—only 4¾ miles—was, regarded as a motor road, beyond the wildest imagination. A canal had burst through its dykes and swamped the road. The water hid the ditches on each side of the road; but Serat was daring and drove by touch. Effe followed in the small car and stuck in a deep rut. We stopped; everyone jumped out and pushed. The lorry swayed and swung from side to side, and we expected to see some of the passengers on the top flung off when it made a particularly violent lurch. But they clung like grim death to the ropes which were tied round the baggage.

Now we stuck fast in the mud; now the bottom of a car stuck on a dyke, and we had to get to work again with spades and pick-axes. Now and then a bit of dry ground rose out of those long road lakes, but the relief was not for long, and the water was soon seething in front of the cars as round the bows of a motor-boat.

When the belt of cultivation, with its canals, its water, and its dangerous bridges, had finally come to an end, another obstacle rose in our way—a level, barren sand dune of con-siderable size. The long narrow rope mats were spread under the wheels, the engines worked with a will, we gained a few yards and stuck fast in the sand till the mats had been moved forward a little way.

When we had at last overcome this obstacle, and had learnt that there were five places like it on the way to the grottoes, we called a halt, took counsel, and decided to mobilize carts and oxen—no horses were to be had. It was black night already. The tent was put up and camp no. 116 pitched. In two hours' time two carts and nine oxen arrived. The latter were to help the cars on their return journey to Tun-hwang.

On the following day we got into the carts and drove south-west between patches of *yardang* about 3 feet high and strips of drifting sand dunes. A fresh breeze was blowing in our faces, and the dust which whirled through the air soon hid the mountains.   For the motorist it is no fun being drawn by oxen.   The honest, phlegmatic beasts take a step forward now and again ; they go with bent heads and noses to the ground, and make no attempt to hurry.   We took six hours to cover 9 miles.

At last we reached a dry river-bed, along which we proceeded SSW.   Immediately to our right we had a perpendicular stone cliff, eaten away in times past by river water. Here were the first grottoes—black gaping holes in this wall of rock.   We drove past them and reached a little fenced-in enclosure in which tall poplars and other trees grew.

In a shelter, empty and abandoned when we saw it, Chinese pilgrims from Tun-hwang are received when they attend certain religious ceremonies at the place on the eighth day of the fourth month.   Three Taoist priests lived there. The chief priest, Wang by name, was not at home, but one of the two others received us and led us to a guest-room in a temple, consisting of two large ruined halls whose only adornment was three statues of Buddha without altar or sacrificial vessels.   Our host, the Taoist priest, who seemed depressed and absent-minded, told us that his home was at Kanchow and that he had taken up his present post four years earlier.   He was unmarried, although marriage was not forbidden in his community.   The temple owned land and leased its fields to farmers, who obeyed and supported the priesthood.   They also bought millet from Tun-hwang. There were two lama monasteries at the place ; their seven monks were Chinese from Kansu.

The priest affirmed that there were 1,800 grottoes, but he had only to perform *k'ot'ou*, or fall on his knees with his forehead to the ground, in nine of them twice daily.   As twilight was coming on, we only had a look at one or two of the nearest grottoes, on whose walls were painted pictures of gods.   These were quite without interest ; they had been painted after the revolution (1911).   Our friend the priest told us that they intended to collect money for the restoration of all the faded or badly damaged pictures more than a thousand years old.   This would entirely destroy their historical and artistic value.   Of the famous library, which was once preserved in the grottoes at Ch'ien-fo-tung and was examined by Stein and Pelliot in 1908 and 1909, not the tiniest manuscript roll remained. What remained after the bulk of the manuscript rolls had been taken away to London and Paris had been stolen by officials or sold to the first bidder. Only a few years ago there was a regular trade in similar rolls in Chinese or Tibetan, or in Indian languages ; they could be bought freely, for example, in the bazaars at Suchow. A number of them are preserved in the National Library at Peking.

Our journey to Tun-hwang had, as I have said, quite another object than a visit to " the grottoes of the thousand Buddhas ". These had been thoroughly examined, described and copied by experts, and there was no possibility of my finding anything new in them. I visited them partly out of curiosity and partly because it seemed absurd to have been at Tun-hwang without having seen the famous grottoes. It would be like going to Agra and not seeing the Taj Mahal.

Nor will I make any attempt to describe that multitude of square rooms cut in the hill-side, with vaulted curbroofs, with religious paintings on the walls and sculptured figures of gods and patrons, of Buddha and his disciples, and with narrow entrances facing eastward. We spent the best part of the anniversary of Gustavus Adolphus' death in wandering along the façade of that strange river terrace, perforated by the gaping black mouths of innumerable grottoes. The bottom-floor grottoes are on a level with the ground outside. I visited twenty-one of them. As a rule each grotto has a main group of images in the middle, opposite the entrance, and three pictures on each side wall. In the background are a couple of animals resembling dogs or gryphons, guardians of the place, and three wooden vessels for incense and offerings.

One ascends by a ladder to the row of cave-mouths on the second floor, some of which have wooden doors facing the valley, while a newly built outside stone staircase leads to the third floor. Horizontal posts are stuck into the outer wall of the cliff here and there, showing that a balcony or verandah ran past the entrances to the grottoes in former times. At other points only the holes made by the posts remain. It is sometimes rather a breakneck performance getting into the sacred places, but a number are connected with each other by doorways inside.

A little farther south we found, in front of the façade of the grottoes, a newly built temple in the Chinese style nine floors high, containing a giant image of Buddha.

On the whole Ch'ien-fo-tung, " the grottoes of the thousand Buddhas ", was a disappointment to me. I had expected something finer and more distinguished, not a monotonous uniformity, neglected and allowed to fall into ruin by the men of latter days. What is impressive is the multitude of grottoes, and the work and patience that were required to excavate these rooms and niches in the hard rock. The men who gave their time and their strength to this gigantic work must have had a burning faith in the power of their gods. The tall Lombardy poplars before the façade of the grottoes and around the temple of Buddha help to lend a touch of beauty and poetry to this curious abode of religious mysticism.

Another place in the same part of the world was of much greater interest to our expedition. Its name is Hsi-ch'ien-fo-tung, " the western grottoes of the thousand Buddhas ", and it lies about 22 miles south-west of Tun-hwang, where the river Tang-ho makes a sharp bend through a little chain of hills. These grottoes were discovered by the inhabitants of the district about 1928. Some shepherds at Tun-hwang told Dr. Birger Bohlin about them, and he went to the place on June 18, 1931.

Bohlin found the grottoes just to the north of the little chain of hills, on a conglomerate slope 56 feet high to the left of the river ; the grottoes are only about 18 feet above its present bed. They consist of a row of niches covering about a hundred yards of the slope, and are clearly the last relics of something on a much larger scale which has been destroyed by the erosion of the river. The most westerly of these grottoes are the best preserved and are in part connected with each other. Of the middle ones only the inner walls remain. The eastern grottoes are well preserved, but isolated from one another. The walls of the grottoes are whitewashed and covered with paintings which obviously date from different periods. In places Bohlin found two layers of paintings, one above the other, and the older incomparably more beautiful than the newer. He found the temple in the charge of Taoist priests, who lived in a little grotto west of the real temple grottoes. Bohlin made plans of the most important grottoes and took more than twenty photographs of them.

The English women missionaries, the Misses E. and F. French and M. Cable, visited Bohlin's grottoes in the spring of 1932. To judge from their excellent travel book, *A Desert Journal*, they were unaware of Bohlin's visit a year earlier.[1]

We had tea and cake in the afternoon, and the solitary Taoist priest received three silver dollars for his hospitality. Then our light luggage was packed on carts, we got in, and the sluggish horned philosophers began their slow return journey northwards, while the strong north-easterly wind rustled through the dry fallen poplar leaves in the valley and set them dancing. When we had once come out into more open country, flying sand enshrouded our creaking carts, and we sought protection against its unashamed caresses by drawing up our fur collars as high as we could.

We passed a small temple in a state of threatening collapse, in which there had been neither priests nor lay brothers for years past. And yet the temple bell was clanging heavily, and the waves of sound were borne from the metal far over the desert. Was it a trick of the spirits of the air as they swept by? No, it was Chia Kwei and Li, who had gone on ahead and now greeted us with bell-ringing as we passed the temple with the solemn slowness of a funeral procession.

The low hills disappeared in whirling clouds of sand, and we could not see where we were going. A couple of carts loomed up through the mist, one drawn by two horses, the other by a horse and a mule. Their drivers had been ordered by the mayor to meet us and help us back to Tunhwang by the same road that we had covered in the cars two days before. The flood water had risen and spread far

[1] See *Harvard Journal of Asiatic Studies*, Vol. I, 1936.

and wide, and he had feared that the oxen would not be able to get us back to town without our getting our feet wet.

We transferred ourselves and our baggage to the new conveyance, and off we went. Twilight fell. The wheels cut deep into the high sand dune close to camp no. 116, and in a short time we reached the flooded area. In western countries the roads are best in and round the towns; but in Sinkiang and Kansu it is a relief to get away from the cultivated belts with their irrigation canals, breakneck bridges, dykes and flooded roads out into the desert, where the ground has not been ruined by human hands. The fragment of our journey that still remained, only 2 or 3 miles, was in truth rich in sensations and effective pictures in sombre colours—all in a pitch darkness which was partially dispelled by a guide's torch.

Our beasts splashed through the water that washed about their legs. At times they stuck fast in the soft mud and had great difficulty in getting free again. The carts on their two high wheels rocked and swayed from right to left, and often threatened to overturn. We reached the first farms, where dogs barked and old trees loomed up like spectres out of the darkness. The torchlight was reflected in the water and faintly lit up the surroundings.

On its return journey two days before the motor-lorry had damaged two of the rotten wooden bridges which led over a couple of fair-sized canals. The lorry itself had got over without breaking an axle. One of the bridges had been repaired to some extent, but a large black hole still gaped in the other. Nevertheless, Kung, Chen and our two servants, who were in the first cart, drove ahead. One wheel slipped down into the hole up to the axle with a tremendous crash—it was luck that none of them was thrown into the canal! The horses were taken out, and our combined efforts succeeded in getting the cart up and pushing it off the bridge.

Yew and I followed in the second cart, whose wheels were to be carefully guided one on each side of the hole. But instead the horse in the shafts tumbled down awkwardly, with all four legs in the hole, and was left hanging. It was unharnessed and lifted out, but had taken such a dislike to

N

the place that it galloped off through the darkness, plunging and splashing, and disappeared. The mule was more careful. It picked its way past the gaping abyss, and the cart followed, jolting and swaying like a boat in a rough sea.

At last the wall of Tun-hwang was discernible to our left. We knocked at the eastern gate of the outer town. After a long wait we heard the watchman turning his great key ; the bar fell to the ground, the gates were opened and we rolled through the pitch dark archway. Then followed the inner town with its eastern gate and its now silent streets, where only one or two lonely wanderers were trudging about with lanterns, and oil lamps burned in shops not yet shut.

November 7 was full up with work of all kinds in connexion with the impending journey—buying sheep, flour, rice and eggs, and consulting with one or two people whom Chen had met on his journey with Hörner three years earlier. A *bek* from Turfan, Ayip Ahun, had been working at Tunhwang for twenty-seven years ; another, Emin Ahun from Charkhlik, had settled there and started business only three years before. They knew of no other roads north and west than the one we had taken from Hami to Anhsi and the road through the desert to Charkhlik, along which Marco Polo had come and, forty years ago, my old friend, not long dead, P. K. Kozlov. Of the roads which specially interested us—the desert road to Lop-nor and Lou-lan, used by Sir Aurel Stein and by Hörner and Chen, or possible caravan routes in the Pei-shan mountains farther north—they knew nothing. Nor had they any knowledge of the direct road to Turfan, now very seldom or never used, but they knew a Torgut named Bughra who had travelled by that route. Unluckily he was away at the moment. The talk we had heard in Sinkiang of refugees, especially merchants, now and then making their way through the Kuruk-tagh to Tun-hwang and Anhsi to get away from the unrest in their own province must have been considerably exaggerated, for no one in those cities knew anything about it.

We met a Tungan who said he knew a by-road to Hami to the westward. It ran north from Tun-hwang, swung to the north-west through the Pei-shan, and then went

Catching fish in the shallow water of Lop-nor

Author on Lop-nor

Departure from Lop-nor

Well-preserved mummy in the Lop-nor desert

Sadik. 27 au t, ong-kel

My boatman Sadik

Cars in the desert between Ying-p'an and Yardang-bulak

Bergman and Author on the Kum-daria : Georg Söderbom in canoe

A coffin found by Bergman in the Lop-nor desert

Wooden monuments at Ördek's burial-place

Camp at Hwang-chi-chiao, south-west of Anhsi

" Grottoes of the thousand Buddhas ", near Tun-hwang

Robbers at Tao-tao-shui: Serat and Jomcha in background

Sand dunes in the Ghashun-gobi

" Sui-Sin-bulak ", newly discovered spring in the Ghashun-gobi, December 6, 1934

Mesa resembling ruins of an old castle : Lop-nor basin,
December 10, 1934

Mesa formations in eastern part of Lop-nor basin, December 10, 1934

north again towards Hami. There were springs and fuel along this road.

No one had ever heard of Altmish-bulak and Lop-nor, or knew of any roads to Korla and Kucha but those via Hami and Turfan or Charkhlik.

This faulty information, and lack of communications with the country to the westward, is quite natural. To the westward extends one of the most savage deserts in the world, a God-forsaken country, a barrier to all human commerce. That is why Tun-hwang is a blind alley, the farthest point on the old Imperial Highway, while Anhsi is a through station on the road from Hami to Suchow. In time of war, as in 1934, those towns and oases fare best which lie far from the beaten track.

Our friend and host the mayor was therefore a lonely man, who enjoyed the visits from the outside world that were so few and far between. He had all the more cause to be pleased on this occasion, because Yew and Kung were from the same province as himself—Kiangsu. He never wearied of telling us about the life and conditions in his town. An interesting question he touched upon was that of the volume of water in the rivers. He declared that a hundred years ago there was so much water in the Su-lo-ho and Tang-ho that they were navigable for canoes and boats. Since then the volume of water had diminished year by year, which cannot have been due to increased irrigation, least of all in war-time, when agriculture runs to waste like everything else.

When we crossed the Su-lo-ho on October 30, it contained only some 13 cubic feet of running water. Its bed, which was some 30 yards wide and 6 feet deep, was muddy, but at the time frozen. There is no bridge over the Su-lo-ho at Anhsi, but at Tun-hwang there is a twelve-span bridge over the Tang-ho, about 6 feet above the water and 75 yards long. It rests on posts $15\frac{1}{2}$ inches thick. We were soon to have an opportunity of becoming more closely acquainted with this primitive piece of architecture.

XVI

TO THE MOUNTAIN MAZE OF THE PEI-SHAN

NOVEMBER 8 was another day of departure. All our baggage was carried out into the outer court-yard of the *yamên*, where a large crowd had collected and a couple of policemen were keeping the inquisitive at a distance. The air was thick and the sun was trying in vain to break through a thin veil of mist. Pigeons were flying to and fro over our heads; light whistles are fastened to their tail feathers, which produce melodious sounds as they fly. A Tungan had been engaged to act as our guide for the first day or two, but he failed us at the last moment and the mayor gave us instead a Chinese, who was said to know the country immediately to the westward.

We rolled through the eastern gate of the inner town, passed the drum-tower and the southern gate of the outer town wall, and then swung northward to the long bridge over the Tang-ho. Its vertical poles, driven into the river-bed, support a bottom layer of huge beams, and on them rest cross-pieces and rough planks, covered with earth and rubble. The small car got over easily enough, but the motor-lorry was too heavy, and all the baggage was taken across in carts, to be loaded on to the lorry again on the left bank.

There was now much more water in the river than the day before. Ten canals run out of the Tang-ho in the neighbourhood of Tun-hwang, and are used in regular order. When a farmer wants to use his canal for a certain time, the other nine have to be kept shut. On the previous day a canal above the bridge had appropriated the whole volume of water, so that only a tiny trickle had then been passing under the bridge. On November 8 it was the turn of a canal situated below the bridge, and the whole volume of water was therefore passing under the bridge.

And now we really started from Tun-hwang. We had 250 gallons of petrol on the lorry. The two cars needed two gallons in all to cover 6 miles. The distance as the crow flies was rather more than 240 miles. If the road had been straight and good, 160 gallons would have been enough to get us to Altmish-bulak and back. But here we miscalculated. Our route was crooked and the road was bad, as my story will show.

We drove to the north-west through villages, past farms, walls, ploughed fields and temples, along avenues and over canals. We met peasants with carts drawn by oxen or horses and small caravans of donkeys laden with stems and roots of dried tamarisk, which are sold for fuel in the town. Here a flock of sheep was grazing, there a number of camels. Black pigs grubbed in the ditches, dogs barked, and now and then a cat darted across the road.

For long stretches the road was sunk as much as 9 or 10 feet in the ground, testifying that it had been worn for a thousand years past by cart-wheels, the hooves of horses and oxen, and the feet of fifty generations of walkers.

We drove through a belt of steppe and reached the village of Pa-tze-chang, on its farther side. Wherever we went the cars created the greatest sensation, which was not surprising, for in those parts a vehicle that ran along the road without oxen or horses had never been seen. Peasants who met us stood dumb with amazement; people rushed out of the farms to the road, unable to believe their own eyes. Horses shied and flung off their loads, but donkeys and oxen took the unknown monsters with philosophic calm.

We camped on a plain outside Pa-tze-chang, whose name means " shooting-range ". Our neighbours crowded round us to enjoy the strange spectacle. They wore shabby sheep-skin cloaks, which had once been white, or the blue clothes usual in China. Some were bare-headed, others wore fur caps, turbans or simple bandages round their foreheads. There were no Tungans, only Chinese. Some had a thick growth of beard, indicating an intermingling with Turki elements. If they had thought that we belonged to Big Horse's rebel forces, they were reassured by our Chinese guide, who after some parleying induced them to sell us

Withering tamarisk on the edge of the desert.

fuel and carry water to our kitchen. All night carts ground
and creaked past our camp, belonging to the people who
earned their daily bread by collecting fuel on the steppe and
selling it in Tun-hwang.

In the night the temperature fell to 13·8 degrees. We
drove across level steppe covered with tussocks of hard
yellow grass and occasional tamarisks. Serat shot an antelope. We crossed low vegetation-clad dunes and again
approached the broad low bed of the Tang-ho, which did
not contain a drop of water, but was full of soft sand.
Here we needed all the patience we could muster. Both
cars stuck fast in the sandy bed, and it was only with the help
of rope mats that we were able to get them across the scrub-
clothed dunes on the right bank. Here it soon became
clear that we could go no farther. We spent hours toiling
and moiling and moving forward a few yards at a time.
But at last some men came along with half a dozen camels
and two ox-carts. The baggage was loaded on to these
—more valuable means of transport in such country—and
carried to firmer ground on the steppe. Last of all the oxen
had to drag the cars through the stiff sand of the dunes.

Then we went on NNE along a softish steppe track, separated from the bed of the Tang-ho only by the narrow belt of dunes. We passed Hwang-tun-tze, " Yellow Tower ", the ruins of an old abandoned place ; there are two temples there, one with three arched doors, in a state of decay, the other still inhabited by a solitary priest. Strange that there should be places of worship in that desolate region, to which hardly a human being finds his way except the fuel-gatherers. But devout people probably visit them on religious festivals. At the shrine of Shen-hsien-miao two Taoist priests lived ; one of them was at home, while the other had gone to a temple on the Su-lo-ho or Pei-ho, " North River ", as the water-course is called in those parts.

Beyond an old watch-tower, Chien-tun-tze, the vegetation grew scantier and the clay desert flatter and harder. Startled antelopes dashed away from the track at frequent intervals. That road through the wilderness was not completely dead ; even there one or two fuel-gatherers were about, with camels or donkeys.

The road led northward, so that we were not approaching our destination, Altmish-bulak, which lay to the westward. We sought vainly for some track turning off in that direction. The guide the mayor had given us, an unusually burly, heavily built fellow, seemed to have an unconquerable aversion for the country farther west. There was nothing there but sand- and gravel-beds, he declared—impossible ground for our cars. He seemed to be afraid that we meant to lure him to Sinkiang, where there was war and one might be shot. For that matter he knew only two roads, to the north-west and NNE, both running over low passes in the outer chain of the Pei-shan, and the latter the easier of the two. However that might be, our road did, in fact, lead us a good way farther north before we found it possible to turn off to the westward.

Camp no. 120 was pitched in the wilderness. The road itself was the only sign of human life ; there were no temples, no ruins. Pitching camp is a simpler affair on a motor trip than when one is travelling with a large caravan. All one needs—tent, sleeping-bags, kitchen gear and the travellers' personal belongings—are made fast to the top of

the car and can, according to their nature, be thrown overboard or lifted down with care.   The quickest off the mark
was always Chia Kwei, the cook, who set up his cooker,
filled the pots and jugs with water, and lit his fire while Effe
and Li were pitching the tent which Yew, Kung, Chen and I
inhabited.   Inside the tent the sleeping-bags were unrolled
in their usual places, with each man's box by his pillow, and
the portable stove lighted just inside the tent-opening : this
stove was in fact nothing more than an empty petrol tin,
with its iron nozzle protruding from the tent-opening.   We
sat down cross-legged on our beds and had not long to wait
before Chia Kwei had our tea ready, with bread and butter,
cheese and jam.   Then each of us wrote up his diary and
recorded his observations, and the three Chinese completed
the map of the day's journey.   Meanwhile Effe, Serat and
Jomcha were busy with the two cars.   A couple of hours
later dinner was served—soup, a meat dish and coffee.   At
night Effe and the two Mongols shared the kitchen tent with
Chia Kwei and Li.

A strong lamp with a glass shade hung from our tent-
post.   The industrious Chen was the last of our party to go
to bed.   The tent-opening, left on account of the stove-
pipe, formed a coal-black triangle, while the white tent-
cloth shone bright in the rays of the lamp.   But after the
lamp had been put out the interior of the tent became pitch-
dark, with the opening a pale triangle in the faint starlight.
Through it the mysterious spaces of the sky looked in on us
—infinite, majestic, silent.

The faint sound of bells was heard far away.   It became
stronger and approached nearer and nearer, till at last the
bells grew loud and clanged heavily in time with the camels'
steps as a little caravan passed our camp.   Then the sound
grew fainter again and died away in the distance.

On the morning of November 10, after 16·3 degrees in
the night, there was a light veil over the sky, but the sun
was visible as a yellow disc that shed a misty light.   The
mountains to the north were very faintly visible.

After a short consultation with the faint-hearted guide we
decided for the time being to follow the road north to the
Su-lo-ho.   The ground was fairly hard, with deep ruts left

by cart-wheels. Small terraces, falling away to the north-ward, were often seen in the clay soil. The road crossed an almost flattened river-bed among luxuriant tamarisks. Tien-chen-kung was a small brickworks with a house for the workmen. On a low hill behind it was a niche that formerly contained an image of Buddha.

As the road was taking us too much to the north-east, we decided to leave it and steered north-west over steppe with a fairly thick growth of tamarisks. We had not got far before the ground became impassable, soft and rough, and with too many tamarisks on mounds of earth. So we turned back and followed the road, keeping a look-out west and north-west all the time.

The well of Tien-shui-ching, "Dripping Water", justi-fied its name, for the water in it was very scanty and defiled with camel's dung, dust and rubbish. Nevertheless, the caravan, whose bells we had heard in the night, had en-camped there. It consisted of nineteen camels, bound for Hami with flour and rice. The men in charge of it were Tungans. When we questioned them, they replied that they did not know the road, which they were trying for the first time. They dared not take the ordinary road from Anhsi to Hami because robbers often raided it. Our guide knew all about them, and declared that they knew this westerly road just as well as the easterly route.

Tamarisks grew in scattered belts in hard clay soil. We often passed spots where the bushes had been destroyed by the fuel-gatherers' axes and only the stumps remained. A little farther on both clay soil and vegetation suddenly stopped and were succeeded by fairly hard *gobi*, or utterly barren dark grey desert, in which the road stood out as a gently winding light grey ribbon. The surface was covered with a thin layer of fine shingle resting on yellowish-grey sand. The desert looked as level as the sea, but soon began to undulate almost imperceptibly.

The outline of the southernmost outer chain of the Pei-shan became clearer. We stopped for a while at a little stone cairn and looked out westward. We had risen 650 feet from our last camp, no. 120.

We had already crossed the bed of the Su-lo-ho without

taking any particular notice of the river. The almost flat bed across which we had driven at Tien-chen-kung, and which did not bear a trace of a watercourse, was nothing else than this same Su-lo-ho, though when we crossed it at Anhsi we had found it a clearly defined river, certainly with little water in it, but still a current. The bed of the Tang-ho we had found equally dry and disused. It looked as if many years had passed since water had run along those beds.

We were now indeed at the parting of the ways. Should we turn off sharp to the westward and try the old Silk Road? I had gone that way, one day's march only, on February 6, 1901, from Achik-kuduk (103 miles west of Tun-hwang) to Toghrak-kuduk, before steering north through the Pei-shan mountains. Stein had gone there on his journey of 1906–08, and Hörner and Chen in the winter of 1930–31. The short stretch I had covered—9 miles—consisted partly of fine dust, in which the camels left deep tracks, partly of sand and queer-shaped clay terraces. Farther west Hörner had found country which he described as " very loose alluvial gravel ". Moreover, this desert contains very little water. At Toghrak-kuduk, " Poplar Well ", the water was drinkable, but trickled in slowly.

The mountain route, on the other hand, had certain advantages ; we could expect to find hard, firm ground among the low crests and ridges of the Pei-shan, and also water. Lastly, the mountain route was attractive because it would lead us into absolutely unknown country, where no European had set foot. The only known track, which we should cross farther west, was the one I had mapped in February, 1901, when I went north with my camels from Toghrak-kuduk across the crest of the Pei-shan as far as latitude 41 degrees 29 N, and thence turned off west, then south-west, and then west again to Altmish-bulak. Although thirty-three years had passed since then, I remembered clearly that we had not been held up by sand dunes and that the ground was comparatively hard and good going for camels.

I freely admit that the old, insidious *desiderium terræ incognitæ*, which had so often before decoyed me into reckless adventures, was now again a factor in my decision in favour of the mountain route. And as we were searching for a

motor road suitable for traffic, and had well-founded reasons
for mistrusting the desert road, it was a clear case. So we
did not turn off west for the time being, but held on our
course towards the foot of the Pei-shan.

We were soon in among the mountains and were following a clearly defined old road, marked by numerous cairns
and a watch-tower on a low hill.

At the mountain foot on our left were a little stone wall
and a watch-tower. Shih-pan-ch'üan, " Rocky Spring ",
at the base of a little ridge, was an open basin of clear spring
water, 6 feet 6 inches by 5 feet in size and 2 feet 4 inches
deep. Here we poured away the inferior water in our
receptacles and filled them with the beautiful new spring
water.

The road, still marked by small cairns, led on to the
NNW between low mountains and small isolated peaks.
The ground was hard and the gradient quite insignificant.
Here and there a tussock grew. We crossed a minor ridge
and encamped on a gravel plain 4,875 feet above sea-level.

The next day's journey took us northward between low
dark ridges. We followed a broad valley with hard ground.
The guide was alarmed at our plans and said that the next
pass was impossible for cars. A cairn to the left marked a
spring which was now dry, but carried water after occasional
rain. The " impossible " pass was low and easy, about
5,750 feet high, and to the north of it wide views opened up.
We passed through a defile only 10 feet wide and came out
into an arena-like valley, where tussocks of vegetation were
more numerous, dry and thorny. Old cart-tracks were
visible, indicating that the road, which without doubt led to
Hami, was practicable for vehicles. There were cairns
everywhere ; once we counted ten from one point. Here
and there we passed traces of old camps ; at one of these lay
the skeleton of a camel. The relative height of the hills
was insignificant, 150 or at the most 300 feet.

A fresh pass was 6,080 feet high and was crowned by a
big cone-shaped cairn made of small stones. On the other
side was another arena-like valley quite surrounded by low
hills. A snowflake or two fell, but the sun, a rare visitor,
shone out now and again over the wilderness. It was cold,

and those who were riding on the top of the lorry put on their fur coats. A few tamarisks grew in the middle of the valley. At Ming-shui, " Clear Water ", there was neither spring nor well, but we got water there by digging in the bottom of the valley. Above it appeared the ruins of a stone watch-tower, 21 feet square and 9 feet high.

The valley we were following contracted and at last became so narrow that the cars could only just get along. It led to a pass with a cairn, 5,850 feet above the sea. The descending valley wound among low hills, which gradually became higher and were rounded like dolphins' backs.

It had been snowing lightly, but in the afternoon a regular snowstorm came rushing up from the west. We collected fuel for the evening in a place where tamarisks grew. The whirling snow pattered against the windows of the car ; the whole country grew white; we were in full winter. Yellowish-grey tussocks peeped out here and there from under the pall of snow.

We were on a narrow winding track, and could not see how the land lay ahead of us. Scouts were accordingly sent on ahead before we dared proceed. The country with its crests, ridges and peaks was like a disturbed sea of stiff frozen wave-crests. We were only about 40 miles from the road from Hami to Anhsi along which we had been driving a fortnight earlier. We went on now through narrow tortuous passages, now through valleys, across small open spaces with moist ground and some vegetation, and past hills on whose slopes sage reflections had been inscribed in Chinese characters with patterns of white stones upon the soft dark soil.

We reached the northern foot of that chaos of hills and halted at a well which the guide called Ma-lien-ch'üan, " Horse Lotus Spring ". This camp, no. 122, was only 24 miles from the last, and yet most of the day had gone. The everlasting search for a practicable route, the state of the ground, either soft or covered with gravel and boulders, and the taking of bearings for the map explained, as usual, this slow progress.

Ma-lien-ch'üan was a little open spring basin at the mouth of a cleft formed by erosion, scarcely a yard in diameter.   A well about 70 yards below the spring was 3 feet deep, and the surface of the water was nearly a foot below the level of the ground.   All our receptacles were filled with water for eight days.   The snow which had fallen during the day disappeared quickly; only white strips remained in sheltered gullies and crevices.

Our gallant guide confided to us that he dared not return to Tun-hwang alone and begged to be allowed to stay with us.   When this wish had been granted he became—quite of his own accord—most communicative, and told us that he had formerly been an opium smuggler for some years. Anyone could export opium from Sinkiang to Kansu, he said, but the export duty was so high that people preferred to take or send it out by secret channels.   These routes were well known to the smugglers, who were also skilled in the art of finding water in the desert.   Our man himself— Li was his name—had gone south from Hami by a secret track farther west and knew three springs containing bad water west of Ma-lien-ch'üan.   He used to transport his valuable wares by camel and preferably in winter, when the beasts could get snow-water.

After 13·8 degrees in the night we started on November 12 through a valley, which at last allowed us to steer a course to north-west and west.   No road led that way, but we soon crossed an old track leading north.   The ground was moderately soft and cut by numerous erosion gullies. Tamarisks and tufts of scrub occurred in places.   No traces of wild animals were to be seen, but there was dung of camels, horses and oxen, probably from the caravans of refugees or smugglers who had been using this by-road between Hami and Tun-hwang.   We drove along the foot of the mountains we had crossed the day before ; they were now a mile or two away to the southward.   Countless small erosion gullies ran out of them to the northward, trying our patience and compelling us to drive slowly.   Our guide knew a spring in the hills south of our route called Hung-liu-ch'üan, " Tamarisk Spring ".

We had hardly covered 12 miles of our day's journey when we saw nine camels grazing peacefully among hillocks immediately to the right of our track.   A traders' caravan going to Sinkiang, or refugees coming the other way, we thought, and held our course. Next moment we saw a man with a gun a hundred yards ahead of us. Astonished at hearing the noise of a car in parts into which honest folk never stray, he stopped short, swung round on his heel and disappeared in the rough ground by the roadside as quickly as he could run.

To the south-west a watch-tower stood on an eminence. Before we had reached it we perceived, immediately to the right of the road and half hidden by the crown of a hillock, six men in shabby East Turki clothes. Two of the men held their muzzle-loaders at the ready. We were right on top of them before they noticed us, for the cars had been hidden in the small ravine we were following. But when they caught sight of the small car, with the lorry just behind it, they were taken aback and were obviously uncertain as to what they should do. One of them rushed off and disappeared among the nearest hillocks to the eastward, while two others ran away northward, first throwing off their fur coats so as to be able to run faster. The three others, who had not made up their minds so quickly, stayed where they were and crouched down on the ground.

We stopped abruptly and shouted to them : " Come here, we want to speak to you ! " The three nearest came forward slowly to the car, and in a short time the three others returned. Two of the former wore soldiers' uniforms under their Turki fur coats and were evidently marauders from Yolbars Khan's troops at Hami.

When I spoke to them in Turki, they gathered outside the car window.

" What are you ? " I asked.

" We are hunters from Hami."

" What are you hunting in this desert, where there isn't a sign of game ? "

" Yes, there are wild camels here. We haven't found any, but we are going on looking for them, north and west of here. We shoot them for their flesh. We are hunting foxes too, for their skins."

One of the men went off and returned with a couple of fox's skins, which he showed us.

"How many of you are there, and how large is your caravan?"

"Eleven men, with eleven camels and thirteen donkeys."

"Where are the rest of you?"

"Three of them have gone west to look for camel's tracks, the others are quite near, to the northward."

"Where's your camp?"

"Here, at the Tao-tao-shui well."

"Which way did you come from Hami?"

"By the Tao-shui, Ku-shih and Ottun-kösa wells."

When we asked how far west one could travel by car, they replied that they did not know the country for more than a short day's journey in that direction, and that it was hilly and difficult for vehicles all the way. They had reached Tao-tao-shui the evening before and meant to return to Hami if the hunting was a failure. Our sudden appearance in that God-forsaken wilderness astonished them, and they could not hide their nervousness. They evidently had bad consciences, and probably were afraid it was just them we had come out to search for. One of them, a tall, strongly built Turki, asked cautiously where we intended to go. My answer that a new road was to be made to Korla, and that we were reconnoitring the ground, made no visible impression on him; he probably regarded it merely as a blind to conceal our real intentions.

During the conversation, which lasted half an hour, Yew took care to photograph the "hunters" from Hami. We then parted in an atmosphere of mutual mistrust, we regarding them as a robber band, while they believed us to be the spies of justice and the law.

We proceeded westward over a steppe covered with scrub and lined with wearisome shallow erosion gullies, leaving the watch-tower on the hillock to the left 2 or 3 miles away to the south. We were on an old road, a track well-worn long ago, and passed a biggish but ruined cairn. To the right we saw the ruins of a little house, or perhaps an ancient watch-tower, by a little depression in which were yellowed reeds and four trees. The ground fell slowly to the westward. We had descended 650 feet from camp no. 122. The ground was absolutely barren and fairly hard;

the car-wheels left their tracks plainly behind them. If anyone wanted to pursue us he would have no difficulty in finding us. The width of the valley varied from a quarter to three-quarters of a mile.

A patch about a hundred yards wide was covered with dead tamarisks, each on its mound; here was fuel in abundance. The watch-tower by the Tao-tao-shui well, where we had surprised the gang, was still in sight, and must in its time have been an excellent landmark, commanding as it does the country for miles around. The old track was still visible as a slight but clear depression in the ground. Once or twice we saw fresh marks of horses' hooves. An eagle hovered over the scene of desolation—the first sign of local animal life we had seen for a couple of days.

After driving 27 miles we encamped near a cairn scarcely 3 feet high. Here, in the midst of the wilderness, we could not help observing the course of an ancient road, probably made by the trampling of camels' feet. In places where the bottom of the valley is very narrow and the soil hard, and where the nature of the ground prevents erosion gullies from being formed, such a track, trodden into existence by the pads of innumerable camels, can remain in existence for a very long time. It was pretty certain that the watch-towers, the ruined stone house, and the cairns on the more conspicuous hillocks, had not been erected in modern times. And this mountain region was doubtless as desolate, barren and weatherworn 2,000 years ago as it is now. The road itself, and its guide-marks and towers, are perhaps relics of the time when Lou-lan flourished, and when the silk caravans from China—or at any rate many of them—preferred to travel in summer through the higher and cooler mountain regions rather than march through the level, suffocatingly hot desert. Moreover, in the mountains there was a better supply of water in springs and wells, for even if this contained salt in places, the camels drank it. On the other hand, the track we were following was probably never used by carts.

At camp no. 123 we calculated that we were just 240 miles from Altmish-bulak and 90 miles from the northerly route I had taken in 1901.

When we had settled down in our camp that evening, our guide Li appeared and told us, still slightly agitated, that the eleven East Turkis we had surprised in the valley were a well-known robber band. He himself had once been attacked and robbed by the band when he was leading his smuggling caravan through the Pei-shan. He recognized two of the men with whom I had talked, and one of them had recognized him and turned away when their eyes met. Li was convinced that all their camels were stolen from one or more caravans which they had attacked, and said that they probably had stolen goods in their lair somewhere in the mountains, perhaps at Tao-tao-shui itself.

Li knew from his own experience how they went to work. They lay in ambush, rushed out and stopped a passing caravan and demanded a fixed payment, saying that they were in the Sinkiang Customs service. When they had made sure that the caravan men were unarmed, while they themselves had rifles, they said nothing more about a fixed payment, but looted everything of value, including the very camels, and sent the caravan men away stripped of all they had. Li thought that our robber band would now not dare to remain at Tao-tao-shui for the night, but would decamp hastily for fear lest we should have been held up by difficult ground and should quickly return; in which case, having perceived them to be evil-doers, we might make things unpleasant for them.

XVII

THE SAND DUNES OF THE GHASHUN-GOBI

ABOUT 1,200 yards south of camp no. 123 there was a well, which the guide called Lo-t'o-ching, or " Camel Well ".

On the morning of November 13 Kung went there and came across one of the members of the robber band. The fellow told him that two of their donkeys had bolted, and that he and two other men were out searching for them. They had heard the noise of our engines in the evening, and had therefore made their way to our camp during the night. He did not think we should find any water for ten days' journey to the westward.

The well was, properly speaking, a spring, with water, rather salt, but drinkable at a pinch, oozing from five crevices. The melted water from the blocks of ice by the spring was quite fresh. Lo-t'o-ching would be an important base for us. The night temperature was already as low as 10·2 degrees.

Brilliantly clear air, blazing sun, silence of the grave! We soon lost ourselves among hillocks. Three robbers had climbed up on to the highest to watch us. The landscape continually changed its aspect; now we drove through narrow valleys with low rounded hills, now across small patches of steppe, where scrub and tamarisks grew. The older bushes were dead and made the most excellent fuel; the younger were still living. Two men on horseback appeared ahead; on seeing us they vanished hurriedly to the southward. We seemed to be shadowed by dubious characters.

The ground was soft, and the lorry often got stuck. Spades and rope mats then came freely into play. To find harder ground, we steered north-west and came into more

open country.   Wild camels' dung was frequently seen, and
also fresh tracks of wild asses and antelopes.   The wild
beasts know all the open springs ; there were multitudes
of tracks round Lo-t'o-ching.

Our course became westerly again.   To northward the
country was extraordinarily open and flat, to southward we
saw low hills a long way off.   Now we drove over soft
barren soil, whose surface was covered with fine grey
shingle, now over patches of yellow clay which had been
washed down by rain—as hard, shining and smooth as a
floor in a palace.

In the afternoon we came out into a broad gully between
erosion terraces 10 feet high.   We followed this welcome
stream-bed for several hours and hoped that it would long
help us on our way.   It fell imperceptibly to the WSW, and
its soil was hard and level.   Low hills rose again at some
distance from the gully.

The lorry stopped and Serat jumped out with the gun.
A solitary wild camel was moving slowly along to our right.
He stopped short, raised his head, stood for a moment as
still as a statue, and then set off to the north and vanished
as swiftly as the shadow of a cloud.   I was glad that no shot
had been fired at the king of the desert.

Twilight came on at 5 p.m., and electric torches were
produced for the compass bearings.   A little later we
pitched camp after a drive of nearly 36 miles.   The difficult
going during the first days had made severe inroads into our
supply of petrol.   One gallon lasted us for hardly more
than 2 miles.   We buried 35 gallons at camp no. 124
for our return journey, and then we had 135 gallons with
us.   Our plan was to keep together for 140 miles till we
reached some suitable place where we could leave the lorry,
and go on in the small car for the last 60 miles to Altmish-
bulak.

On November 14 we continued along the same splendid
gully, but after the first few miles its bottom grew narrower
and soft, and went winding to the WSW between low
pinkish hillocks splashed here and there with black.   The
hills sometimes assumed a reddish tint, and now and again
we passed a patch of white quartzite.

The large gully became less well defined and ended in open country. The lorry led the way; Serat was an excellent pilot, and no one could judge the difficulties of the ground better than he. Sometimes his car disappeared; then he was down in a hollow. If he was in sight for a long time we could be sure that the ground was firm; if he suddenly stopped we knew he had got stuck in a soft place. We who followed in the small car were, therefore, kept in a continual state of tension. Here and there solid rock was exposed—porphyry, gneiss or granite. The gully was still plainly traceable between rounded hillocks; its breadth varied from 100 to 200 yards. Otherwise we were now quite surrounded by undulating steppe patched with scrub; only to the south-west was a low mountain ridge visible a long way off. Our course was westerly. The ground fell very slowly in that direction.

It was half-past three, and we had covered nearly 36 miles, when the kindly gully suddenly stopped or disappeared under low sand dunes. The motor-lorry had got stuck and could not move a yard. From its roof we examined the ground in every direction through glasses. Sand, sand, sand everywhere: a sea of dunes west, north-west and north. The small car went ahead like a scouting vessel to look for a place where we could get through. But none was found, and we turned back eastward for 9 miles and pitched camp. We would reconnoitre next day from that point. It was the Ghashun-gobi, one of the most savage deserts on earth, which had stopped our advance westward.

The evening was clear, and the stars shone like electric lamps; not a soul was to be seen, no trace of wild animals, no plants except the few dry tussocks which stood round the tents. On all sides lay the vast mysterious desert.

Reconnaissances to north and south on November 15 led to nothing. That cursed gully the day before had been a deceiver, and the advance into the Ghashun-gobi had deprived us of a considerable part of our supply of petrol. We saw six wild camels, but did not interfere with them. Once or twice we passed little dried-up salt lakes, as white as snow. Several times we saw paths trampled up by the wild camels, leading to springs which only the wandering

ships of the desert knew.   There was not a trace of organic
life.

We returned to our old wheel-tracks.   Would the wild
camels dare to cross those mysterious, deep-cut furrows in
the ground, a quite new and unknown feature of their
peaceful home ?   They knew every stone, every hillock and
every watercourse between the heights, but they had never
seen the tracks of a car before.   They might well wonder
what the marks signified, and whether it was some kind of
trap set to catch them on the way to their salt springs.

We returned eastwards in our own tracks with the intention of making a new advance westward south of the outer
range of mountains.   At camp no. 124 we dug up again the
petrol cans we had left there.   Then we covered the stretch
to Lo-t'o-ching in the twilight and darkness.   We went
quicker now that we were not losing time over the everlasting compass bearings for the map.   The temperature
fell ;   the night minimum was 7.3 degrees ;   winter was
approaching.

Yew and I left the spring and well of Lo-t'o-ching, where
our camp no. 126 now was, in the small car with provisions
for one day, and steered towards the mountains to the southward.   We followed a clearly defined track through a line
of low hills, marked by cairns, and crossed a valley running
parallel with the mountain chain from east to west.   Then
followed low ridges and ravines, fairly broken ground.
Cairns were erected on all the dominating heights.   We saw
tracks made by a couple of the horsemen belonging to the
robber band.   A herd of antelope fled.   The tracks of wild
camels and wild asses all led westward, where there must
certainly be an open spring.

We lost the old road on the utterly barren plain.   After
some search we found another cairn which showed us the
way into a narrow stony valley, leading south and south-
east to a pass 6,000 feet high over a crest of red granite and
black porphyry.   The valley from that point was impassable, and we turned back to the plain and were at Lo-t'o-
ching again late in the evening.

So this push too had been fruitless.   Not even the
small car could get forward through the narrow valleys

between steep rock walls, still less the motor-lorry. We examined the maps of the routes we had already covered, and measured the distances from Lo-t'o-ching to Altmish-bulak and Anhsi. As regards the western part of the Pei-shan mountain region the maps were white and blank—except for my 1901 route. It was decided, therefore, that Yew should return to Anhsi next day with the lorry. The distance to Anhsi was 115 miles, a considerable way in a roadless country with difficult going. Yew was to have Effe, Serat and the boy Liu Chia with him, as well as the guide Li, with whom we were now dispensing. Six hundred gallons of petrol were to be brought to us by Georg in the other lorry. Our supplies, too, were to be reinforced with sheep, eggs, bread, sugar and a lot of other things.

Certainly, for a journey in unknown country without a single base one needs provisions, water, petrol and lubricating oil. But one needs something else as well, without which everything else is worthless—patience, angelic patience!

When Yew and his companions left us on the morning of November 17 we, who remained at Lo-t'o-ching to await their return, needed patience indeed. They were going to steer due east to the village and spring of Hung-lin-yuan on the main road from Hami to Anhsi, and thence turn off south-east to the last-named town.

Kung, Chen and I inhabited our usual tent, Chia Kwei, Jomcha and Li the kitchen tent. I had given Yew five days; he ought to be back on the evening of November 21, bringing Georg and 600 gallons of petrol on the lorry which was always called "Edsel". He had taken letters and telegrams to be despatched from Anhsi, and was to bring us news from the world outside. Anything might have happened during our absence. Perhaps orders had arrived for us to return to Nanking without delay, and, if so, the new road to the Lop basin for which we were searching would remain as unknown as it was at that moment.

Kung, Chen and I went back to our tent, where a fire was crackling in the stove. As usual, we studied our maps and calculated the distances. Then I got into the small car to read and write. I was surrounded by the impressive silence,

the wonderful quiet of the desert.   Only a light south wind
set the little Swedish and Chinese flags on the cars flapping
and cracking.   A *terra incognita* extended on every side.
No European had ever set foot there.   To westward the
only route ever travelled was our own—66 miles to the sand
barrier which the Ghashun-gobi had raised in our way.
The sand had beaten us ; next time we must go south of it,
and *then* we must succeed.   One of the last blank spaces
on the map of Central Asia was to be crossed.   No one had
been there before.   Not even the robber bands withdrew
farther than Lo-t'o-ching.   In the west, where the horizon
drew its even line from hillock to hillock, I felt that a gate
stood open—a gate leading into the unknown land.   At the
point where we had turned back we were 30 miles from my
route of 1901, the only one that had crossed the blank space.

The thermometer had been below freezing-point all day,
and as soon as the sun had set it grew cold.   The temperature was 11·3 degrees as early as 8 p.m., and during the
night (November 17–18) it fell to 0·7 degrees.   The next
day was brilliantly clear ; only far to southward light white
clouds hung over the low hills.   Our camp was the central
point in a big slice of the earth's crust, one of the most
desolate in existence.

On the morning of the 19th we decided that Chen and
Kung, with the small car and Jomcha as driver, should make
a short reconnaissance to find a practicable route over the
low hills to southward, where we had vainly endeavoured
to get through three days before.

Chia Kwei, Li and I were now alone in the camp.   The
expedition was scattered to all the winds that blow.   Georg
and two servants were at Anhsi ; Yew, Effe, Serat and Liu
Chia on their way to that place ; Kung, Chen and Jomcha
reconnoitring to the southward, and we three at the
Lo-t'o-ching well.

At half-past twelve Chia Kwei and Li went to the well to
fetch water with empty petrol tins on their backs.   They
had dug a new well for the purpose in a deeper hole.   I was,
therefore, quite alone in camp, and missed the dog Tagil,
who had scented trouble and bolted when we set off from
Urumchi.   The silence of the grave prevailed ; only the

gentle murmuring of the wind was to be heard ; there was not a sign of life on the earth, not a bird in the sky.

Just after one I heard three gun-shots in succession from the neighbourhood of the well, which was hidden by the hillocks close to the camp. " The robber band ! " I thought. " They have found that some of our fellows have gone east with the lorry. Their scouts have also told them that some have gone south with the small car. And finally, they have noticed that two of the others have left the camp. They have attacked them at the well, and then they can easily capture the sole survivor here in the tent."

I took out my revolver and went up on the nearest hillock to have a look through the glass. Nothing was to be seen or heard, so I continued my work in the tent. In half an hour the two boys returned with water. It was they whom I had heard—blazing away at a wild ass.

It was not long before Kung, Chen and Jomcha returned too, having gone 48 miles south-west over firm, practicable ground. They had used 4½ gallons of petrol, and declared that the road they had found was possible for the lorry as well.

November 21 was the fifth and last day which I had given Yew. But almost the whole day passed without anything being heard of him. What were we to do if he did not come ? If he had not come in two days' time, we should know that something had happened to him. Perhaps he had been detained by the authorities at Anhsi, though Georg and his two men and " Edsel " ought to have been hostages enough for us. Both the mayor of Anhsi and his colleague at Tun-hwang had insisted that we should take an escort of three soldiers, but we had obstinately excused ourselves on the ground that the cars were so heavily loaded that they could take no more people. Now we had been away twenty days, and no one knew what we were doing. If Yew, Effe and Serat were detained, the rest of the expedition would doubtless be compelled to return.

The western horizon was tinted a deep glowing red, and the full moon rose silvery white out of the mist in the east. This gorgeous display, the fantastic wealth of warm fiery colours on one side and the cold silent silver sheen on the other, reconciled us to the nakedness of the desert. But soon the flaming hues to westward paled, as when a steppe fire is quenched by night, and the moon assumed sole sway over the wind-worn hillocks.

We were sitting in the tent chatting, and the lamp was just going to be lighted, when Chen cried, " A car ! " and hurried out. We followed him up to the viewpoint. There it came ! Only *one* lorry—a bad sign ! Georg ought to have been there too, bringing " Edsel ". Perhaps Yew was coming with a message that we must all return, probably on orders from Nanking.

The travellers jumped down. There were Yew, Effe, Serat, the boy San Wa-tse and the Mongol Chokdung. We were now eleven strong at the Lo-t'o-ching well. Georg and Liu Chia were the only absentees.

" Are things all right at Anhsi ? " I asked.

" Perfectly," Yew replied.

" Where are Georg and ' Edsel ' ? "

" Georg dared not risk the lorry in the dark. So we drove on and left him, but he's coming to-morrow."

In the tent, Yew discharged at us a crackling broadside of news. There was a new war in Sinkiang. Eastern Turkistan had rebelled against Sheng Shih-tsai. We had got away at the last moment. If we had stayed one day longer we might have been caught for a quite indefinite time. Nothing was known of Ma Chung-yin, Big Horse, but he was believed to be at Khotan. An army of two divisions of Tungans was said to be moving west, to Anhsi and Sinkiang. We should very likely meet them on the Silk Road and lose our cars for the fourth time, and for good. The Minister of Railways at Nanking, Ku Meng-yü, under whose orders we were, had sent us a wireless message giving us liberty to carry out our plans.

High spirits, therefore, reigned in the tent ; a thousand questions and answers were exchanged—Yew's store of news from the outside world seemed inexhaustible. The whole day was spent in discussions and plans.

At 9 o'clock that evening what sounded like a loud detonation was heard 2 or 3 miles away. Had Georg been attacked, or had his petrol exploded, or was it simply a

landslip ? Effe advised us to have rifles and revolvers
ready. But no further suspicious sounds were heard, and
the night passed quietly. Tracks of mounted men were
seen in the neighbourhood, especially where our cars had
passed. Yew, Effe and Serat had heard at Anhsi that the
robber band we had come across at Tao-tao-shui had killed
many travellers and plundered their caravans.

The whole of November 22 passed, and the following
night, without anything being heard of Georg. When he
did not appear on the morning of the 23rd, it was clear that
something had happened to him. Had he been detained at
the last moment, or broken an axle on the way ? He was
already twenty-four hours overdue. I decided to organize
a search myself, accompanied by Yew, Effe and Jomcha.
The small car was got ready ; we took only fur coats and
some food.

We started at 11.20. As we were not now delayed by
map-making, it did not take us long, following our old
tracks, to reach the " robber well " at Tao-tao-shui. This
time there was no one there. We stopped a little while to
fetch water for the radiator, which was boiling—the fresh
breeze was behind us. In another two hours we were at
the Ma-lien-ch'üan spring, whose name the discarded guide
had given us. At Tao-tao-shui the predominating rock
was crumbling granitic gneiss, at Ma-lien-ch'üan rough,
yellowish-white marble. Chao-pi-ching was a well and an
open spring surrounded by reed-beds and brushwood.
Then we followed a river-bed 13 feet deep, and crossed
innumerable watercourses and a plain where the tamarisks
grew thick, almost a small wood.

The sun sank blood-red and the shadow of the earth rose
clearly defined over the eastern horizon. The darkness had
gathered when, hardly 6 miles from the Ta-ch'üan spring
on the Hami–Anhsi road, Effe slackened speed and said,
" Two men ! " But they were not robbers, for now
" Edsel " too loomed up in the darkness.

We stopped a few hours with Georg and Liu Chia, who
were almost frantic ; one or two bearings in the engine had
seized and refused to work. This had happened on the
morning of the 21st, so that they had been there three days

and their food supply had run out. It was impossible to repair the damage without certain tools which were in Serat's lorry. If Georg had accompanied Serat and Yew on their night drive from Anhsi on November 20, the trouble could have been quickly remedied. But now, owing to his dislike of the dark, he was stuck there helpless, cut off both from the tools and from our camp. He had just decided to send Liu the 54 miles to us, a distance which the young Chinese, walking and running, ought to have been able to cover in fifteen hours.

Two hours later, Georg having received the small food supply we had taken with us, we returned the same way as we had come to bring the help he required from the camp at Lo-t'o-ching. It grew cold in the car; the temperature was down to 15·8 as early as 8 p.m., and the night minimum was 2·7 degrees.

We stopped a little while at Ma-lien-ch'üan to get water. We heard men talking in the scrub. We hunted for them in the moonlight, but they vanished like shadows.

We proceeded. The car lamps were lighted. In their bright glare the tamarisks emerged from the darkness like white ghosts with outstretched arms. Effe declared that he saw a man's head sticking up over a hillock; but it was only a road-mark.

It was past one in the morning when we reached our tents at Lo-t'o-ching. Our fellows were all so fast asleep that we had to wake them up with the motor-horn. Our late supper and long discussions kept us up till 4 a.m., while the winter cold held the outside world in its grip.

XVIII

THROUGH THE WILD CAMELS' HOMELAND

ON November 24 both cars left for the scene of Georg's breakdown. Serat and Chokdung drove ahead in the lorry; Yew, Effe and Jomcha in the small car. For us who remained behind at Lo-t'o-ching a fresh period of waiting began that tried our patience sorely.

After 32 degrees of frost in the night, Sunday, November 25, was radiantly fine and clear; late in the afternoon the thinnest veil of clouds was drawn over the sky.

At six in the evening the cry of " Lights to eastward ! " was heard from the kitchen tent. It was Serat and Chokdung coming back with 230 gallons of petrol from " Edsel ". We had 270 gallons in the camp. Yew and Effe had stayed with Georg only an hour and then gone on to Anhsi. Serat and Jomcha had helped Georg with his repairs, and I had ordered Georg now to return to Anhsi and there await our arrival.

On the 26th Kung set out on an important reconnaissance. He had with him Serat, San Wa-tse and Chokdung, half our petrol supply, four drums of fresh water and six of saltish water for the cars; a fortnight's provisions, a tent and sleeping-bags. He was to be away five days. This time there were four of us left in camp—Chen and I, Chia Kwei and Li. The two latter put out saltish well water every evening to freeze and in the morning skimmed off the ice, which was used for making tea and soup.

On the night of November 26-27 we had a temperature of —10.8 degrees. One was not long out in the open air and the biting west wind before one's fingers began to stiffen and one longed to get back to the stove. Our long stay at Lo-t'o-ching had enabled us to make a pretty reliable estimate of its height above the sea—4,390 feet. At

Altmish-bulak thirty-three years earlier I had found the height to be 3,360 feet. So, generally speaking, the ground fell slowly to the westward.

We had plenty to do. Chen was never unoccupied for a minute; he worked out his calculations, took meteorological observations and worked on the map of our route. I made notes.

At 5.30 on the morning of November 28 I was awakened by the sound of a car, and woke Chen. We lit the lamp. Yew came in, and Effe, when he had poured away the water out of the radiator, also appeared. While Chia Kwei was preparing food and tea for the travellers, and Li was lighting the stove, Yew reported that all was quiet at Anhsi. He brought welcome telegrams from my home.

It must have been a disappointment to Georg to be unable—for the second time—to accompany us to our desolate mountains. But the trick " Edsel's " engine had played us on November 21 was a warning to us to be careful. Our general experience had been that Ford's four-cylinder 1933 trucks stood the Central Asiatic country better than his eight-cylinder 1934 trucks. If any serious accident had happened to this car on our journey to the Lop-nor depression, we should have had to leave it there for good and all. It certainly played us several unpleasant tricks on our way home from Anhsi to Sian, but it reached Peking safe and sound and, in the late autumn of 1935, had the honour of taking part in the motor journey which Sir Eric Teichman,[1] Secretary to the British Embassy, made over our old ground —through the Gobi to Hami and on via Ku-ch'eng-tze, Urumchi and Korla to Kashgar. Sir Eric, like ourselves, found Ford trucks " strong, fast, powerful and reliable ", and he adds : " Only the strongest machines will stand the strain of Gobi travel—and the nature of some of the ground that has to be crossed must be seen to be believed."

The 2,550 miles' journey from Sui-yuan to Kashgar took thirty-eight days. At the start Sir Eric Teichman, like ourselves and so many other travellers in the Gobi, had invaluable help from Georg Söderbom. Of the connection

[1] See *The Silk Road*, Appendix, pp. 295 ff.

between our motor journey in 1933–35 and his own in the autumn of 1935 Sir Eric Teichman says :

My transport consisted of two Ford trucks, one new and one old, the latter having already done some thousands of miles of expedition work for Dr. Sven Hedin the year before. The old truck suffered several mechanical breakdowns and had eventually to be abandoned 500 miles short of Kashgar ; the new one reached the end of the journey in perfect condition, and had the distinction of being the first motor vehicle to be driven through from the Chinese border to Kashgar. The moral is that only new machinery is good enough to stand up to the strain of Gobi travel. My native staff of six included two Mongol driver-mechanics who had been with Dr. Hedin on his last journey. One of these was the Mongol Serat, whose invaluable services I obtained through Mr. Georg Söderbom of Kwei-hwa-ch'eng. Serat was my right-hand man throughout the journey. Starting as a youth in the service of Mr. Larson, he had spent his life wandering across the length and breadth of Inner and Outer Mongolia. Subsequently he made two expeditions with Dr. Hedin to Sinkiang, and he can now probably claim to know more than anyone else about the routes and practical details of motor travel in Mongolia and Chinese Turkistan. . . .[1]

This high testimony to Serat's qualities is in no way exaggerated. As long ago as 1928 he received from the King of Sweden the gold medal for loyal service. I know no one, either Asiatic or European, whose knowledge of the roads of Central Asia, above all Mongolia, can be compared with his.

November 30 was the 216th anniversary of Charles XII's death. I celebrated it by telling Yew and Chen about the king. They thought his story wonderfully romantic ; indeed, its echo impressed them almost as strongly as the actual events had impressed others long ago, when they astonished the Turks and the whole Mohammedan world of Asia.

We passed the day writing, making plans and waiting.

[1] *Geographical Journal*, April, 1937, pp. 297 ff. In the spring of 1939 the sad news was received that our faithful Serat had passed away.

Kung and Serat were to be away five days, and November 30 was the fifth day. Their task was to find a route fit for traffic westward to the Lop depression.

It was nearly three when we heard the noise of a car and hurried out. There came Serat and Chokdung with the lorry safe and sound; they brought a letter from Kung reporting that they had advanced 90 miles south-west and west over fairly difficult ground to a depression where they had found water by digging. Thence they had proceeded for another 12 miles till stopped by impenetrable dune sand. They had therefore returned to the new well, which they called " Kung-ching " (Kung's Well). There Kung and San Wa-tse had remained, while Serat and Chokdung returned to us. In his letter Kung begged us to come quickly in order to find a more southerly route westward from " Kung-ching ".

On December 1 we packed and loaded the baggage again. It looked a hopeless task to find room for all the stuff on our only lorry. There stood, in picturesque disarray, whole rows of petrol drums, provision boxes and packing-cases, and there lay the rolled-up tents and sleeping-bags. Sacks filled with ice and old petrol tins containing fresh water also required space. The lorry's load would certainly be more than two tons.

We had now 270 gallons of petrol. There were 120 gallons more with Kung. We thought it too risky to leave a store of petrol for the return journey, as we did not know whether we should come back that way or another. Four superfluous empty drums were filled with sand and set up as a road mark. This " cairn " would probably excite the suspicions and fears of the wild camels and wild asses which came to Lo-t'o-ching to drink, as a scarecrow frightens birds; but if a robber band visited the place in the future our monument would probably not be left in peace—iron drums are useful for carrying water.

It was already past noon when we started and passed the well, where the fragments of ice from the skimming still lay glittering in the sunshine. The region was cut by numerous camel-tracks. We followed one of these to the south-west. Here, too, an older road ran, marked by many cairns erected on conspicuous hillocks. Occasionally we saw solid rock, a light granite; here and there quartz occurred in white patches. We drove through narrow valleys and over low hillocks often broken by small level spaces strewn with rather coarse, sharp stones, about three-quarters of an inch across and spread evenly over a layer of the finest sand or dust. The sun set ahead of us like a glistening diamond, and the afterglow shed its light over the silent desert. Generally speaking, the district was quite barren, but in places dried tussocks and tamarisks grew on their mounds of earth. In such a region as this we pitched camp no. 128. We had covered only 15 miles; map-making, and the soft, uneven surface, accounted for most of our time. Orion shone above the tents, and not a sound disturbed the silence of the night.

Next day we found a gully a hundred yards wide between terraces 6 feet high, offering an excellent road south-west. The ground was as level as a floor. Here, too, lay gravel, small stones an inch or so in diameter, disposed with incredible evenness on the loose, light-yellow dust, in which our scouts' wheels had made deep ruts. This black and white gravel lay spread on the surface of the ground with almost geometrical exactitude, seldom or never so close that the different stones touched one another. Dr. Hörner, who has studied the formation of the ground and the nature of the soil, can no doubt tell us why the heavier gravel does not sink down through the fine light dust, but floats on the surface like corks on water.

Now and again a dark chain appeared on our left a few miles away; it grew clearer as we approached it. In places the ground ran in low undulations and was cut by annoying, tiring little gullies. They were only a few yards apart. The car heaved and pitched like a boat in a seaway. When there were 20 yards between two gullies one had a pleasant restful feeling. They ran from south to north. To the right rose low hills of a light pink hue, while the mountain chain to the southward was almost black. According to Dr. Erik Norin, who examined the specimens of rock I took home, the mountains in this region are of crystalline limestone, with a strong intermixture of slate, and marble.

After 42 miles' run we pitched camp no. 129 in a place where there was a supply of tamarisk wood.

Although the depth of winter was coming on, with its continental cold, and we were in the heart of the great continent, far from all the world's seas, we had no reason to complain of the frost; a temperature of 5·7 degrees on the night of December 2–3 did not worry us at all. The winter remained kind to us, and not one single storm tormented us with its clouds of dust and flying sand.

We followed the same delightful gully. It fell towards the south-west, the direction in which we were going, continually varied in breadth between 40 and 120 yards, and was flanked by terraces 10 feet high, above which rose desolate, weather-worn hills and crests. The height above the sea was 3,640 feet, or 975 feet higher than Lop-nor.

A kingdom of death surrounded us : not a beast, not a track, not even the skull of some old wild camel which had dragged itself here to die in solitude. Just now and again we saw a dried-up tussock in a gully. They seemed dead, but they may have had in them a latent spark of life which allowed them to revive for a few weeks after a local downpour of rain.

To the SSE we could make out three mountain ridges, of which the nearest, quite low, flanked the valley we were following, while the farthest seemed fairly big and was only a pale mass dimly visible in the distance; probably it was the outer and southernmost chain of the Pei-shan complex. Farther on our valley cut through dark grey porphyry cliffs. Where these had been split by the frost the surfaces were fresh, not brittle and weathered. Then our course went winding between little black ridges, a labyrinth of low hills, gullies and passes. Here fine-grained gneiss, crushed very small, predominated, along with fine-grained amphibolite.

Far away to the south we could faintly discern, like a desert mirage, the outline of a mountain chain with snow on its crests. This was the Astin-tagh, the border mountains of north-eastern Tibet, 108 miles away. Our eyes hovered over the belt of desert between the two mountain systems, where no human beings live, and animals and plants are very rare visitors. The last tentacles of the Su-lo-ho disappear in this belt of country, and there lies the Kum-tagh (Sand Mountains) desert, which I crossed in February, 1901.

We followed another valley, less clearly marked, between red and black cliffs. It gradually opened out and became an undulating plain, bounded at some distance by low hills.

After a 30 miles' run we reached the place where Kung and San Wa-tse were waiting for us. They came running to greet us, delighted to see us again, and to feel that they were no longer cut off and alone in the wilderness. Three-quarters of a mile north of their camp was " Kung-ching ", the well dug by Kung, a depression where tamarisks and reeds grew. There we pitched camp no. 130, 3,410 feet above sea-level, 750 feet above Lop-nor and 880 feet lower than camp no. 129. Diabases and diabasic porphyrites formed solid rock in the neighbourhood.

The water in the well was saltish, but it was perfectly drinkable when frozen and then melted. The first foot down was a stratum of saliferous loose earth resting on a stratum of sand 8 inches deep, and below this again was solid rock. The new well was 13 inches deep.

Relying on the maps we had with us, we reckoned that from camp no. 130 it was 174 miles to Altmish-bulak and 210 miles to Anhsi. We must still be 60 miles from the route I had followed northward in 1901. The point where we had turned back the first time, at the sand dunes of the Ghashun-gobi, ought to be due north of camp no. 130.

It was decided to devote the next day to reconnaissance towards the north-west. Serat was our pilot, and only the small car was used. I remained at camp no. 130. At 6 p.m. the lamps shone out in the darkness and our scouts returned, having consumed 9 gallons of petrol in going 46 miles and as much on the return trip, or 92 miles in all. They had found an open salt spring with the skeleton of a camel (probably tame), camel and horse dung, and faint traces of an old encampment. They had been on the farther edge of a belt of sand 2 miles wide, which they did not consider to present any obstacle to the lorry.

Everything that could be dispensed with was left at camp no. 130, where San Wa-tse and Chokdung had to stay with one of the tents, sufficient food and 160 gallons of petrol.

The lorry was therefore a good deal lighter when we started on December 5 in brilliantly clear and pure air.

We drove westward through absolutely barren country, an undulating plain of black gravel, with loose earth under it. A cairn was built on a hillock where we rested for a short time. We wondered whether some traveller of days to come would find it. The ridges between which we drove consisted of porphyry and porphyritic tuff.

To south-west and west the country opened out and resembled a sea. The dry bed of the Su-lo-ho was plainly visible to the south-west, and beyond it, to the south, we could see the ground rising gently to the foot of the Astin-tagh. There were no ridges or low hills between us and the Su-lo-ho; the ground fell slowly to the river-bed.

We steered south-west through low broken country. Sand dunes were seen at a distance in the direction in which we were travelling; we passed a single tamarisk and a small withering reed-bed. We saw the quite fresh tracks of two camels, which had not been there the day before when the reconnaissance went out.

The scenery was most confusing. To westward, ahead of us, it appeared to be level, but we had not got far before we lost ourselves in shallow ravines and were then among hillocks again. Driven sand had collected here and there in crevices. Not a blade grew there. We came upon narrow stretches of sand which we were able to go round. High dunes appeared to the north. The wheels, which hitherto had made ruts an inch to an inch and a half deep, now sank in 2·3 inches.

We came to dunes 4 feet high and left them on our right. We looked out time after time from the tops of hillocks and so found a narrow winding passage through the belts of sand. When we had made our way through the fine yellow sand we reached coarse dark sand rippled by the wind. The bed of a little salt lake appeared not far to the right. A river-bed ran into this lake, with a hard bottom which offered us a firm road. We pitched camp (no. 131) at sunset, having covered 33½ miles.

We had a temperature of 3·2 degrees in the night. Our camping procedure was simplified to some extent. Washing was forbidden—we had to save water. Instead of breakfast being served in our tent, the tent was to be struck and loaded on Serat's lorry while we breakfasted in the kitchen tent, greeted by Chia Kwei with a jovial "*god morgon*" in perfect Swedish.

We proceeded along the dry bed, where a rock 13 feet high had long ago been cut off sharp by the flowing water. An old cairn stood on its summit. A thin layer of crystallized salt covered the surface of the bed. In one place a number of dried tamarisk stems had been washed down and piled up in the bed, on whose bank we passed two thick masses of live tamarisks.

We drove, as through an open door, into a sharply defined valley that cut through the hills with a cairn on each side. Just there we found in the river-bed itself an open but shallow salt-water spring. The left, or eastern side, had a pronounced erosion terrace, on the right the hills fell steeply to the river-bed. The spring had two vents, the upper close to a little stone barrier which formed a basin, now covered with ice. We took the ice with us. Several empty drums were filled with water so that we might find them frozen on our return. Tamarisks and reeds grew in abundance about the spring. The place was pleasant and inviting, a regular oasis in that melancholy mountain desert.

Dry wood for three camps was loaded on to the two lorries. Wild camels' tracks crossed the region in all directions, and we often saw their fresh dung. The reason why we so seldom saw the animals themselves was no doubt mainly that the noise of the cars frightened them away. It was otherwise in the old times, when my caravans were composed of their own tame relations, padding through the desert as silently as themselves. The wild camels' senses are extraordinarily developed. They smell the petrol and hear the noise of the engines at a very great distance, and make off in good time. Only their tracks remain, easily recognizable in the soft earth.

Kung was right in saying that the wild camels' tracks could easily be distinguished from those of the tame beasts. The latter are larger and make a deeper impression. But when he tried to persuade us that, on looking at a tame riding-camel's tracks, one could tell whether the rider was a man or a woman, we could not help asking if one could not say whether she was married or not, and how many children she had.

The valley swung north-west and west, and finally ran into a plain, bounded at a long distance by low hills. A herd of six wild camels had passed by. Cairns were common, always erected on conspicuous hillocks. One of them consisted of four stones, the others of stones and slabs of varying sizes piled up in conical heaps. This had without doubt been a well-known and often-used summer route. There was grazing for camels, and perhaps a few fresh-water springs or wells just off the course we were taking. The camel caravans, which in ancient times carried Chinese silk to the western countries, were in all circumstances better off and more comfortable—men and beasts alike—in the Pei-shan mountain region than down in the flat scorching desert. In all probability, too, there were depressions among the mountains where tolerable water could be found by digging. At the spring I mentioned just now, and a hundred yards down the valley, water was to be found 18 inches down, a shade less salt than the water of the spring. Perhaps caravans innumerable, with precious loads, camped there 2,000 years ago. Then the place had a name, which the desert winds had swept away. We gave it the name of Sui-Sin-bulak, after the two provinces of Sui-yuan and Sinkiang. Quartz-bearing gneisses and hornblendes, and also tuff containing quartz and porphyry, were found by the spring.

When the river-bed became untraceable, we ascended over low hills to a little watershed, 520 feet above our last camp; from the watershed the ground falls again to the north-west. We were bound to cross my northerly track of 1901 somewhere in this region. But time had effaced the impression in the soil left by my camels' pads. Thirty-four years had passed since then, and many storms had swept over the desolate mountains. I exhorted all our men to keep their eyes open. In some depression sheltered from the wind, a faint trace of an almost obliterated track might possibly be found. But we searched in vain; our tracks had disappeared as completely as the furrow of a ship at sea.

The waves had met in the course of my old ships of the desert too, and the ever-wandering particles of sand and dust, driven by violent storms, had hidden the ephemeral characters which our caravan had inscribed among the hillocks. How little I guessed, as I sat in the saddle on my white horse, or perhaps walked to keep myself warm, that at a certain moment I was passing a point which I should revisit thirty-four years and ten months later, and, after one fleeting second, leave again!

On February 6 and 7, 1901, I had encamped at Toghrak-kuduk, "Poplar Well", on the old desert road, a place which the silk caravans between Tun-hwang and Lou-lan used to pass in winter, and which I found to be 2,670 feet above sea-level. Thence I marched 6 miles to the north-ward and on February 8 encamped at the foot of the mountains, 2,685 feet up. My next camp, on February 9, was 12 miles north of the last, and the height there was 3,665 feet. We had then crossed the border mountains and were in the southern part of the Pei-shan. Another 13 miles northwards brought me to camp no. 143 on February 10, and there I was 4,760 feet above the sea.

To judge from the heights and the lie of the mountains, it must have been on the section between camps nos. 142 and 143 that we now crossed the old route on December 6, 1934. Unfortunately we carried out no astronomical observations on this motor trip westward, and the wireless apparatus had been confiscated and at the same time spoilt by the Russians at Korla. We had thus only dead reckoning and the cars' speedometers on which to rely.

Meanwhile we proceeded westward along a gully that ran that way. Its yellow clay bottom was hard and even. It always looked as if it was coming to an end, but continued again round the next corner. A few tufts of vegetation here and there were still fighting for their lives. Between red clay terraces, often white with salt, that admirable gully swung away to south-west and south, down towards the desert. We therefore left it and went through a valley 50 yards wide to a low ridge and thence down into an equally slight valley to the day's camp, no. 132, where the height was 4,225 feet. We had covered rather more than 30 miles.

We pitched camp in the darkness of the night, and the tents were put up by the light of the headlamps. When we came out into the open air next morning, the rising sun was shining over a landscape which we did not recognize. But it was not so very difficult. We were in a shallow valley between hillocks. Then, a little farther west, we were driving between sharp-cut low cliffs. No cairns were to be seen here; we had lost the old high road in the dark the evening before. The country was utterly barren. We saw the tracks of two camels, going north-east. The mysterious beasts that had made the tracks did not show themselves; they had doubtless fled on hearing the distant noise of the cars.

The valley we were following ran between two rock gateways of red and grey gneiss and diabase. Several boulders were lying on the ground, but without blocking the way. The rock was hard, and weathering affected it little. We passed a ridge about a hundred yards long, hardly 3 feet high, with a curiously regular shape, like a defence work made by human hands. To our right rose a bright tawny-coloured peak.

The road was rather soft, and Serat and his lorry got stuck. Li jumped off to push behind. Serat got free again, and Li hastened to clamber up on to the load; but as he did so the lorry lurched sharply and the boy lost his hold, fell to the ground and lay there. We, in the car behind, saw what had happened and were terribly anxious. Effe, our driver, put on speed and drove up to the injured boy. We jumped out, wondering if he was crushed to death. But it was not very serious. Li rose into a sitting position. One of the back wheels had gone over his left foot. We took off his boot and stocking. His foot was painful, and tears came into his eyes when I felt it to make sure that no bones were broken. By the greatest good fortune the ground at that spot was sandy and soft, so that his foot had only been pressed down into the sand. If the accident had happened on hard clay soil, Li would have had his foot crushed. But, again, on hard ground the lorry would not have got stuck and would not have required help. Kung, good fellow, changed places with Li, who was now thoroughly

coddled and allowed to drive with us in the small car. He
was let off work for several days and had soon quite
recovered.

On we went westward through a valley between hillocks
from 15 to 30 feet high, where the silence of death reigned.
Black and red were the prevailing colours. After a time
the country opened out. The view westward was infinite.
We saw no more bushes for fuel, no more tufts of vegetation, and there were no more springs. It was with a feeling
of awe that we penetrated that God-forsaken country.
The ground fell as we drove along a gully flanked by red
terraces, here and there white with salt. We were 2,700
feet above sea-level.

Far to the westward, very pale, we could see a new mountain ridge. To southward the country ran in a number of
very slight undulations, and beyond and over it rose the
dim outline of the Astin-tagh.

The ground became softer and softer. Serat turned off
to the south between low black rounded hills. A gully
ran south-west. The lorry toiled and groaned, and the
wheels sank deep into the soil. Then, through a last gate
in the hillocks, we drove out into absolutely open, flat
country. Only to southward was a hardly noticeable ridge
belonging to the Kum-tagh. Effe cast an astonished look
over the boundless even desert, and cried : " Why, we're
driving right down to Lop-nor ! "

He was right. Ahead of us, to the WSW, lay the
" wandering lake ". But the distance was too great for us
to see it. To the WSW in particular the horizon was as
level as the sea. And a lake which lies in such country is
completely hidden by the curve of the earth. According to
the altimeter we were 2,600 feet up ; most likely about a
hundred feet higher, for we had previously estimated the
height of Lop-nor to be 2,665 feet.

At last we drove down between two low and flat, but very
clearly defined banks, and pitched camp no. 133, after a 43
miles' run, on the coast of that dried-up sea the sole relic
of which is the " wandering lake ".

XIX

TO THE END OF THE ROAD

OUR camping-ground no. 133, where we pitched our tents on the evening of December 7, 1934, was extremely interesting from a geographical point of view. We had crossed and left behind us the outer and last border chain of the Pei-shan mountain system, and were on the northern edge of the belt of desert 84 miles wide which separates the Pei-shan to the north from the Astin-tagh to the south. To the top of the outermost chain of the Astin-tagh system the distance was 102 miles. It is this desert which the East Turkis call the Kum-tagh or " Sand Mountains ", so named because of the huge sand dunes in its interior, piled up like mountain chains.

While the Kum-tagh desert separates two mountain systems, it also forms a connecting link between two great desert regions—to the west, the Taklamakan's sea of sand in the Tarim basin, and, in the east, the Gobi desert proper.

From camp no. 133 we reckoned that we were about 66 miles from the nearest point on the eastern shore of the new Lop-nor, to the WSW, and Altmish-bulak was a hundred miles away to the WNW as the crow flies. As already state, we were probably a little farther west than we thought.

When December 8 began to dawn over the deserts and mountains, we were confronted by the question whether, from camp no. 133, we could discover a practicable route to Altmish-bulak either by going straight WNW—probably impossible, because we had to cross the wide north-eastern creek of an old dried-up extension of Lop-nor—or by making a detour to the north so as to get round this creek. The dry lake-bottom, which dates from a time when Lop-nor was probably six or seven times as large as it is now, consists of what the East Turkis call *shor*—saliferous mud, which when it dries becomes as hard as brick and rises in ridges and crests of an average height of 1 foot 8 inches. I had made the acquaintance of this awful country in my crossings of the Lop desert; it is extremely trying for any kind of transport and even for walkers, and I knew that on technical grounds it was absolutely out of the question for motor-cars.

Hörner and Chen, at the cost of great hardships and privations, had crossed this fearful *shor* all the way from their camp no. 61 to the eastern bank of Lop-nor. Their camp no. 61, according to their map and our dead reckoning, was only 15 miles SSW of our camp no. 133. A motor road to Eastern Turkistan could in no circumstances follow their track, which in any case led straight to the lake. The only possibility would be to follow the southern foot of the outlying mountains of the Pei-shan to their western extremity, which was quite near, go round this and then steer north-west and north, leaving the dry " *shor* creek ", which runs north-east, on our left.

To begin with, a reconnaissance was to be made. The Chinese drove south-west and west in the small car with Serat as driver. If the ground in this direction was practicable, we would all set out with both cars.

But the reconnaissance did not last long. I could see the car all the time from the camp as it slowly approached the end of the outlying mountain chain to the south-west. It stopped there for some time and then returned to camp. The whole reconnaissance had lasted only an hour and a quarter and had led to an absolutely negative result. The scouts' report was short and to the point:

Absolutely impossible! To south-west and west the ground gets softer and softer—fine, loose, gypsum-bearing earth. At last the car got hopelessly stuck in it, and the only thing to do was to turn back. We had a job to get the car out. From that point we could see irregularities, like *yardangs*, some way off to the westward. In some places, too, the ground looked like turning into *shor*. Four miles to the WSW we saw the track of a path, only slightly sunk but quite clear, and we found a cairn on what must have been a piece of the bank of the old Lop-nor, or a small *mesa*.

That was all we needed to know. The desert road was definitely shut to us. Where the light small car could not get through, it was out of the question for the lorry to force its way. But who had taken a caravan past the western end of the mountain range, and who had set up the cairn on the bank of the old Lop-nor? It could not have been done in ancient times; the soil was much too loose for that. Stein had gone that way, but twenty years had passed since then, and the tracks could not have remained so long in such soil and in open ground, exposed to every storm. But Hörner and Chen had encamped close by at Christmas, 1930, and it was possible and probable that the tracks of their caravan could have remained for three years and ten months. If this assumption was correct, the reconnaissance had after all been of great importance; it enabled us to link up with Hörner's and Chen's map.

Nils Hörner says in his book *Resa till Lop*:

> On December 28, 1930 . . . we left what had once been a promontory of the lake coast and made our way out over the dry, hard, bumpy salt crust of old Great Lop-nor. Although the ground was hard, dry and firm under our feet, we nevertheless felt as though we were putting out to sea. We now followed the west-north-westerly course which should take us to Lou-lan, the ruined city, although we had to reckon on finding a barrier in our way—the water of the new lake. But the new lake was just what we were looking and longing for. Everything was still as hopelessly dry as anything possibly could be—salt as hard as stone. As at sea, we had only the compass to steer by; there were no longer any landmarks.

Hörner told me that a belt about 30 miles long immediately south of the outer chain of the Pei-shan and in the neighbourhood of our camp no. 133 was composed of " very loose alluvial gravel " and was " impracticable ". He says of the same region, in his book, that it was " heavy going " for the camels. He says of the *shor* that it is like a field heavily ploughed and then frozen hard—a very telling simile. The crests and ridges formed in it are composed of salt crust and lumps of salt and clay, and are from 8 inches to 1 foot 8 inches high. Farther west he found a sharply defined boundary between the hard " new salt ", as smooth

as a floor, and old *shor* salt—a boundary which marks the
maximum of the lake's expansion since 1921, when it returned to its old bed.   Many of the illustrations in Hörner's
book are very instructive, and give a clear idea of this
extraordinary ground.   The *shor* surface which marks the
outline of Great Lop-nor, and which Hörner and Chen
crossed at the end of 1930 and the beginning of 1931, when
they went for a fortnight without finding water, forms a
long, roughly isosceles triangle with one angle pointing
WSW (Kara-koshun), one ENE towards Hörner's camp
no. 61, and the third north-east.   I had crossed the last
named on February 17, 1901, not far from its end and at a
point where it was hardly 12 miles wide.   In 1906 the
American Ellsworth Huntington went right across the salt
crust, and in 1914 Stein crossed the two triangular snippets.[1]
But no one has investigated this curious old lake-bottom
more thoroughly than Hörner on his journey of 1930–31 in
Chen's company.   ·

In any case, at camp no. 133 we had come into contact
with the Lop depression again and had left the area of the
Su-lo-ho river behind us.   In other words, we had crossed
the ridge which, according to Hörner, excludes the possibility of the Su-lo-ho being connected with the Lop-nor
depression.   Hörner says in his book :
" The Su-lo-ho never runs into the Lop-nor depression,
and a number of the gullies which have been thought to be
watercourses are clearly of quite different origin."   And
farther on he says : " The alleged connection between the
Su-lo-ho and Lop-nor simply does not exist, and never has
existed in the history of man."

Let us now return to December 8, 1934.

When the patrol had come back with the news that the
desert road south of the outer chain of hills was impracticable for cars, we decided to carry out a reconnaissance
northward through the mountains.   We had 140 gallons of
petrol with us and, for the return journey to Anhsi, a further
20 at " Sui-Sin-bulak " and another 160 at " Kung-ching ".
We had, therefore, no cause for anxiety as regards fuel.

To begin with we followed our old tracks, having on our

[1] See map at end.

right a black ridge which pushed out into the low ground, like a cape on a sea-coast. We steered north, driving between red, rose-coloured and black ridges and over gravel-covered ups and downs. Not a sign of wild beasts, not a blade of vegetation. A low crest barred our way. We tried to go round it to the north-east, but several low black slate ridges prevented us. We observed the lie of the land from hills that commanded a view. To northward and westward the country looked hopeless.

While Serat waited with the motor-lorry, we made a re-connaissance with the small car to the north-east, north and north-west. We were stopped now by steep ridges, now in narrow valleys blocked by fallen boulders. A broad gully strewn with red gravel opened the way to us. Little plains extended between low red and black hills. We nosed our way forward in a zigzag course ; at times we even left the small car and sought a way forward on foot through that labyrinth of ragged little hills—whose general line, how-ever, was from east to west. We had passed the watershed of the border chain of hills and the ground seemed to be falling again towards the Lop depression. But we were still about 425 feet above camp no. 133. We were clearly approaching the creek I spoke of, which runs north-east from the old dry *shor* surface of Great Lop-nor.

A detour to north-east and east brought us near the edge of this creek, which resembles a great bright yellow plain, cut by darker streaks here and there and by *yardang* belts and *mesas*. Later in the afternoon a gully showed us the way down to the level ground of the basin. Three modest tussocks grew in the gully, and we saw tracks of antelope and wild camels. Creatures which can exist on so scanty a diet must be easily satisfied. Here, too, we saw a clearly marked shore-line or a low rounded terrace.

After a patrol of 45 miles we returned to Serat and pitched camp no. 134. The rugged hills we had passed during the day's journey consisted of porphyry, gneiss and slate.

The night of December 8–9 was unusually mild, with a minimum temperature of 20·3 degrees. Again we left all superfluous baggage in camp to make the lorry as light as possible.

The dead landscape lay bathed in sunlight when we started on our last forward move. We followed in the main our tracks of the previous day, avoiding difficult passages and trying new ones. There were shades of red in the soil, the low hills were usually dark ; patches of quartzite shone here and there. The ground was unfavourable. The lorry often stuck and had to be freed with the help of spades and canvas mats. We wandered about in various directions.

The part of the Pei-shan in which we then were forms a peninsula which shoots out like a huge tongue with several points, a promontory pushing out westward into the Lop depression. The difficulty was to find any spot suitable for crossing it. The whole day passed, and at dusk we pitched camp no. 135.

The evening hours were spent in keen discussion of our plans. Our food supply was running short, and we had water for three days only. The situation was a complicated one. It would have been the easiest thing in the world to leave the lorry, its crew and all the baggage at camp no. 135, while Yew, Kung, Chen and I, with Effe as driver, made the last push to Altmish-bulak. If the ground were favourable it could be done in one day. The distance was probably less than 84 miles.

But was it wise, was it advisable, defensible even, to stake everything on one card ? When I proposed that I should make the final push alone, with Effe as driver, I was certainly expressing a personal desire, but my real attitude was that I was not morally justified in parting company with the expedition. It was fairly certain that reports of our prolonged absence on a journey to the westward had been spread abroad in Anhsi and had thence been conveyed via Hami to Urumchi. We had fetched fresh supplies of petrol and provisions from Anhsi more than once ; it could be guessed, therefore, that our journey was a long one. We had had all the trouble in the world in finally obtaining permission to leave the province of Sinkiang—and now we were suddenly returning to it six weeks later and without permission. General Sheng Shih-tsai would have been justified in suspecting our intentions, sending frontier

Mesa on edge of Lop depression.

patrols to the Lop-nor country and treating us as spies.
We might in that case have been taken prisoners at Altmish-
bulak, conveyed to Urumchi and kept there for months, or
years.   And meanwhile our comrades who were waiting
for us at camp no. 135 would have finished their provisions
and their water, and would have been obliged to return to
Anhsi to escape death by starvation.

Even if the scouts in the small car succeeded in reaching
Altmish-bulak without coming into collision with frontier
guards, their position might have been desperate if any
accident had happened to the car at or near the spring, and
rendered it unserviceable.   This would have meant a 300
miles' march back to Tun-hwang, without food or water,
fuel or sleeping-bags, a winter walk which would have
killed the strongest man.

If I had been alone I might have staked all on one card.
But I was responsible for all the members of the expedition
and their families, and I was in the service of the Chinese
Government.

As long as we had the lorry with us we could have gone

on westward for another two days.   But the ground we
had explored on December 9 was such that the lorry could
not traverse it even if lightened.   In such a case neither
spades nor canvas mats were of avail.   Every tenth yard
the lorry stuck in the soft, tenacious loose earth, and it
might take an hour to get it out again.

We therefore decided to leave the motor-lorry, Serat and
Jomcha at camp no. 135 and ourselves make quite a short
trip in the small car down to the level bottom of the Lop
depression.   We would do this the next morning, December 10, and, when we had reached it, turn back and all return
to Anhsi together.

We started in a WNW direction at 10.17 a.m., and in
three minutes were down in the depression, whose soil was
covered with gravel and in places white with incrustations
of salt.   Behind us was the mouth of the little valley we had
followed, and before us the level plain . extended.   The
ground sank imperceptibly to the west, and we drove over
one or two faint indications of an old coast-line.

After a twenty-three minutes' drive on ground which
could only just bear the small car and compelled us to drive
slowly, and in which the motor-lorry would have got hopelessly stuck, we came to a *mesa* some 50 or 60 feet high and
astonishingly like the ruins of an old castle—a huge block
of clay with sides quite vertical in places ; the stratification
was generally horizontal, at times somewhat irregular.   We
stopped there for a little while, took one or two photographs and made hurried sketches.   At close quarters thin
white strata of gypsum appeared in the reddish-yellow
deposit.   The white strips were only an inch or less thick,
the reddish-yellow from 4 to 8 inches.

Immediately to the west of this stately monument, a
mighty relic left by erosion in the late tertiary period, we
found four more *mesas*, all smaller in size and not so picturesque as the first.   Erosion remains, weathered by the
storms of thousands of years, were to be seen at one or two
other points.

We spent three-quarters of an hour in that impressive
archipelago of gigantic blocks of clay, which stood up like
rocky islets out of an open sea, and then proceeded west

Last *mesas* on eastern edge of Lop depression.

and WSW. The ground was not absolutely horizontal.
We noticed long, smooth undulations, whose shade of
colour grew lighter the farther off they were.

When we had driven for several minutes longer in the
direction S 70 degrees W, several more red fragments of
mesas appeared several hundred yards away on our right.

Steering westward, we passed a few more smallish remains of *mesas*. We crossed in eight minutes a belt whose
surface was sprinkled with sheets of gypsum, glittering in
the sun. Small rudimentary dunes were to be seen here and
there.

We stopped at a quarter to twelve after a 9 miles' drive.

We got out of the car and let our eyes roam round the
horizon. Towards S 15 degrees W we saw small, gently
rounded hills, the extreme westerly slopes of the peninsula
which we had crossed, and which belong to the southernmost outer chain of the Pei-shan. To south-west and WSW
the line of the horizon was as level as that of the sea, and it
was just in that direction that Lop-nor should be. To the
WNW, very faint and low down, was the outline of a
mountain chain—it must have been the Kuruk-tagh—and
to the north-west, north and north-east also bluish mountains were to be seen.

The point where we turned back was 19 miles south of

my route of February, 1901, and about 25 miles east of the creek that ran north-east from the dry *shor* of Great Lop-nor. The description of the march of February, 1901, in my book, *Central Asia and Tibet*,[1] Vol. II, page 94, gives an idea of the nature and appearance of the ground in this " creek ". It shows how serious an obstacle the *yardang* formation was even to camels, and what an absolutely in-superable barrier to cars this creek of the old-time lake presented.

On the 17th of February [1901] our position began to look most serious. It was ten days since the camels had had any-thing to drink, if we except the few mouthfuls of snow they picked up a week ago. Their strength would not hold out for ever.

During the course of the day we passed successively the two desert ranges which we had crossed over on our way north. They ran towards the west and both alike disappeared in the sand, and so could not be directly connected with the Kuruk-tagh, although they belonged to the same orographical system. We saw the chains of the Kuruk-tagh a long way to the west, but they were higher and altogether bigger than these. As there was far greater likelihood of our finding water near them than in the desert, we decided to make for them. . . .

Turning my back on the outliers of these mountains, I soon reached the level plain, composed of saliferous clay, but diversi-fied by ridges and swellings, not more than 6 feet in height. The desert was perfectly open both south-west and north-east, and resembled the long, narrow bay of an ancient sea.

After tramping for five hours, I stopped to wait for the caravan. The country now changed, and became worse than any sandy desert I ever traversed. It consisted of *yardangs*, or clay ridges, like those I have described [in the Lop desert], only here they were 20 feet high and 30 feet to 40 feet across the top. North and south they stretched in endless succession. Had it not been for the small gaps broken through them, we could not possibly have progressed, for their sides are per-fectly perpendicular. An advance of 10 or a dozen yards some-times necessitated a sweep round of a furlong or even of a quarter of a mile. . . .

At length, however, I succeeded in finding a way out of the wearisome labyrinth.

---

[1] *Central Asia and Tibet*, London, 1903.

When we then crossed the north-eastern snippet of the bed of old Lop-nor the ground consisted of *yardang* ridges, not of salt *shor*, as in the region where Hörner and Chen crossed the bed thirty years later. The *yardang* " creek " probably does not extend so far to the north-east that cars cannot easily get round it.

Having completed our observations at this point, the end of our second advance into the Lop depression, we returned in our own tracks, past the line of tawny *mesas*, to camp no. 135. We had secured no real link-up with Altmish-bulak, but we had seen so much that the missing 84 miles of our motor reconnaissance between Korla and Anhsi would not present any great obstacle to the making of a motor road, if the question should one day become actual. To make 12 miles of *yardang* country as level as a floor is no great achievement in a day when one tunnels through the hardest rock to improve communications. Of the 516 miles which, as the crow flies, separate Anhsi from Korla we had driven 432 by car. The remaining 84 miles were the only part of the whole section which could not be covered by lorry—because the ground was too soft. But I am convinced, from my experiences of 1901 and 1934, that it will be possible to find a practicable way round from our turning-point to Altmish-bulak as easily as in the parts of the Pei-shan we had put behind us. I would undertake at any time to conduct a light motor convoy the whole way from Sian via Lanchow, Liangchow, Kanchow, Suchow, Yü-men, Anhsi, Altmish-bulak, Korla, Kucha, Aksu and Maralbashi to Kashgar, a distance of 1,920 miles as the crow flies. We ourselves had shown that the route to Kucha via Turfan was practicable, both by the Etsin-gol and along the Imperial Highway. The section from Kucha to Kashgar has been covered by many Russian Amo cars and recently by Sir Eric Teichman. The road from Anhsi to Korla via Hami and Turfan is 810 miles long. The desert road through the Pei-shan which we reconnoitred is 300 miles shorter, and follows the track of the famous Silk Road.

A monument composed of eight empty petrol drums was erected at camp no. 135 ; three of them were filled with sand

to give stability to the pyramid-shaped sign.   Travellers or
road-builders of days to come will find it, for no one else is
likely to come and take it away.   The wild camels, which
now and again wander to the place like Flying Dutchmen,
will stop dead when they see the black spectre that was
never there before, snuff the air, turn about and disappear
like the wind in another direction.

We were on our return journey, free from the time-
wasting map-making, and passed one of our old camping-
grounds after another.   On the 11th we had not got far
when the small car's front spring broke.   It had been made
in the garage at Urumchi and had held out for 1,902 miles.
Luckily a reserve spring had been manufactured at the same
time.   This, and all the tools, were in the lorry.   The
repairs took a full three hours.   If this misadventure had
taken place on a dash to Altmish-bulak, when the lorry was
not there to give help, both the small car and its passengers
would have been done for.

Serat drove ahead.   It was so dead still that the clouds
of dust raised by the car lay like a mist above the track.   We
were on roads we had travelled several times.   How long
would the track we had ploughed remain visible ?   Certainly for some years, and probably much longer.

At " Sui-Sin-bulak " we collected the ice which had
formed in the empty vessel during our absence.   A little
way off a wild camel had followed the track of the car for
a good way, without daring to cross it.   His own track
formed a zigzag line.   Time after time he had reached the
track, had sheered off again but quickly returned, impelled
by his curiosity.   He had been afraid, and had not been able
to pull himself together and take one decided leap over the
two deep ruts in the ground.

In the evening we reached " Kung-ching ", where San
Wa-tse and Chokdung were anxiously and uneasily awaiting
our return.   The former had driven a stake into the ground
by the well Kung had dug and fixed to it a piece of board
with the following announcement in Chinese characters :
" Kung-ching, station on the Sui-Sin motor expedition.
Ministry of Railways."   Only the spirits of the air could
profit by it, for the wild camels, donkeys and antelopes can

read no other writing but that which Nature herself has inscribed on the face of their desolate homeland.

On the morning of December 12 we had another keen discussion about a new push to westward by a route north of that which we had already tried. We could get petrol and food supplies in Anhsi, as before. The most serious obstacle to the carrying out of such a plan was the worn-out state of our cars. They had already done about 9,000 miles in the most trying country, and would not stand a new journey at high pressure in the Pei-shan mountains. For a fresh advance completely new equipment was required, and the plan was therefore dropped.

We continued on our way, passing camps no. 129 and no. 128, and the horrible stretch between them where small transverse gullies occurred every 2 or 3 yards, and we swayed and jolted till we nearly had our insides shaken out of us. When Effe sang, as he usually did, it sounded as if he had got hiccups.

At 8 o'clock in the evening a big light-grey wolf suddenly appeared not more than 50 yards ahead of us and stopped dead, paralysed, hypnotized and blinded by the car's headlights.

" Full speed, run over the brute ! " we cried. But Effe lost his presence of mind and missed his chance. He did the wrong thing in the circumstances ; he stopped dead like the wolf and clutched at his gun. Then the spell was broken ; the wolf came to its senses and disappeared in the darkness out of the beam of light.

During the night we passed Lo-t'o-ching, Tao-tao-shui and Ma-lien-ch'üan, and next day we drove by Ta-ch'üan on the Hami road and encamped for the night on the north bank of the Su-lo-ho.

On the last morning, that of December 14, we were awakened by an east-north-easterly storm which drove dense clouds of dust and sand over our tents at the rate of 35 miles an hour. The three arms of the river were frozen. The first held under the small car, but when we were crossing the second the ice broke under the front wheel. The car suffered no damage. We crossed on firmer ice lower down and soon afterwards were at the town gate of Anhsi, where half a dozen soldiers in fur coats and high fur caps stopped us. A few minutes more, and we were sitting talking to the pleasant mayor. Presumably Yew had initiated him into our mysteries; if not, it must be owned that he showed extraordinary delicacy and tact in not even asking us what we had been doing in the western deserts for six long weeks.

Since November 12, when we had so unexpectedly run into the arms of the robber band at Tao-tao-shui—that is, for over a month—we had not seen a living soul but Georg. We had been dwelling in a part of the world to which men never stray, and where there are no roads. The only signs that here, too, life once beat in veins long calcified are the cairns erected on hillocks, terraces and mountains to show merchants and caravans the way along the old Silk Road. Many of the cairns, no doubt, marked roads running from north to south, of which the maps show at least three between Hami and Tun-hwang. We crossed these roads at many points. But the men who built the cairns have slept in their graves for 2,000 years, and these graves are spread all over the interior of Asia and China.

The traveller who in our time journeys over these obliterated tracks hears only in fancy the echo of the caravan bells dying away in the distance, and the camel drivers shouting at their beasts.

XX

THE WANDERING LAKE

DURING my travels in the heart of Asia I have had the opportunity of mapping a number of previously unknown lakes, among others the whole chain of lakes situated in the most northerly east-to-west valley of the Tibetan highlands between Eastern Turkistan and Tsaidam, as well as the chain which recurs at the northern foot of the trans-Himalayan mountain system.

Not counting the Sea of Galilee, with its sacred Biblical memories, four of the lakes of Asia lie nearer my heart than all the others.

On Chargut-tso, in the heart of Tibet, I was out in a cloth boat in rough weather for several days in the autumn of 1901, while the Tibetan militia, called up for the purpose, sought me in vain on its shores.

At the end of 1906 and the beginning of 1907 I was walking or driving, in a sledge drawn by *ladakis*, backwards and forwards over the hard frozen surface of Lake Ngangtse-tso in order to take soundings through gaps in the ice. On the eastern bank my road was barred by the governor of the province of Naktsang, but after long negotiations he opened to my caravan the gates of the Forbidden Land and the holy monastery of Tashi-lunpo, where that ecclesiastical dignitary the Tashi Lama resided.

The third Asiatic lake which has played a momentous part in my life is the holiest of all the waters upon earth, Manasarovar, a lake which is sacred to hundreds of millions of Hindus and, under the name Tso-mavang, equally sacred to the people of Tibet. It lies shining in the sun on bright summer days and blinding white under the winter ice and snow—between the holy mountain of Kailas or Kang Rimpoche to the north, Siva's paradise and Brahma's heaven,

and to the south the mighty Gurlamandata system, under
its armour of shimmering blue glaciers and gleaming white
snowfields.   In stormy and in still weather I have sailed and
rowed over this lake and sounded its depths, and have been
a guest in its eight monasteries, which lie set like jewels in
a bracelet of bluest turquoise.

But more deeply than any of these three has Lop-nor,
" the wandering lake ", entered into my life and by the force
of circumstances been linked with my destinies.   Forty-one
years have passed since I first pitched my tent on its shores,
and three years since I listened for the last time to the whis-
pering of the spring wind in its reeds and, as I have described in this book, navigated the northern part of it in a
canoe.   And through all the years which lie between these
two dates I have followed the pulse-beats of the river Tarim
and Lop-nor as a doctor examines a patient's heart and
circulation, in part myself, in part through exploratory work
by members of my expeditions.   And now at long last our
combined efforts have been able to solve the sixty years' old
problem of the wanderings of the mysterious lake, and
discover the physical causes of its capricious conduct.

The oldest account of the Tarim and its terminal lake
dates from the first century B.C. and is preserved in the Han
annals.   According to these one stream flowing down from
the Pamir joined another from the Kun-lun which ran into
the P'u-ch'ang sea, or Lop-nor, a salt lake 300 li long and
as many broad.   As a result of the misinterpretation of an
old text the Chinese believed then, and for 2,000 years later,
that the river which ran into Lop-nor came up to the surface
of the earth again in north-eastern Tibet to form the great
river of the Central Empire, the Hwang-ho.

As all the Chinese maps which existed before 1137 have
been lost, the map drawn on a stone slab and preserved in
the Sian museum is the oldest which includes the Tarim and
Lop-nor (the P'u-ch'ang sea).

A most interesting fact is that a European who lived in
the days of the Han dynasty, the Greek Marinus of Tyre,
obtained a description of this river and lake system which
corresponds with that given in the Han annals.   Marinus
himself had obtained his knowledge from merchants and

agents whose caravans had travelled along the Silk Road. His version was adopted in the second century A.D. by Ptolemy, who marked on his map of Asia, in the extreme north-east, the name Serica, or Silk Country, and the river Œchardes, formed from two sources and ending farther east in a lake at the foot of a mountain range.

On Ptolemy's map we find, south of the Œchardes, another river, *Bautisus fluvius*, likewise formed from two sources and ending in a lake. Many geographers have identified the Bautisus with the Tsangpo-Brahmaputra in Tibet. In my book *Southern Tibet*, Vol. I, I tried to show that the Bautisus also represents the Tarim and that the lake in which it ends is Lop-nor, which thus occurs twice on Ptolemy's map. And why? Because neither Marinus nor Ptolemy had any idea that Tibet existed. On Ptolemy's famous map we find a mountain range running from west to east, which to the west is called *Imaus mons*, in the middle *Emodi montes*, and to the east *Serici montes*. *Imaus* is the Himalayas, *Serici montes* the Kun-lun and Nan-shan, or the mountains that bounded on the south the Silk Road of which the merchants of ancient times had heard. Ptolemy did not know that a whole world of immensely high mountains extended between the *Imaus* to the south and *Serici montes* to the north. Tibet did not exist for him. And the explanation of the Tarim and Lop-nor being marked twice on the same map is simple enough. The information about the Tarim and Lop-nor came from two sources, and neither Marinus nor Ptolemy realized that the descriptions applied to one and the same river and lake.

It may reasonably be asked : how is it possible that a lake which lies hidden away in the heart of the world's greatest continent and surrounded by the world's greatest desert, farther from the sea coast than any other lake—except the Ebi-nor, a lake whose existence became known to European geographers only in the seventies—could be known to a handful of Western geographers 2,000 years ago? That Ptolemy, about A.D. 150, knew that a great river formed of two confluent streams ran from west to east and, like the Kum-daria described in the first chapters of this book, ran into a lake which lay in the northern part of the desert and

in the same place where we found Lop-nor during our
expeditions in the last ten years ?

And how is it possible that after Ptolemy's time Lop-nor
vanished like a shooting star in the night, and that an
impenetrable silence then shrouded the mysterious lake for
more than 1,500 years ?

It is true that a European traveller heard the name Lop
spoken in 1273.   This traveller was the merchant of Venice,
the immortal Marco Polo.   He understood the meaning of
the name as little as we.   Through the wonderful account
of his journey the name Lop became known in Europe for
the first time.   But Marco Polo does not say a word about
Lop-nor; he only speaks of the great Lop desert, which he
embellishes with fairy stories of wizards and ghosts.

In the sixteenth century the name Lop appears on European maps—for example, on Jacopo Gastaldi's map of India
and Central Asia, published in 1561 ; on it we read the
words " Diserto de Lop ".

Can it therefore be said that Marco Polo had no knowledge of Lop-nor, or at least of the existence of a lake ?   No,
for it may be supposed that he had seen or heard of one or
more lakes with reedy banks to the left, or north, of his
route from Charkhlik to Tun-hwang, and that he simply did
not think it worth while to say anything about his discovery.
After all, he travelled from Kashgar through Yarkend and
Khotan to Charkhlik without once mentioning that he had
one of the highest mountain ranges in the world on his
right all the way.

One century after another passed, and still the capricious
lake succeeded in keeping its secret.   When, in 1603, the
Jesuit Benedict Goes began his adventurous journey
through Asia, he passed through places situated on the
lower Tarim, but unhappily he died of sickness at Suchow
in 1607, and hostile Mohammedans burned all his notes.
The little the Jesuits in Peking learned of his route afterwards was communicated to them by Goes' Armenian
companions, and these communications were inadequate.

In the sixties of the eighteenth century the Emperor
Chien-lung sent the Jesuits, Hallerstein, d'Arocha and
d'Espinha, to Eastern Turkistan to fix by astronomical

observation the position of certain points in the newly
conquered countries in the interior of Asia. But these
learned travellers have nothing to tell of Lop-nor.

And yet Marinus of Tyre and Ptolemy of Alexandria were
so well informed as to the existence, both of the lake and of
the river which keeps it alive, that they inserted them on
their maps twice over!

Their knowledge was without the slightest doubt due to
the great silk trade. The caravans carried the lordly silk
along the longest and oldest of all the world's trade routes,
from the land of the Seres, the Chinese, via Tun-hwang,
through the desert whose acquaintance we had just made,
along the northern shore of Lop-nor and the Kum-daria,
and on via Korla, Kucha and Aksu to Kashgar. Commer-
cial travellers from the West travelled along it too, and told
of the countries, lakes and rivers they had seen. So the
knowledge came to Marinus and from him to Ptolemy, and
it was the silk trade alone that early geographical science
had to thank for its first knowledge of the famous lake and
its river system.

Not far west of the northern part of Lop-nor the town of
Lou-lan lay on the Silk Road. About A.D. 330 there was a
revolution in the course of the Tarim and in the situation of
Lop-nor. After having flowed due east for, probably,
many centuries and formed its terminal lake in the northern
part of the desert, the lower Tarim—i.e. the part of it which
we now call the Kum-daria—left its old bed and broke a new
course for itself through the desert to the south-east and
south, where, in the southern part of the desert, it formed one
or two new lakes. At the same time the old course and the
old lake dried up, and the town of Lou-lan was abandoned
by its inhabitants and consigned to total oblivion.

Marco Polo, Benedict Goes, Hallerstein, d'Arocha and
d'Espinha had none of them any idea that the " wandering
lake " had moved from north to south, even if they had seen
the newly formed lake. And—what is stranger—neither in
ancient nor in modern times have the Chinese realized that
the lake they knew 2,000 years ago under the name of the
P'u-ch'ang sea was, and is, a wandering or, as Hörner calls
it, alternating lake. On all the maps, even the important

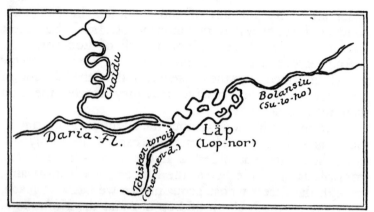

Lop-nor and its rivers on Lieutenant Gustaf Renat's map, Stockholm, 1733.
As on the Chinese maps, the lake is located in the northern part of the desert. The
Su-lo-ho is represented as entering Lop-nor from the east.

Wu-chang map of 1863, the river is shown running due
east, and Lop-nor lies at the eastern end of it. Not even
the makers of the Imperial map of 1928 have been quite able
to free themselves from the old classic idea.

The well-known Paris cartographer, Delisle, includes in
his excellent atlas of 1706 a " Carte de Tartarie ", which adds
some new names to those that previously figured in the
maps. We find on it Cachgar, Ugen, Conche (= Konche),
Cucia (= Kucha), Yuldus, and the river Kenkel, which
corresponds to the Konche-daria, but not Lop-nor. The
wandering lake still succeeded in preserving its incognito.
The whole of the interior of Asia he calls " Tartarie Indé-
pendante ", and knows that it consists of vast sand deserts.
Between Acsu (= Aksu) and Cucia he places a great meri-
dional mountain range—probably a successor of the meri-
dional range *Imaus*, which in Ptolemy's map divides *Scythia
intra Imaum montem* in the west from *Scythia extra Imaum
montem* in the east.

In 1730 a remarkable map of northern and central Asia
appeared in Stockholm, made by one of Charles XII's
officers, Strahlenberg, during his captivity in Siberia. His
idea of the Tarim agrees with Delisle's, but he knows of
Kara-shahr too, and the Khaidu river, which according to
him does not join the Tarim. Lop-nor is still absent.

The map of Gustaf Renat, another of Charles XII's warriors, is of still greater interest as regards our area. His representation of Lop-nor and its rivers is substantially correct, except that he too includes the Su-lo-ho in the same hydrographic system. He makes the winding Khaidu join the Tarim and along with that river run into the lake, which he calls Läp—a corruption of Marco Polo's Lop, nearly 500 years older.

In the same year in which Renat's map appeared, 1733, d'Anville's great map of the interior of Asia, based on the explorations of the Jesuits in China, came out in Paris. His version of the river system and Lop-nor is much less correct than that of Renat, who obtained his information from Dzungarian sources.

For another 140 years Lop-nor remained an unsolved puzzle. When, in 1870, the Englishman Robert Shaw came home from his meritorious journey to the western part of East Turkistan, people in Europe had very confused notions about our rivers and lakes, and Shaw did not succeed in obtaining any reliable information about them. In his account of his journey he only says:

> The skirts of the deserts are occupied by Doolans, a Mussulman tribe of semi-nomadic and predatory habits. Beyond them again, and amongst the lagoons and lakes (the chief of which is Lob Noor), formed in the midst of the desert near the district which is called Koordam-Kâk, where the united watercourses from Eastern Turkistan vanish in the sand, there are vague rumours of a savage tribe who live on fish, and dress in the bark of trees, but I never found a man who had seen them.[1]

Shaw learned, on the other hand, that " the antelopes go in large herds, as do also the *wild camels* (?) in the great desert to the eastward. This desert is the subject of strange superstitions." Shaw puts a query mark after the wild camels, whose existence he seems to doubt.

So, as late as 1870, there was no more reliable information about Lop-nor and the wild camel than the learned Carl

[1] Robert Barkley Shaw: *Visits to High Tartary, Yarkend and Kashgar*, London, 1871.

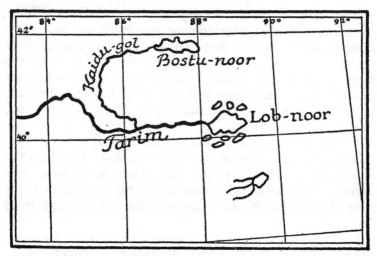

Lop-nor as shown in Stieler's Hand Atlas, 1875. Here too the lower Tarim is, generally speaking, in the same position as the Kum-daria now, i.e. it flows due east to the terminal lake.

Ritter, who writes in Part VII of his *Erdkunde* (page 27) apropos Kashgar, Aksu, Kara-shahr, etc. :

> As regards the course and connection of the great Turkistan river system, the steppe river which ends in Lop-nor, we know of no special account by an eye-witness who has travelled along its banks whereby this connection, which is generally assumed, could be established as an indubitable fact.

Of the expanses of the Gobi desert he writes :

> This place, if any, is the home of camels and horses, in a wild state or in a state which nearly approaches wild life. Wild camels and wild horses are often spoken of. On the steppes around Bogdo-Oola, and on mountain heights, an eye-witness, an old and experienced lama, said that there were still wild camels just like the others (the tame ones) except that their two humps are scarcely visible. Those which are captured young are easily tamed ; no one troubles about the old beasts. (*Erdkunde*, VII, p. 381.)

As late as 1875 nothing more was known of Lop-nor and the wild camel than Ritter had known forty years earlier. On the sheet " India and Central Asia " in Stieler's Hand Atlas of 1875 the Tarim is shown going due east and form-

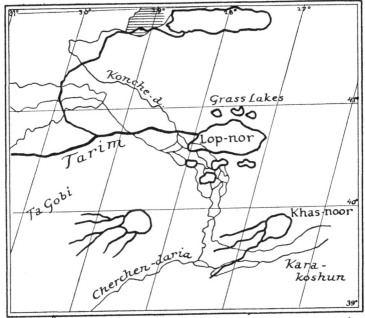

Lop-nor and the Tarim with its tributary the Konche-daria as represented on Chinese maps, e.g. the Wu-chang map of 1863.

ing at its eastern end the lake Lop-nor, which is thus placed in the northern part of the desert, as it is in all the Chinese maps. On this, as on all other European maps, the lake is placed 287 miles from the nearest mountains to the southward.

But now the time had come to rend the veil of mystery that had hung over Lop-nor for 2,000 years. The Russian, Colonel Nikolai Mikhailovitch Prjevalsky, born near Smolensk in 1839, had already made his name famous by his first great journey through unknown parts of Central Asia. Between August 12, 1876, and July 3, 1877, he made his second journey of 2,654 miles through largely unknown country.

It was on this journey " from Kulja by the Tien-shan and Lop-nor to the Altyn-tagh " that Prjevalsky discovered that the Tarim, far from flowing due east, in reality turned off south-east and south to form, in the southern part of the desert, a double lake, Kara-buran and Kara-koshun, situ-

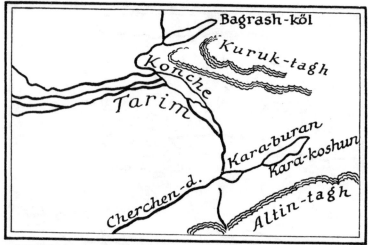

Prjevalsky in 1877 identified Kara-koshun with the old historical Lop-nor.

ated one geographical degree south of the place marked from ancient times on Chinese maps.

He found, too, that the terminal lake, which he identified with the Lop-nor of the Chinese, was only 38 miles distant from the southern mountains. This involved a radical change of the map of the interior of Asia.

As he did not turn aside from the routes known and used by the inhabitants, he never managed to see the wild camel, but he acquired a hide from a native hunter and confirmed the fact, previously doubted, of the royal beast's existence.

Prjevalsky's discoveries on this journey created an extraordinary sensation in the geographical world. When the first telegram containing his story was flashed over the world, the geographer, Dr. E. Behm, wrote in Petermann's *Mitteilungen*:

> So at last the darkness which surrounded Lop-nor is put to flight, and we shall soon see the lake on the maps as it really is. But who could have guessed that there was a high mountain range to the south of it? Our ideas of the Gobi desert are about to be revolutionized.

Professor Baron von Richthofen considered the journey to be " one of the most important things that have been

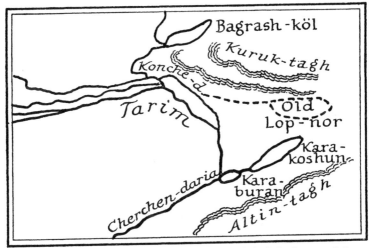

Situation of old Lop-nor according to von Richthofen's theory, 1878.

done in recent years ", and Dr. August Petermann wrote in his *Mitteilungen* :

> Prjevalsky's journey is a most interesting and important, exceedingly meritorious geographical achievement. . . . It sets the coping-stone on a fine piece of exploratory work in Central Asia, and links up our modern exploration with that of Marco Polo 600 years ago and other journeys of still older date. The line thus drawn on the map of the globe is as important as any could be, for it goes right through the region of Central Asia which has remained the least known up to the present day. . . . The main outlines of Central Asia have by Prjevalsky's journey been given fairly definite shape, a firm skeleton ; and an important desire of geographers is thus realized. In this respect Prjevalsky's journey ranks equally with the solution of such famous problems as the crossing of Australia, the reaching of the North Pole or Timbuctoo, the discovery of the sources of the Nile, and Stanley's journey down the Congo. . . . Prjevalsky's journey to Lop-nor is a model achievement in the geographical field.

The year after the Russian colonel's return Baron von Richthofen subjected his alleged discovery of Lop-nor to a critical analysis as thorough as it was acute. Its object was to prove that Prjevalsky had discovered not the historic

R

lake Lop-nor, the P'u-ch'ang-hai or Yen-tse (" salt sea ") of the Chinese, but a newly formed lake. A terminal lake, in which a great steppe and desert river has during centuries collected all kinds of steppe salts, must inevitably be salt ; indeed, it was called " the salt sea ". And now the first European eye-witness, and one possessing singular powers of observation, says that the terminal reservoir of the Tarim is a fresh-water lake !

Von Richthofen seeks for various explanations, among others " that the Tarim, which often alters its course and position, has left its old reservoir and emptied itself into the present one, which in that case would be comparatively new ".

Von Richthofen considers the most probable solution to be that Prjevalsky, when travelling among the various branches of the Tarim, overlooked a branch which, as shown on the Chinese maps, continues eastward to form a lake in the interior of the desert, a prolongation of the Tarim, the real, historic, Chinese lake Lop-nor. He concludes with the words :

> However highly we must value Prjevalsky's work on the exploration of Lop-nor, we cannot regard the problem, for the sake of which he underwent such great hardships, as completely solved.

Prjevalsky, in the course of his reply, said :

> My view is that no change of such magnitude (as that the Tarim in recent times has taken another and a south-easterly course) has occurred in comparatively modern times, but, on the contrary, that the markings of the lower Tarim and Lop-nor on the Chinese maps, and the descriptions of them, can quite simply be attributed to the misleading and inaccurate information about these regions which the Chinese themselves possessed. . . .
>
> As to the possibility that another branch exists, through which, as Baron von Richthofen assumes, the Tarim sends a quantity of its water to the eastward to form there the real lake Lop-nor, such an assumption finds no support in the evidence hitherto obtained. Apart from the fact that the natives would quite certainly have known of such a channel and a lake of such size, and sooner or later would have told me about it, we

followed the bank of the Tarim and could not discover the smallest watercourse crossing our route. If one had been there it would not have escaped our attention, for the channels were always troublesome to cross. . . . Finally, I consider it my duty to repeat that the natives frequently denied the existence of any other lakes in the surrounding deserts except that by which they lived.

That the volume of water in the river diminishes as one goes downstream is due, according to Prjevalsky, to the fact that a large part of the water is diverted into canals which are used for irrigation and for fishing. The reason for the freshness of the water in Kara-koshun is, according to him, that the current of the Tarim runs far out into the lake, while the relatively stagnant water close to the banks contains salt in many places.

It was, perhaps, not so strange that Kara-koshun was a fresh-water lake. In its north-eastern part I found on the banks lagoons whose water was slightly salt. And perhaps, as Hörner supposes, there was a terminal recipient containing salt water north-east of the fresh-water lake. If so, Kara-koshun was not a terminal lake, and therefore was fresh.

On his fourth journey also (1883-85) Prjevalsky visited Kara-koshun and spent two months on its banks. He says in his narrative :

As to the existence of another Lop-nor formed by a prolongation of the Tarim . . . I should like to say that we now thoroughly cross-examined the Lop-nor people about it, and that they unanimously denied this. They declared that, as far back as local tradition went, the lake on whose banks they lived had always been in its present position.

Such are the main outlines of the controversy between the great explorer Prjevalsky and the great geographer von Richthofen ; and so it was that the Lop-nor question remained an unsolved problem from the historical and geographical standpoint. With the knowledge we now possess of the wandering lake, we must greatly admire the acumen of the two antagonists and admit that both were right in some respects, but wrong in others.

Von Richthofen was right when he maintained on theoretical grounds that Kara-koshun, Prjevalsky's Lop-nor, was a newly formed lake and that the classical lake must be found as a prolongation of the Tarim to the eastward ; but he was wrong in his supposition that as late as 1877 a branch ran to the old lake of the Chinese in the northern part of the desert.

Prjevalsky was wrong in his categorical affirmation that the lake he had discovered was identical with the Lop-nor of the old Chinese maps, P'u-ch'ang-hai, but right in his assurance that no branch ran out to a desert lake to the eastward. He denied just as categorically—and rightly—the existence of such a lake.

Prjevalsky's discoveries excited great interest in Sweden also. In the spring of 1884 Dr. Carl Nyström gave a lecture on Prjevalsky's travels to our geographical society, and I —then still at school—had the privilege of drawing a gigantic wall-map to illustrate the lecture. This was my first contact with Prjevalsky and his doings. On Vega Day, April 24, in the same year, the great Russian, who was then in the interior of Asia, was awarded the Vega medal. Nordenskiöld, who had lately returned from his famous voyage round Asia and Europe, admired the man who had penetrated and explored such important areas of the great continent. I myself dreamed of having the good fortune to take part some day in one of Prjevalsky's expeditions, and I remember how deeply the news of his death in 1888 grieved me. In January, 1891, I made a pilgrimage to his grave on the Issyk-köl and published in the same year the story of his travels in Swedish, with a preface by Nordenskiöld.

The travellers who after Prjevalsky visited the lower Tarim and its terminal lake—the Englishmen Carey and Dalgleish in 1885, Bonvalot and Prince Henry of Orleans in 1889, General Pjevtsoff in the following year, and Littledale in 1894—followed his footsteps religiously, without penetrating into the interior of the desert, and therefore made not the least contribution to the solution of the riddle.

On the other hand, Lieutenant Kozlov, on his journey in the northern part of the Lop desert in the winter of 1893–

94, discovered the dry river-bed running eastward which the East Turkis called the Kuruk-daria, "the dry river". Kozlov touched it at two points, but did not realize its significance.

One of the objects of my travels through Asia in 1893–97 was to contribute to the solution of the Lop-nor problem. In March, 1896, I crossed the upper part of the Kuruk-daria near the point where the old dry bed broke off from the Konche-daria, and called it on my map "old dried-up bed of the Konche-daria". I did not then know of Kozlov's discovery of the old river-bed farther east, two years earlier, for nothing about it had as yet been published.

I then followed the eastern bank of the intricate course of the Tarim delta to find out whether any branch, as von Richthofen had supposed, left the river and ran away into the desert. No such branch existed; so on that point Prjevalsky had been right.

Instead I found a chain of lakes, through which arms of the Tarim ran, and considered them to be the last distorted remains of the ancient lake Lop-nor. Von Richthofen shared this view; but I subsequently had to abandon it on the ground of new discoveries. Even then, more than forty years ago, I applied to Lop-nor the term "the wandering lake".

My lecture to the Imperial Russian Geographical Society in St. Petersburg on October 27, 1897, led Kozlov to write a pamphlet, of the dimensions of a small book, in which he disputed my arguments point by point. He certainly admitted that the Kuruk-daria was the old bed of the Konche-daria, but declared that this old river had made its way to Kara-koshun by a roundabout route to the eastward. He was anxious to defend Prjevalsky's honour at all costs, and ended by declaring:

> The only conclusion I can draw from the above analysis is that Kara-koshun is not only the Lop-nor of my unforgettable master N. M. Prjevalsky, but also the ancient, historic, genuine Lop-nor of the Chinese geographers. So the lake has been for the last thousand years and so it always will be.

It was to be shown three years later that this conclusion

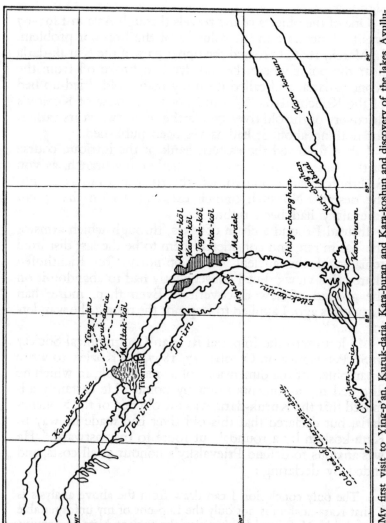

My first visit to Ying-p'an, Kuruk-daria, Kara-buran and Kara-koshun and discovery of the lakes Avullu-köl, Kara-köl, Tayek-köl and Arka-köl, which twenty years later nearly dried up.

was premature. In 1900 I returned to the disputed region, followed the dry bed of the Kuruk-daria as far as it was visible in the Lop desert, and found it to be in general about 100 yards wide and from 12 feet to 15 feet deep. These considerable dimensions made it probable that the whole Tarim, with its tributary the Konche-daria, had in ancient times flowed along this later dried-up and abandoned bed.

From the Altmish-bulak spring I crossed the whole Lop desert to Kara-koshun and on March 28, 1900, discovered, in the northern part of the desert, the ruins of the town of Lou-lan. Our water supply was insufficient, and we could not stay more than twenty hours. Perceiving the importance of this discovery, I returned to Lou-lan at the beginning of March, 1901, by the eastern roundabout route through the Pei-shan—described in the previous chapters—and spent a week in archæological excavations which produced important results.

I then carried out a survey from Lou-lan southward, which showed the existence of a depression in the northern part of the desert. The difference in height between my camp at Lou-lan and the northern shore of Kara-koshun was hardly more than 6 feet. Thus the Lop desert, as a whole, proved to be almost as horizontal and even as the sea. It was covered with sediments of different ages deposited in lakes and modelled by the wind into the curious *yardangs* I have already described. Wide areas of old lake-bottom consisted, too, of *shor*, or salt-bearing clay, stiffened into slabs and ridges as hard as brick.

After I had mapped the dry bed of the Kuruk-daria, investigated the neighbourhood of Lou-lan, navigated most of the channels and lakes of the Tarim delta to the point at which the reed-beds became impenetrable, and crossed the most north-easterly creek of the old Lop-nor depression, I had obtained an experience of the region, and a general grasp of it, which enabled me to frame the following theory:

In a desert country, whose surface is practically as level as that of the sea, running water must be extremely sensitive even to the smallest changes of level. During the (geologically speaking) short periods of 1,500 years with which we are here concerned, changes of level produced over a

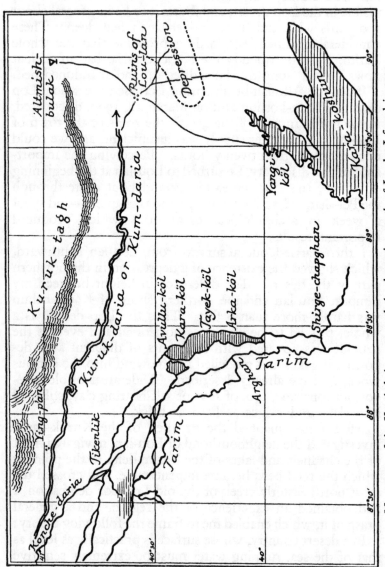

My survey of the Kuruk-daria, 1900, and the depression south of Lou-lan I found in 1901.

long period by movements of the earth's crust cannot play any perceptible part. The periodical movements of the terminal lake between the northern and southern part of the desert, or its alternative occupation of beds to the north and to the south, must depend on another factor, i.e. swifter changes on the earth's surface.

These factors are the ceaseless transportation by running water of solid material, both organic and inorganic, and the power of the wind to erode the surface of the soil and by its disintegrating force to loosen and carry away ordinarily firm elements of that surface.

Thus the southern lake, Kara-koshun, whose average depth I found to be 2 feet 7 inches, is filled with flying sand and dust from the air and with decomposing vegetable and animal remains—for example, withered and broken reeds, shells of molluscs, fishes' skins, scales and skeletons, shells of birds' eggs, excrement of various animals, etc.

While this filling-up process is going on to the southward, the arid desert regions to the northward are eaten away by the extraordinarily violent east-north-easterly storms, and while the level of the ground in the northern parts of the Lop desert is falling, the bottom of Lake Kara-koshun rises and becomes higher and higher. The immediate consequence is that Kara-koshun is slowly silted up and its water, continually renewed by fresh supplies from the Tarim, is inclined to enlarge the area of the lake and overflow its low banks. As the ground rises imperceptibly from the southern shore to the foot of the Astin-tagh, while the ground on the northern shore is level in a northerly direction, ephemeral lakelets are formed north of Kara-koshun.

The ultimate effect of this alternation between north and south, which has been proceeding uninterruptedly for centuries, is that the—relatively—deepest depressions lie in the northern part of the desert and that the river and lake *must* of necessity return to their old, previously dry beds, while the south-going portion of the Tarim shrinks to nothing and the southern lake, Kara-koshun, speedily dries up, since the powerful evaporation is not replaced by fresh water flowing in.

This theory is no *esprit d'escalier*, evoked by subsequent

movements, apparently capricious, of the "wandering lake". It was formed in the years 1900 and 1901 in the dry bed of the Kuruk-daria, during my survey work, and on the shores of Kara-koshun. It recurs in my book *Central Asia and Tibet*, where I say, *inter alia*:

> During the last few decennia—that is, since the time of Prjevalsky's visit—Kara-koshun had clearly shown a tendency to dry up. The reeds encroached upon it more and more every year, and the marsh grew less in area. I am convinced that in a few years' time the lake will be found in the locality where it was formerly placed by the Chinese cartographers, and where von Richthofen proved by an ingenious deduction that it must once have been. . . . Now these changes of niveau are deter-mined by purely mechanical laws and local atmospheric con-ditions ; consequently the lake, which serves as the terminal reservoir of the Tarim system, must be extremely sensitive to their influence. It is a matter of mere physical necessity that the water should overflow and run towards the relatively lower depressions. Then vegetation and animal life, as well as the fishing population, inevitably accompany the water as it migrates, and the old lake-bed dries up. In the future the same phenomenon will be repeated again, but in the reverse order, although the laws dictating it will be precisely the same. It will be only then, however, when there exist more abundant materials to go upon, that the length of the period of oscillation will admit of being determined. All that we now know for certain is that in A.D. 265, in the last years of the Chinese Emperor Yuan Ti, Lop-nor lay in the northern part of the desert. In fact, Lop-nor is, as it were, the weight which hangs on the pendulum of the Tarim river, and even though a single oscillation should stretch over a thousand years, still, measured by the clock of geologic time, that is comparatively speaking little more than one of our seconds.

In my work *Scientific Results of a Journey in Central Asia, 1899–1902* (Stockholm, 1905) there is a chapter " Migra-tions of the Lop-nor ", in which the whole migration problem is thoroughly discussed. I there say :

> In the light of the knowledge we now possess of the levels that exist in the Lop desert, it is not too daring to affirm that the river *must* some day go back to the Kuruk-daria. . . . It is only a question of time when the country round about (the

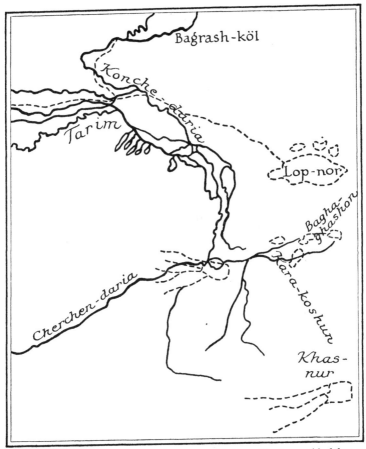

An attempt to reconcile the Wu-chang map with the real hydrographical data as they were in 1901. The dotted line shows the representation on the Wu-chang map.

lower Tarim and Kara-koshun) will become so full of alluvium that the river will be forced to return to its northern bed.

In the same book is a sketch which shows how the lower course of the Tarim and the terminal lake oscillate between the Lop-nor depression to the north and the Kara-koshun depression to the south.

My predictions, on the face of it too daring, that both river and lake would soon return to their old beds excited no particular attention among geographers. Prophecies of geological changes in the surface of the earth are generally of doubtful value; it may be thousands or hundreds of thousands of years before they come true—even if they are correct at all. And then the prophets and their writings have long been forgotten.

I hope that the term " the wandering lake " will not give the reader the false impression that it is primarily the lake Lop-nor that wanders, while the watercourses remain more or less where they are. In reality there is a conspicuous parallelism between the migrations of the watercourses and the lake. If the lower Tarim had not left its old bed, presumably in the Karaul region, above Chara and Yangi-köl, and, combined with its arms Ugen-daria and Inchike-daria, run east to the Konche-daria in the neighbourhood of the Chong-köl and then, at Tömenpu, entered the old bed of the Kum-daria, Prjevalsky's lake, Kara-koshun, could naturally not have moved north to form the lake Lop-nor which we discovered near Lou-lan. Strictly speaking, therefore, it is the migration of the river which takes the principal place in the chain of events; but the cause is always the same—erosion by the wind and filling up with solid material.

As far as I know only *one* explorer, Sir Aurel Stein, criticized my theory on any material point. I cannot go into his argument in detail here, especially seeing that later events have robbed it of its significance. In his excellent work *Innermost Asia*, Vol. II, page 761, he says:

An examination of this region appeared to me all the more important on account of the theory that Dr. Hedin had put forward, after his explorations of 1900–01, as a solution of the so-called [!] " Lop-nor problem ". According to this theory the Kuruk-daria was supposed to have carried the whole drainage of the Tarim, including that of the Konche-daria as an affluent, into the " old Lop-nor " lake located by him south of the Lou-lan site, until the Tarim's diversion into its present course in comparatively modern times. This theory could not be reconciled either with what my surveys had shown of the well-defined delta of the Kuruk-daria traceable over a considerable area to the south and east of the Lou-lan site, or, what seemed even more significant, with early and definite data regarding the hydrography of this region furnished by an im-

My caravan in March, 1900, went along the bed of the Kuruk-daria, then dry for 1,600 years past—the same bed down which we passed in canoes in April and May, 1934.

portant Chinese record, not accessible to Dr. Hedin when his theory was formed. I mean the very interesting account which M. Chavannes has extracted and translated from Li Tao-yüan's commentary on the *Shui ching* in the "Note additionelle" to his masterly analysis of the Wei-lio's notice of the "western countries".

Chavannes' brilliant translation and Stein's acute analysis of Li Tao-yüan's commentaries were, a few years later, with regard to the capacity of the Kuruk-daria, to receive the strongest possible contradiction—an answer to all unsolved questions, itself calling for no commentaries—a new pulse-beat in the life of the lower Tarim and Lop-nor. Then Nature herself betrayed her secrets and laid them before our eyes like an open book, a document which—in contrast to Li Tao-yüan's writings—allowed of no misunderstanding or false interpretation.

XXI

THE LAST PULSE-BEAT

ON February 20, 1928, my great expedition was in old Turfan staying in Hodja Abdul's house. Here, as usual, I thoroughly questioned a well-informed merchant, Tokta Ahun, about trade and its routes, and other conditions in the district.

Tokta Ahun told us, among other things, that he went to Tikenlik every year to buy sheep, which he sold in the bazaars of Turfan. When I asked which route he took and where he spent the nights, he gave us the names of his camping-places and said that at Ying-p'an he used the ferry "which conveys travellers and their goods across the river because the water is too deep to wade".

I asked Tokta Ahun what had happened, for when I was last at Ying-p'an, in 1900, the old river-bed had lain dry. He replied that the water now took quite different routes; seven years earlier, in 1921, the Konche-daria had left its old course and entered the dry bed of the Kuruk-daria, so that it ran fairly near the ruins of Ying-p'an, south of which a ferry colony had been established. He did not know how far the river continued to the eastward; the only person who could tell us about that was the camel-hunter Abdu Rehim.

I was thunderstruck at the news. It meant not only that my theories put forward twenty-eight years earlier were right, but also that my prophecy that Lop-nor and the lower Tarim would soon return to their old beds in the north had already come true.

I have never so thoroughly pumped a native about his knowledge as I did on February 20, 1928. I realized at once that the day would be one of note in the history of Central Asiatic exploration. It gave us the solution of the riddle of the wandering lake. Here was the answer to the polemics between von Richthofen and Prjevalsky, Kozlov and myself, and light on Huntington's and Stein's discoveries and statements.

I had occupied myself with the geographical problems of Lop-nor since 1896. The old Silk Road had run along its northern bank and along the Kuruk-daria. Lou-lan was its chief place in this region. When the river and lake moved south about A.D. 330, the Silk Road had been cut, Lou-lan abandoned and forgotten. Now the water had come back into its old beds, and new prospects of historic significance were unrolled before our eyes. Drought, the silence of death and oblivion had enveloped this region for sixteen centuries, but now it had suddenly come to life again, and it was reserved for our expedition to fasten together the links in the chain. Behind lay the 2,000 years in which Lop-nor had been known to the Chinese, and before—we grew dizzy at the thought of the countless shadowy years to come in which new arteries of communication—motor roads, railways, strategic roads—would be created in the heart of Asia, and new posts and towns would grow up in a desert region which for 1,600 years had been so poor that it could not provide a home even for scorpions and lizards. Only the wild camels had now and then wandered into it from their salt springs in the Kuruk-tagh —but now, when the water had returned and men were approaching, these wandering ships of the desert would see with consternation the frontiers of their ancient sanctuary curtailed and withdrawn.

How hard and tiring those marches along the bed of the Kuruk-daria had been, twenty-eight years ago! I recalled in memory the aspect of the river-bed, broad, deep and winding, but dried up, with the dead timber on the banks. There stood the trees like tombstones in a cemetery, grey, split, dead for 1,600 years, and as brittle as though made of clay. No life, not a drop of water in that bed, where a mighty river once ran and the desert wind murmured in the summits of leafy poplars. A town had been there, with a richly ornamented temple and tower-like *stupas* [1] erected in

---

[1] A *stupa* is a Buddhist monument of masonry for the preservation of relics.

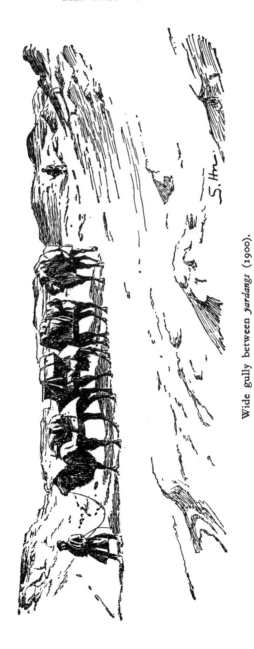

Wide gully between yardangs (1900).

Two of my camels in a wind-eroded gully between *yardangs* (1900).

honour of Buddha. A strong garrison had been kept there
for defence against barbarians from the north, and traders
from western lands, from India and China, had carried on
their business in the caravanserais and market-places. The
costly Chinese silks, in which the courtesans of Imperial
Rome had adorned themselves for the dance, had been
transported on camels and in ox-carts, made up into bales
or sewn up in sackcloth.

Yes, so it was in 1900. In 1921 the river had returned to
its old bed, and in 1928 I received the first news that my
prediction had come true. That I was the first educated
man in the world to learn that it had happened was indeed a
dispensation of Providence, so strange and improbable that
it would have seemed out of place in a work of fiction.

Meanwhile we went on from Turfan to Urumchi, the
capital of the province of Sinkiang, where we were
hospitably received by the governor-general, old Marshal
Yang Tseng-hsin.

Erosion terraces on right bank of Yarkend-daria (1899).

But Tokta Ahun's oral descriptions were not enough for us. Orientals possess a fertile imagination, and truth is to them a very elastic thing. We ourselves must make sure, with our own eyes and instruments, that Tokta Ahun's statements were accurate.

I obtained without difficulty Marshal Yang's permission to send our geologist, Dr. Erik Norin, down to the resurrected river at once.

Norin started from the hamlet of Singer, in the Kuruktagh, on April 11, 1928, and soon saw, 6 miles away to the southward, the waters of the new river glittering in the sun. So long as the bed lay dry it had been called Kuruk-daria, the " Dry River ". Now the East Turkis use the name Kum-daria, the " Sand River ", which is employed all the way from Tömenpu down to Lop-nor.

Norin was the first European who saw the Kum-daria winding like a blue ribbon through the pale greyish-yellow desert. He followed the river eastward for 140 miles to a point about 12 miles NNE of Lou-lan, mapped its course as well as he could from the bank, and found that, generally speaking, the great stream ran in the same bed which I had mapped twenty-eight years before. On the upper part of its course the new river was 100 to 150 yards wide, of a considerable depth, and had a velocity of about 3 feet per second.

North of Lou-lan Norin found the river split up into an inland delta, which prevented him from pushing forward as far as the ruins of the city itself.

Even then huge luxuriant reed-beds grew on the banks. Fresh tamarisks were taking root, and the seeds were being carried by the stream farther and farther into that desert which in my youth had been as dead and desolate as the surface of the moon. Now there were antelope and hares ; wild pig rooted among the reeds ; on the blue lakes there were swarms of duck and geese, and storks and herons sought their food in the marshes.

Accompanied by our young astronomer, Dr. Nils Ambolt, Norin completed his exploration of the Kum-daria in February and March, 1930, and followed the river to longitude 90 degrees E, or 25 miles NNE of Lou-lan. The

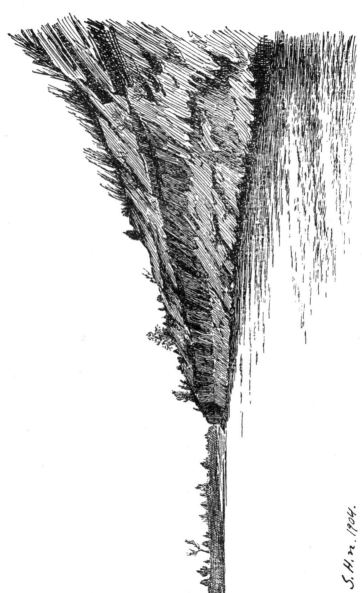

Steep sandy erosion terrace on right bank of Yarkend-daria (1899).

S.H.n. 1904.

My boat on the right bank of the middle Tarim (1899), not far from the mouth of the Aksu-daria.

map of the Kuruk-tagh and parts of the country to the south of it compiled by the joint labours of Norin and Ambolt is marked by an exactitude rarely found in the mapping of similar desert areas.

In the autumn of 1928 I vainly sought permission to visit the Kum-daria from the new governor-general of Sinkiang, the obstinate and narrow-minded Chin Shu-jen. I was anxious to make use of the winter, when the watercourses were frozen, to push forward to the terminal lake, the new Lake Lop-nor. The lake should lie in the same bed as the classical P'u-ch'ang-hai of the Chinese geographers and maps—Norin and Ambolt had not been able to reach it without boats on account of the lateness of the season. Moreover, their branches were different, Norin being primarily a geologist, while Ambolt specialized in geodetic and astronomical observations, and I had agreed with them that the search for Lop-nor should fall to my lot. But that plan had to be given up on account of the governor-general's disapproval.

On the left bank of the middle Tarim; boat drifting downstream (1899).

It was then, in December, 1928, that Professor Hsü Ping-ch'ang, Dr. Hummel and I went to Nanking to complain of the governor-general's intractability. Marshal Chiang Kai-shek promised us his support. I was then diverted by the force of circumstances to a new task, and Lop-nor had to wait for the time being.

We were clear as to the main features of the problem; only the terminal lake was not yet explored. Five members of our expedition had in 1928 travelled through the delta of the lower Tarim, where Prjevalsky had first set foot, and where I twenty years later had also gone by camel, canoe or boat. Two of these five, the archæologist Folke Bergman and the meteorologist Dr. Waldemar Haude, sent me reports on their journeys and observations. They found the lower parts of the Tarim and the Konche-daria almost dried up. Only at flood-time could a small quantity of the water at the most find its way into their beds. According to Bergman's observations, not a drop of running water had reached Arghan since 1924. Only pools of stagnant water were still to be found in the abandoned bed of the Tarim.

It was, therefore, clear that both the Tarim and its tributary, the Konche-daria, had by 1928 altered their course and entered the old dry bed of the Kuruk-daria, now called the Kum-daria. This proved the correctness of my theory that not only the Konche-daria, but also the main arm of the East Turkistan river system, the Tarim, had since 1921 gone over to the old bed of the Kuruk-daria. As long ago as my visit to Ying-p'an on March 12, 1900, I realized that in ancient times the *whole* of the Tarim had flowed through that bed, the deepest part of which still contained a salt pool. In my account of the visit (*Central Asia and Tibet*, Vol. I) I wrote :

> Even the natives saw that we were on the ancient course of the river (the Tarim). But the moisture does not extend farther east ; the bed lies as dry as tinder till it disappears in the equally dry basin of the old Lake Lop-nor.

To establish, definitely and for all time, the Swedish priority in the discovery of the latest migration of Lop-nor and the lower Tarim, I was able, when my book *Åter till Asien* was ready for the press in the summer of 1928, to insert two pages on the subject and relate the events which had taken place since 1921, so far as we knew them. The book was published in Stockholm in October, 1928. The German edition did not come out till the spring of 1930. The English and American editions were not ready till 1931, which had the advantage that I was able to introduce into them a provisional map of the new Lake Lop-nor itself, drawn by Dr. Nils Hörner and Parker C. Chen.

It was to be foreseen that so revolutionary and most extraordinary a transformation of the earth's surface would attract other travellers to the place as soon as it became known. The measures I had taken to provide documentary proof of our priority rights in the discovery soon proved to be justified.

When I was in Stockholm, in June and July, 1928, an Englishman, Colonel R. C. F. Schomberg, had been at

A " mazar " on saint's grave in a wood on the middle Tarim (1899).

Urumchi and at Bogdo-ula, and had met one or two members of our expedition. He had during the previous years
been carrying out a thorough exploration of Eastern
Turkistan on behalf of the Indian Government. In the
Geographical Journal, Vol. LXXIV, July to December, 1929,
pages 573–76, is a note by Schomberg under the heading
" River Changes in the Eastern Tarim Basin ", which says :

> In Urumchi I had heard from members of a Sino-Swedish
> expedition that there had been changes in the rivers of the
> Tarim basin, and Abdur Rahim was able to confirm and
> elaborate this report.
> My original intention had been to follow the river to its end,
> but it was too early in the season to do so. The water, the
> swamp, and the conditions generally made it impossible, and
> the journey was put off till the swamps were frozen and the
> water less.
> The end of Yangi or Qum Darya is said to be a large swamp
> west and north-west of the Lou-lan area, so that the ancient
> site is now only accessible from the east and south, i.e. from the
> Lop-nor direction.

It had not occurred to Colonel Schomberg that the best

Fishermen setting their nets; lower Tarim (1899).

way to study the new river right to its end was to travel by canoe as described in the opening chapters of this book. The information he had received about the position of the new lake was diametrically the opposite of the truth, for, as we know, the wandering lake had placed itself east and south-east of Lou-lan. At the time of our visit in 1934 there was probably not one inhabitant of the Lop country who knew where the lake lay.

The winter trip to the Kum-daria and Lop-nor which Colonel Schomberg had planned does not seem to have been carried out, for in his book *Peaks and Plains of Central Asia* he does not mention any such trip. What he says in the book does not contain much beyond the original note. He says:

> I had heard from members of Dr. Sven Hedin's expedition, whom I was fortunate in meeting in Urumchi, that there were changes in the river of the Tarim basin, and that long dry channels were again flowing. So although I was very peevish over the frustration of my plans, I consoled myself with the thought that there was plenty more to see (p. 123).

He goes on (p. 129):

> We were now about to reach a region where an interesting geographical change had recently occurred. Centuries ago, at the foot of the Kuruk-tagh, and past the town of Lou-lan, a river had flowed to the Lop Nor. Later it had changed its course, and the country near its old channel grew arid and was abandoned. Now, once again, the empty channel was filled; and the Tarim River, which collected the waters of nearly every stream south of the Tien Shan, was in consequence almost dry, thanks to the deflection of its waters to their original course. It was a most interesting phenomenon, bound to affect local conditions by drying up of pastures, destroying fields and compelling the abandonment of settlements; producing, in fact, on this side of the Tarim River what, a millennium ago, it had brought about at Lou-lan.

The change at Lou-lan had actually taken place 1,600 years ago, or about A.D. 330.

On July 30 the English papers in China published several detailed articles about a new expedition to our regions which Sir Aurel Stein was just about to undertake. One of them (*Peking and Tientsin Times*, July 24, 1930) was under the headline " Into the Lop Desert " and had cross-heads " Tarim Basin ", " Lop Desert ", " Lou-lan ", " The Silk Caravan Route ". Another was published in the *Statesman* on June 19 and was called " Expedition to Wilds of Central Asia ". This was accompanied by a sketch of the Lop area, with under it the caption " A map of the country to be explored by Sir Aurel Stein ". It showed the Kum-daria ending in a fan-shaped delta in the Lou-lan region, but forming no terminal lake. On the other hand, Lop-nor is figured north-east of Abdal as before, in Prjevalsky's time.

In his book *On Ancient Central Asian Tracks* (1933) Stein says that in 1915 he was able to find salt water by digging shallow wells in certain deep places in the Kuruk-daria, and continues:

> Hence I could not feel altogether surprised when I learned on my fourth journey in the Tarim basin (1930–31) that a recent great hydrographic change affecting the course of the Tarim had caused the greater portion of its summer floods to meet the Konche-daria much farther north than before and thus to

J.H-n.04

Where the lower Tarim cuts through the sand desert (1899).

deflect the united waters of both once more into the " Dry
River " and towards the area of ancient Lou-lan. The hoped-
for chance of studying this latest change affecting the Lop basin
has, I regret, been denied to me through Chinese obstruction.

The above extracts from the writings of Schomberg and
Stein show that we were not the only people who had their
eyes on the latest pulse-beat of Lop-nor and the lower
Tarim. Erik Norin, as much as two and a half years before
Stein's journey, had cleared up the course of the Tarim as
far as its delta by Lou-lan, while Bergman and Haude had
established that the water had forsaken the old bed of the
Tarim. The only thing that remained was to fix the position of the final reservoir in the desert where the Tarim
water evaporated and disappeared.

I had found, as I mentioned above, that although my
expedition was a joint Swedish-Chinese undertaking, and
among its members were such eminent men of learning as
Professors Hsü Ping-ch'ang and P. L. Yuan, I was quite
unable to get from the governor-general, Chin Shu-jen,

Steep sand dunes on right bank of lower Tarim (1899).

permission to travel to the Lop desert. In other words, all
routes to Lop-nor within the boundaries of Sinkiang were
shut and barred to us. I therefore decided to carry out a
plan that would paralyse this fellow Chin, who had even
ignored Marshal Chiang Kai-shek's orders—and which
eliminated Sinkiang altogether.

We must act quickly. One fine day Schomberg might
carry out his projected trip to Lop-nor, and we knew from
the papers that Stein was on his way to the same lake. I
could not allow others to reap the fruits of the work we had
already done on the Lop-nor problem, and of the close study
and labour I myself had devoted to it.

Two of our expeditions were at work on the Etsin-gol in
1930—Folke Bergman on archæology, Nils Hörner and
Chen on quaternary geology and geodesy. Gösta Montell
and Georg Söderbom were with me in Peking. I sent the
two last with our Ford car via Belimiao through the desert
to the Etsin-gol. They had several errands to discharge,
but the one that most keenly interested me was to seek out

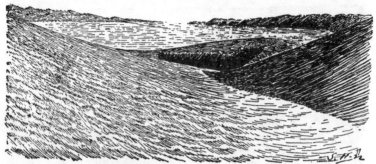

Yangi-köl, one of the lakes along the lower Tarim, looking NNE (1899).

Hörner and Chen and give the former a letter the gist of which was as follows :

Form a strong caravan ; go via Tun-hwang, by the desert road south of the Pei-shan, to the Lop depression ; do not come back till you have found Lake Lop-nor, formed since 1922 ; make a map of it and explore the Kum-daria delta !

Hörner and Chen carried out their task brilliantly in every respect. In the previous chapters I have often had occasion to speak of their journey. Those who—even if more on patriotic than scientific grounds—feel inclined to make a closer study of a great Swedish achievement, should not neglect to read Dr. Hörner's informative and most interesting book, *Resa till Lop* (Stockholm, 1936).

Then followed the motor expedition fitted out by the Central Government at Nanking, which was under my command and lasted from the autumn of 1933 to the spring of 1935 ; I have described it in *Big Horse's Flight* and *The Silk Road*. I there related how the commander of the Northern Army in the war against Ma Chung-yin, the White Russian general Bektieieff, most kindly helped me and compelled the military governor Sheng Shih-tsai to send us, willy nilly, to Lop-nor of all places.

This journey I have described in the present volume, but no one should think that our investigations in the Lop-nor region between the years 1928 and 1934 represent the last chapter in the history of the wandering lake. Certainly we have solved the Lop-nor problem, in so far as it can be solved at present, but the restless lake is no more per-

Bank terrace 15 feet high (1899).

manently established in its bed in the northern part of the desert than it has been during past centuries. Since the changes which have taken place since 1921 have proved the correctness of the theory I propounded in 1901, it is even safer than it was then—indeed, it can be regarded as axiomatic—to affirm that when the period that has now begun has reached its end, and the pendulum has swung back, the lower course of the Tarim and the terminal lake will forsake their present beds and wander back to the south to seek out lower parts of the desert—perhaps the same as in Prjevalsky's time, or perhaps other regions now dry.

The two factors on which the theory rests are the deposit of solid material in the living water and the erosion of the dry clay desert by the wind. That this process takes place is confirmed by Hörner in an essay on "Alternating Lakes", in which he says: "On the whole, the river changes and lake displacements seem to be a function of sedimentation and wind erosion." And it is clear that these forces, during coming centuries and millenniums, will work in the same way as in the past, in line with the events which we have been able to follow in Chinese annals and in the great book of Nature herself.

As to the length of the period which has now begun, it is best to refrain from all prophecies. We do not know for how many centuries the river and lake had been near Lou-lan when they left their beds about A.D. 330. Will the

Camp in wood on the Dilpar (March, 1900).

next great period last 1,600 years? Or will there be intermediate stages, like that which prevailed at the beginning of the eighteenth century? Only the future can supply an answer to these questions.

The most probable thing is that both river and lake will remain in their present beds so long that it will be reserved for a remote future to witness the next swing of the pendulum. But perhaps the Turkis will some day succeed in damming the river and forcing it back into its old bed.

The changes which periodically take place around Lopnor bring with them real catastrophe for plant life, for animals and for men. The danger to men is not so great when a river unexpectedly begins to decrease and after a time dries up altogether. They are warned when the volume of water diminishes and can move elsewhere in time. The higher animals of wood, undergrowth and shore, birds and winged insects can migrate in the direction from which the water used to come. But all the fish, molluscs and insects that live in the water are doomed to

Kalmak-ottogho; an arm of the Tarim which once watered the fields of Tikenlik (1900).

Rich vegetation on one of the arms of the Tarim delta (1900).

Reeds and poplars on the banks (1900).

speedy extinction. The plants can fight against destruction
so long as their roots reach the subsoil water. But their
days too are numbered; we saw that on the journey down
the Kum-daria, when we daily passed dried-up trees and
bushes, white or grey monuments over ancient graves, and
I had seen it on previous journeys around Lou-lan and in
other parts of the Lop desert. Again and again I was
astonished to see the poplar trunks still standing upright
after 1,600 years, though countless storms, bearing clouds of
driving sand, had swept over them. Only the trunks had
held out; boughs and twigs had disappeared long before;
the wood was dried up, light grey and brittle, burned
splendidly and sank in water. The last-named characteristic, which I discovered by pure chance, is presumably due
to the fact that these trunks, after they have lost their bark
and been split, have become impregnated with drift-sand
and fine earth; possibly this helps to preserve and harden
them and increase their power of resistance to the wind.

All this had happened on the Kum-daria and around Lou-
lan about A.D. 330. Even if military and political changes
had been contributory causes of the evacuation of the town,
the removal of the river and lake to the southward presented
absolutely insuperable obstacles to the continuance of

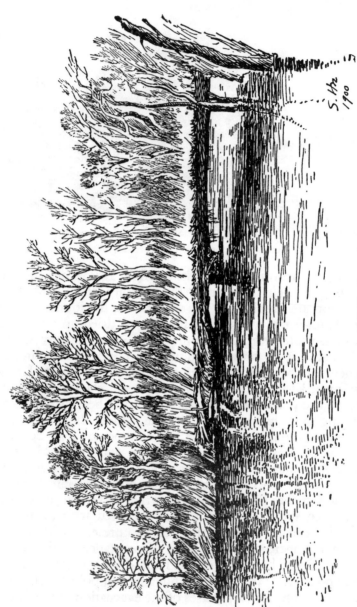

Bridge over Ilek (April, 1900).

human life and all organic life in that region. When, on
March 28, 1900, I was the first to enter the ancient city, I
was surrounded by a landscape which bore in everything the
stamp of death. Only in a few depressions farther south in
the desert, which the water of the Tarim may at intervals have
reached through arms of the delta, were there still one or
two tamarisks which retained a spark of life.

Where there is no water in the desert no life is possible.
When the water returns, life too follows in its track. The
animals that live in the water are the first settlers. The
stream carries seeds of reeds and other plants; they quickly
secure a foothold on the banks and take root. It is surprising to find that the number of live tamarisks increases as
one gets lower down the stream, and that they are especially
abundant on such arms as the channel I described in an
earlier chapter, in the direction of Lou-lan. Perhaps the
subsoil water was nearer the surface of the ground close to
these old watercourses, and this made it possible for the
tamarisks to keep alive during the long interval.

The last to arrive are the poplars, but we found on our
journey that even the poplar, the characteristic tree of
Eastern Turkistan, an outpost on the edge of the desert,
had begun its re-entry into the old desert kingdom from
which it was expelled when the river dried up.

It was with a feeling at once solemn and festal that, in
April and May, 1934, I let the water itself bear me eastward
through the kingdom it had conquered. I felt myself a
guest at a celebration by Nature of one of her own victories;
and the murmuring of the wind in the reeds, and the plashing of the water on the promontories, sounded like the
accompaniment to a triumphal march. In various forms
organic life was returning to the desert so silent only a few
years before, where only death and dissolution had had
their abode. Fresh and newly awakened, the tamarisks
were enthroned on their little mounds, and in last year's
vast yellow reed-beds the green stems and leaves of the new
spring were beginning to shoot up. Far out in the delta
wild pig had already made themselves at home, and in the
northern part of Lop-nor, where the water is still fresh,
fish lived in astonishing abundance. Year by year the reed-

Old poplars (1900).

beds will grow broader and denser, and animal life will develop. If the river keeps its course long enough, the woods on the banks of the Konche-daria will spread right down to the Kum-daria's delta.

Nature in our time plays no triumphal marches on Prjevalsky's old waterways and the lake which he discovered, Kara-koshun. There the silence of the grave reigns. In the last year the animals noticed that the water was diminishing, but their instinct, the inherited experience of centuries, told them that the spring or autumn flood would come as usual bringing a new, fresh stream. When the new water failed to come, the last pools evaporated and fish and molluscs were caught in the mud of the lake-bottom and suffocated.

The reeds are withering, and only stumps remain. The woodland remains alive so long as the roots of its trees can obtain the source of life from the subsoil water. But it is doomed to dry up and die if the water system retains its present form. Its farthest outposts to southward will show in the future, as now, how far the wood succeeded in

Natural canal through the reeds (1900).

extending during the last swing of the pendulum. It never reached Kara-koshun. The shores of this lake have always been bare and open, which confirms the information given me in 1896 at the fishing village of Abdal by Prjevalsky's old friend, the octogenarian chief Kunchekan Bek. He told me that his father, Numet Bek, had lived in his youth by a big lake situated north of Kara-koshun, and that the last-named had not been formed till 1720–30. Prjevalsky's lake had thus evidently gone through intermediary stages before it settled down a couple of hundred years ago in the most southerly depression in the desert.

The fishing population which I found in 1901 in the little villages of reed-huts just above the point where the Tarim ran into Kara-koshun, and which was there till 1921, departed when the lake began to dry up and the water in the river diminished. Most of them went to Charkhlik and became tillers of the soil, others upstream. The whole country now presents quite a different appearance from what it did in Prjevalsky's time; it can safely be said that so radical a transformation is a rare phenomenon on this earth.

S. H. n̄
1904

At the mouth of the Charchan-daria (1900).

It will be an interesting study for geographers of the future to observe the change of scene on the Kum-daria. Chen and I, on our canoe trip, saw only a few shepherds pasturing their sheep on the upper part of the river. Apart from these there was not a human being on the new river, but in the summer large flocks of sheep came to the neighbourhood of our motor-car camp and even lower down the river. There are *satmas* south of the Kum-daria also, but where there is water there is also life, and the life-giving water draws men with it. There have been ploughed fields on the Konche-daria from time immemorial, which are watered by irrigation canals dug from the river. Along the new river artificial irrigation is extremely problematical on account of the unfavourable conformation of the *yardang* landscape, and, if it is carried out, it will require immense labour.

A fishing population of the same modest type as the Loplik tribe on the lowest part of the Tarim will find a means of existence on the Kum-daria also. There, too, are vast grazing-grounds for cattle and sheep.

If the motor road we planned in 1934 ever becomes a reality, this country, now so poor but so rich in water, will acquire an importance it does not possess in our days. And then perhaps even Lou-lan, the sleeping city, will rise from the dead, even if in another place and in another shape.

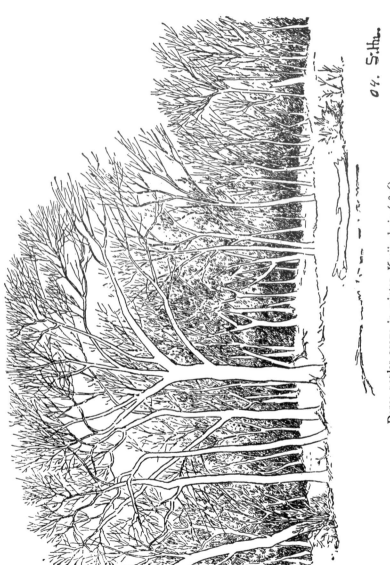

Dense poplar grove in winter, Kerija-daria (1896).

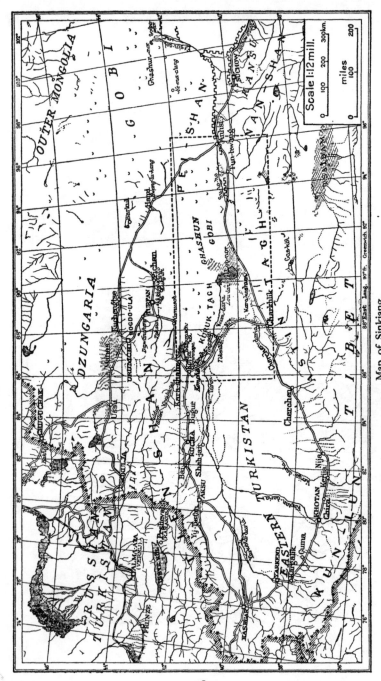

Map of Sinkiang.
(The dotted lines enclose the territory shown on the large map.)

INDEX

INDEX